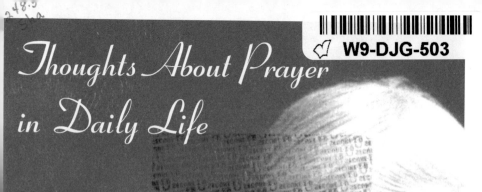

Thoughts About Prayer in Daily Life

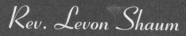

Rev. Levon Shaum

Thoughts About Prayer in Daily Life

Requests for information should be addressed to:
Evangel Publishing House
2000 Evangel Way
P.O. Box 189
Nappanee, Indiana 46550
Phone: (800) 253-9315
Internet: www.evangelpublishing.com

Cover Design by Matthew Gable

ISBN: 1-928915-77-9
Library of Congress Catalog Card Number: 2005933852
Printed by Evangel Press, Nappanee, IN
Printed in the United States of America

5 6 7 8 9 EP 8 7 6 5 4 3 2 1

INTRODUCTION

Prayer is one of mankind's most valuable tools. Prayer gives the privilege of having an audience with Almighty God. Prayer reaches into the daily life of the believer, and with God's Word is a personal guide into the unknown.

These pages will permit prayer to be applied to personal every day circumstances which will be confronted in life's daily walk with the Lord. Prayer must lead the believer into every area of life where most prayer list do not go. Biblical characters and modern day miracles are a daily example of how believers approached the situation and found spiritual victory. Hopefully, the content will allow each reader to apply each particular subject matter to their personal experience. Usually the single subjects are brief and can be read in a few minutes, even as a daily devotional.

The value of faithful prayer was a reality in our home, especially in our work that dealt with boys who were wards of the court. No one was ever approached personally for financial help; no one was contacted for pledges or shares; no one gave us an amount to be matched; nor no one said: "if you have any need, let me know." That means our God would have to meet the need when bills came due. Can our God do the impossible for each one of His children? The author and his wife have been down this road and have had firsthand experience in watching our God fulfill His promises. We marveled how our Lord always supplied in His unique way.

Many contributions have been made in one way or another and whenever possible the source was given credit. Many years in the ministry gave opportunity to make notes, and clip articles and now the source is unknown. These were placed in quotes when the source was unknown. Then, there were those who pored over my handwritten pages, lovingly correcting and giving suggestions. Their many hours were deeply appreciated.

A note about the author. Levon A. Shaum is a graduate of Asbury College and Asbury Theological Seminary and is a retired United Methodist minister of the Ohio West Conference. He ministered in Indiana, Kentucky and Ohio; was conference Evangelist for ten years; and founded 20th Century Home for Boys.

SPIRITUAL SELF ANALYSIS TO PREPARE FOR A VITAL PRAYER LIFE!

What does the Spirit of God say to me about the following?

1. Am I critical just to be critical? _____
Does this concern me? _____

2. Do I blame others for my Spiritual defeats and life's failures? _____
If so, why? Explain

_____

3. Am I jealous? _____ Is this glorifying God? _____

4. Am I envious ? _____
What is this envy doing to me? _____

5. Am I self-seeking? _____
Do I have to have my own way? _____
How does this affect my relationship with the Lord? _____
With others? _____

6. Am I self-righteous? _____
Do I try to impress others with my righteousness? _____

7. Does it give me mental anguish when I am not recognized? ____
How do I handle this, especially when I have faithfully served longer than the one recognized? _____

8. Do I have unforgiveness harbored in my heart? ____
How is this affecting my spiritual life? _____

9. Do these hidden harbored areas come before me when I pray?

_____

10. Am I going the second or third mile in a difficult situation with an irritating person? _____

11. Does my temper emulate God's grace in my everyday life?

_____
Is my answer that which pleases the Lord? _____

12. Is it necessary for me to deal with the unpleasing areas that the Lord has continually revealed? _____
Why? _____

13. Does my pride prevent me from being completely broken so that I can be perfectly molded after His perfect will for my life? _____

14. Do I want His perfect will for my life, more than anything else this world has to offer? _____
Will our Lord accept anything less? _____

15. Is my prayer useless because I hold a grudge against another person? _____
Do I pray for those who despitefully use me? _____

16. Do I find revenge occupying a certain area in my life?
_____

17. Does depression affect my spiritual life? _____
How am I dealing with it? _____

18. Are there animosities that I feel justified in retaining? _____

19. Is there a spirit of hostility and anger occupying my life? _____

20. Is there enmity present in some area of my self life ? _____

How do I handle these temptations? _____

21. Do I justify any ungodly attitude towards those who exasperate me? _____
Am I charitable and kind towards those who are unchristian and have a different viewpoint? _____

22. Do I firmly believe that only the pure in heart shall enter the kingdom of heaven? _____
Does my daily life meet this requirement? _____
Is my conviction based on Biblical Truth? _____
What is meant by heart purity? _____

23. Do I feel justified to speak my mind forcefully when I feel I have been misused? _____

Or when proper attention has not been given to my wishes? _____

24. Am I a constant complainer? _____

25. Do I protect my cold, lukewarm spiritual life? _____
What reminds me of my lukewarm prayer life? _____
List them, _____

26. Am I demanding from others standards I fail to keep
consistently myself? _____
If I do not live these Biblical standards, what does that make me?
_____

27. Is my Christian life more than a profession? _____
Do I see real evidence of sacrificial giving and personal self-denial on
my part to place our Lord first in all of life? _____
I am listing my reasons for my answer.
_____

28. Is a holy life necessary? _____
Is there any other way to please God? _____

29. Would others see a Holy life in the things I do? _____
The places I go?_____ The type of clothes I wear?____
The way I talk? _____ How I treat others? _____

30. Am I cantankerous? ____
Argumentative? ____
Insultive? ____
Rebellious? _____

31. Are there spiritual convictions once held, but that no
longer disturb me? ____
Why? _____
Have I hardened my heart to the appeal of the Holy Spirit? _____
What has happened to my tender conscience? _____

32. Am I willing to acknowledge my forbidden hidden motives? _____

33. Is there any controversy between my soul and my Savior? _____
Between myself and another person? _____

Does answered prayer have a connection with what I do about
this controversy? _____

34. I will go back over these questions answered and carefully compare
my answers. Are my answers all consistent? _____
If my answers are inconsistent, why?
_____

35. Can God's grace, prayer, and obedience solve the questionable areas
in my life? _____
Or do I find the questionable more involved? _____

36. Is my Lord adequate for all the sin problems I
will face in my life? _____ Do I know this to be true? _____

37. Do I actually know real spiritual victory in my life?_____

38. How does all this affect my prayer life?
_____

39. Can I have continual spiritual victory without a daily
vital prayer life? _____

40. If Jesus, the very God, felt the necessity to pray, is it absolutely
necessary that I spend time with God that is far beyond the several
minute routine? _____

41. Is my prayerlessness a grave sin of omission? _____
What does the sin of prayerlessness mean to me? _____
To my Lord? _____

42. What are my prayer concerns? _____
Have I taken the time to make a prayer list? _____

43. Are all my concerns centered around myself and my own little
world? _____

44. What is my concern for lost souls? _____
If everyone carried the same concern I do, what would be the results?
_____

45. Will my Lord hold me accountable for my prayer life? _____

PRAYER IS MAN'S CONNECTION WITH THE LIVING GOD !

Prayer is defined by words, but they have their limitations. But until some thing better is available, Wilhelm von Humboldt's words can give some insight: "Prayer is intended to increase the devotion of the individual, but if the individual himself prays he requires no formula; he pours himself forth much more naturally in self-chosen and connected thoughts before God and scarcely requires words at all. Real inward devotion knows no prayer but that arising from the depths of its own feelings."

Jeremiah places prayer in the Biblical prospective: "And ye shall seek me and find me, WHEN ye shall search for me with all your heart." (Jer. 29:13)

God gave Jeremiah these words for his promise, and Israel as a nation, which now includes all people from every race. But as with all of God's promises, they are given on condition. These words are only a reality when prayer meets God's demand. But, is prayer worth our time and effort? Does God merit this resolve to seek Him, and His will for our daily lives? Is Jeremiah saying, the fulfillment of prayer is to pray, seek, search, if so, He would hear, not only hear, but could be found, providing the seeker would be seeking with their whole heart?

Many people pray but do they follow the conditions that are stated here? Their prayer life is limited almost entirely to some crisis. They appear to be successful; nice home, good bank account, decent family, and more, suggesting that the counsel given by Jeremiah is overstated. Does not this promise imply time, effort, and searching with an obedient heart?

Many professing Christians can quickly compare the worldly person's material assets with those of some prayer warrior who has limited tangible worldly goods. Why then spend that time in prayer, when life's good things come to the prayerless who pray very little or not at all? Prayerlessness is not too disturbing because the careless professing Christian has found little value in the minute or two minute prayer. Usually there is little guilt because long ago that inner voice has been silenced by neglect. The sin of omission is never as biting as the sin of commission. But both are equally deadly disobedience. (James 4:17)

Is materialism the reason why so many who have taken the position of being evangelicals have a hit and miss prayer life? To many, prayer is not missed! They see little difference in their lives, when they pray or do not pray. The religious routine is still continued; church attendance, giving, and sharing when convenient; and maintaining some moral standards, usually made to fit their personal lifestyle.

Or there is the possibility, that the careless praying person has experienced what Habakkuk did, listen to his words: "O Lord, how long shall I cry, and thou wilt not hear? Even cry out unto thee in violence, and thou wilt not save." (Hab. 1:2) This cry is confronting God, yes, even challenging God. Why the silence? What's the use? This kind of confrontation does something to the challenger. It either beats faith into the dust, fills the mind with doubt and defeat, or the despair will crush the soul to deeper submission and utter trust. All too many people live in uncertainty and failure. A defective prayer will reveal a spiritual deficiency that reaches into every area of life. A flawed prayer life can be protected by a religious front that is safely guarded by a pious appearance. A defeated prayer life rests on, "I tried that!" Christians, as well as non-Christians are forced to ride out life's violence. But then come to the conclusion that God has little impact on daily life, so why pray? Modern culture has taught us well. We are told again and again, that we are victims of life's circumstances, so why not eat, drink and be merry. It appears God can't, or won't, do anything about the tragedies that surround us. At least, He hasn't responded the way I prayed.

How does this fickle faithless attitude affect personal relationship with the Lord? Is that difficult to understand? Daily living reveals just how miserable life can be trying to straddle the Spiritual fence. The time we spend in prayer uncovers the inner life and what is valued. When caught in this mode of thinking it is not difficult to consider prayer an inconvenient sideline; limited to a short devotional page and a closing minute or so in prayer. A mealtime prayer can be slipped in. It is as if the Lord ought to be pleased with the little He is given.

A questionable state of mind can understand how little David wanted to explore the unknown. "Little David loved to accompany his missionary father in the pickup on visits to the Indian villages. They crossed the rivers in the High Andes of Bolivia many times when the water was deep and treacherous. Following one particularly dangerous passage, David asked his father: "Dad, can we go back to the other side and cross the river again,"

"Why should we do that?" David seriously replied: "Well, you know how we always pray before we go over, and we made it just fine? It's a real bad one, Dad, and I want to see how we do without praying for once."

Little David was ready to risk the turbulence and rage of the river crossing without prayer. There evidently was no sense of fear. How indicative of life's masses! They can and will brave life's chaotic and disastrous circumstances without asking the Lord's help. A number may have tried facing life this way, and found they have survived. The tempest was overwhelming at times but they hung on by refusing to be swallowed up. Therefore, the need for prayer is further questioned. This self-will victory may not be announced openly, for that would border on blasphemy. But nevertheless, the thought is held in the subconscious that keeps repeating: you are doing quite well without praying, so why get excited now?

I have no desire to go over my life to see how it would have been worked out without the hours spent in prayer. Evidently, great hosts of people see no future consequence in little David's suggestion. He couldn't see God at work, protecting them. God didn't pick the truck up and put it on the other side; nor, did he see God in the driver's seat, or holding back the water. In fact, he didn't see God anywhere when they crossed the river. So, how did God intervene? If he couldn't see God working, why pray? How many people secretly feel the same way!

What would I have missed if I had been nothing more than a prayerless professing Christian across these years? When I use the word prayerless, I mean giving but a couple minutes each day to prayer.

- I would have missed the inner rest and invaluable fellowship and communion with the Infinite mind and soul that is Omnipotent, Omniscient and entirely Holy and righteous; the coming King and Creator of the entire universe, and my personal Heavenly Father.

- I would have missed that Omnipotent power that undergirds and is available to live life victoriously. There is no undertow strong enough to pull me under when I rest completely in His care, no matter how hurtful the trial or the heartbreak.

- I would have experienced the tragic knowledge of living below my Heavenly Father's intended privilege; thus, putting a big question mark on my desire for my only hope beyond this life.

• I would have missed the verification of prayer's miraculous answers.

• I would have missed the leadership of the blessed Holy Spirit.

• I would have missed this glorious privilege of walking daily, in personal intimate relationship with the God who cares about my every need.

Little praying, results in losing faith to grasp the handles of God's promises. Prayer's value is only realized in relationship to the results experienced. If prayer is pursued, prayer's worth is measured by faith in prayer itself. To minimize prayer to a few minutes a day is to disobey the scripture that commands us to be in an attitude of praying without ceasing. If we don't pray, there is an enormous responsibility attached to the sin of omission. If we do pray, we are not relieved from that responsibility to the unredeemed. I must ask myself, HOW IMPORTANT IS A VITAL PRAYER LIFE TO ME?

Do I pray because there is guilt if prayer is neglected, or is the need so compelling that the concern drives me to the prayer closet? If prayer is an imperative, then God's passion must be at the core. There are few things that are less taxing than prayer. Prayer is unavoidable to a Spirit-filled Christian for there is no greater binding force that commands a more intimate relationship with our Infinite God. The Biblical characters that moved history from Genesis to Revelation verified prayer to be the mandatory ingredient in the Spirit-filled life.

The maximum example is our Lord. The very God man felt prayer as an obligatory commitment. Evidently His humanity mandated an audience with the Father, whether it was in the wilderness, or Gethsemane's garden, or when the religious hierarchy attacks His Deity or the burdened weight of the multitude that continually press for attention; prayer was His refuge.

Do we find life any different if we pray, or if we do not pray? If there is no difference, then we have answered the question: why pray? Then, God must not be a definite part of our life, for prayer is our link to the heavenly Father through Christ our Redeemer. Prayer gives direction and purpose to our lives; meaning there is fellowship with the Creator and controller of all, giving adequate grace in the midst of life's tragedies.

Macartney tells of Harold Dixon, one of the three men who drifted on a raft for thirty-four days for a thousand miles. Floating on this four by eight foot raft with no food or water, caught in every circumstance imaginable in the open sea, Dixon spoke of the prayer meeting they held each night: "O there was a comfort in passing our burden to Someone to do the impossible for us in that empty vastness. Further, the common devotion drew us together, since it seems we no longer depended entirely upon each other, but could appeal simultaneously to a Fourth that we three held equally in reverence."

Prayer is a realization that we cannot carry life victoriously on our shoulders without the Power that is bigger than life and all its circumstances. Prayer gives access to that God-given gift. Without this Power active in our lives, we are hopelessly lost in the vastness of life's raging sea.

Three Hebrew men faced life's darkest hour, refusing to bow to Nebuchadnezzar's images and were thrown into the fiery furnace. Did they think, now is a good time to start a meaningful prayer life? If so, they would not have been ready for the crisis. Their prayer time in the past had readied them for the present test. Their intimate prayer relationship gave them confidence to rest their faith in their Infinite God. They were prepared before the plot unfolded. Listen to these men's words: " . . . our God whom we serve is able to deliver us from the burning fiery furnace, and He will deliver us out of thine hand, O King. But if not, be it known unto thee, O King that we will not serve thy gods, nor worship the golden image, which thou hast set up." (Dan. 3:17&18)

Prayer conditions the believer for the unknown. Someone said: "Our adversary introduces us to ourselves." The unknown is filled with untold nameless impenetrables that wait to entrap the prayerless. Suddenly there is confrontation with the unexpected. Only the spiritual soul can deal victoriously with the uncertainties that the unknown presents. Praying over the pages of God's Word, a prayer that is anchored in a faith that refuses to allow anything to separate the prayer warrior from the Lord God gives resting assurance in the darkest night of the unknown. Who but the Lord God can arrest the fears of the unexplored, because there is no unknown to Him. How good it is to expect your personal Savior to be right there when the unthinkable happens, and the circumstance is about to sweep the victim into an uncontrollable torrent. Faithful prayer is that which assures His study hand, His underwritten presence.

PRAYER HAS ITS DISAPPOINTMENTS!

Paul prayed earnestly three times for the Lord to remove his grievous thorn in the flesh. Here was a man who had the faith to heal the sick; prayed and the jail crumbled to dust; prayed life back into a lad who had fallen from the window; but when he prayed to the Lord for his personal healing, God's response was: "My grace is sufficient for thee." (2 Cor. 12:9)

God knew what Paul did not know; Paul accepted that, being content with God's answer. He delighted in God's purpose for his life more than his personal comfort. Did Paul need this thorn in the flesh? The thorn in the flesh was that something that he needed to keep him aware of his continual dependence on the Lord. Is it possible to become arrogant if there is not something in life that keeps the soul humble and at the foot of the cross? Is it not logical that the Father would overrule a legitimate prayer for Paul's personal good?

Another way to identify God's purpose is in the answer the teacher gave to a young lad's question: "Why is it that so many prayers are not answered? I do not understand," the Bible says, "Ask, and ye shall receive, seek, and ye shall find; knock, and it shall be opened unto you; but it seems to me a great many knock and are not admitted."

The teacher replied: "Did you ever sit by your cheerful parlor fire on some dark evening and hear a loud knock on the door? Going to the door, you found no one there, but you heard pattering feet of some mischievous boy who knocked but did not wish to enter, and therefore ran away? Thus it is often with us."

When we pray a number of things come to mind:

- What if God wants me to do something I do not want to do! I run.

- What if God says, you want this, but what about the type of disobedient life you are now living, and you are not willing to face this reality. I run.

- What if God the Father wants me to make something right with a particular person whom I dislike, it would be humiliating. I couldn't take that, so I run.

- What if unbelief was greater than faith! I turn and run.

- What if God says, you come to me now, caught in this overwhelming circumstance, but ignore me when things are going well. The shame causes me to run.

We run because we fear coming face to face with God and His terms when our lives are willfully displeasing; we are caught in our personal goals, and self-centeredness. Our lives are turned wrong side out and we want to avoid what we know that God knows about us. So we run.

Christians in Africa, having no privacy in their huts to pray, would go off into the bush behind their huts to speak with God. Soon, behind each Christian's hut, a little worn track becomes visible, by walking back and forth to his place of prayer. Whenever a track became overgrown with grass from the lack of use, another Christian would comment, "Friend, there is something the matter with your track." Is the grass growing on our prayer track? It is time to check.

There is no service we can render to our Lord greater than time spent in prayer. Our human limitations may restrict our abilities to help another, but all can enter into the prayer arena to seek the Father's direction for our personal lives and for others.

Evidently Satan has a direct conversation with God. It is clearly revealed in Job. 1:12, "And the Lord said unto Satan, 'Behold all that he (Job) hath is in thy power; only upon himself put not forth thine hand.' So Satan went forth from the presences of the Lord."

Satan is a fallen created being with angelic powers. Since he is a created being, he cannot be an equal with his Creator. The Creator is always master of the created. As Adam, Satan had the freedom of choice: to be faithful in the realm in which God had created him, or to rebel. When he rebelled, that revealed a personal arrogance that refused God's demand for obedience. This disobedience has left its permanent brand on Satan, to which there is no repentance, just as Adam's sin has been imprinted on all mankind from his willful disobedience. But for man, at Calvary, God's sacrificial Lamb makes redemption possible for the new birth to ransom lost mankind.

Subconsciously, many see Satan's influence in action, and determine that

Satan is as powerful as the Infinite God. All mankind lives in an atmosphere where they see mounting evidence of an evil take over. People are cheated at the gas pumps, defrauded in business transactions, lied to, and conned. All of the dishonesty and hypocrisy makes evil very real. The question builds up in the subconscious, if God is Almighty, why doesn't He wipe Satan out? He could and will, but only when He decides the hour has come.

Why mention Satan when discussing prayer? The subconscious mind can have a "hang over" during prayer time. If Satan's power is so overwhelming in the subconscious mind it will affect faith in God, automatically intimidating prayer time faith. If the attention is on what Satan is doing, it cannot be wholly on what the Father needs to do, and wants to do. Whether it is realized or not, confidence has a question mark.

It is easy to see the mockers and be astounded at the taunting of righteousness, feeling there is no way this onslaught can be stopped. The futility cries: "why pray?" The odds are too great. Which comes back to, how big is your God? Meaningful prayer has victory or defeat at this point. Is our God who He claims to be, or is He at the mercy of the evil despot. This problem will be met in the prayer closet. The depth of the spiritual life depends on who is winning.

A wounded faith feels war is one thing to avoid. A hiding place is sought, even if the war is confined to the prayer closet. Only spending a minute or two in daily prayer can not circumvent it. It is simple to find a considerable number who are avoiding the combat zone as much as possible. The mind and heart are occupied with less weighty things that do not take the time or the energy. There are always ways to be found where there will be the appearance of spiritual victory. Prayer costs and the price is always paid in the prayer closet. There are no short cuts.

It is a fact, if the decision is to walk the straight and narrow way, "what if" will pop up. What if God calls me to serve among the riffraff that are smelly and obnoxious? What if this complete surrender, which includes my whole family and the Lord, calls my only child half way around this world? What if, the secret closet encounters self ambitions, and reveals material goals that are causing a halting between two opinions, and what possessions must be sold and given to the poor, cutting all ties to follow Him? What if there is a lengthy sickness, everything has been sold, and now there is no way to pay the medical bills, because I sold everything I had?

Isn't the enemy subtlety spreading the "what ifs?" There are endless "what ifs." There is one more, to be added, "what if" the prayer closet loses the battle, and the Lord knocks on the door as He did the rich man that He called a fool whose plans were to build more barns? How many believers would be found building more barns, while the prayer closet is silent because "other things" (possibly good things) have been given precedent?

The prayer of complete faith is that which will bring victory over life's "what ifs." It is the faithless "what if" that has faith killing questions; it keeps stirring the worry pot, ending in indecisiveness and causing mental anguish. Doubt can keep looming larger and larger. The enemy knows the weakest chink in our spiritual armor. Prayer will make us be aware of that fragile point as well.

Being sensitive to the spiritual world is imperative, for that is where humanity will be continually tested, but there is where you will find God. There is an innate awareness that our God has placed in all mankind that reaches far beyond man himself. Since God made human kind a spiritual being, superstition is one of the major chinks the enemy uses to circumvent entire committed faith. Does not superstition leave vital prayer wounded when it comes to winning the battle in the intangible world? The intangible world is where the greatest struggle to satisfy the deep spiritual hunger will take place.

Superstition plays an enormous part if prayer is be effective. When I was small I had heard that if a black cat ran across your path that meant bad luck. I avoided black cats. I was riding my pony, carrying a sharp ax on my way to cut wood and a black cat darted across my path, startling my pony and I found myself on the ground, on my ax. I was fully convinced about the black cat theory. The Lord had to show me years later how superstition can displace faith needed to make my prayer life competent.

If the Christian is living on the theory that good or bad luck is their guiding fortune, they are powerless in their prayer life. Luck has nothing to do with what happens to the Christian. If the Christian is fully committed to the Lord, his life is NOT in luck's hands, but in Almighty God's hands.

Daily prayer warriors have found themselves trapped in superstition or heinous sin? It is in the prayer closet that the spiritual need is met by feeding upon God's eternal manna. He, the living God, placed that eternal spirit in mankind to commune with Him. Refusing to drink the living water is to drink from life's cesspool.

When prayer is considered, it must have a basis for the faith involved in that prayer. If prayer is to be fruitful, and the living God is the source of that fruit, then, who is this God that, for centuries, mankind has dedicated their lives to Him? They must have known something about Him; something made a tremendous impact and transformed them to bury their lives in lifetime service on the fact of an intangible Being.

If prayer is to be effective, it must move beyond reason. From the book, *The Grounds of Theistic and Christian Belief* (p. 43), Fisher writes: "I hear certain proceeding for their lips. What right have I, from these purely physical phenomena, to infer the presence of intelligence behind them? What proof is there of the consciousness in the friend at my side? How can I be assured that he is not a mere automation, totally unconscious of its own movements? The warrant for the contrary inference lies in the fact, that being possessed of consciousness, and acquainted with its effects in myself, I regard like effects as evidence of the same principle in others. But in this inference I transcend the limits of sense, and physical experiment. In truth, in admitting the reality of consciousness in myself, I take a step, which no physical observation can justify. Were the brain opened to view, no microscope, were its power immeasurably augmented, could discover the least trace of it."

Human reason must stop at the door of the spirit world. Human reason deducts and analyzes, but prayer transcends reason. How can reason analyze that which cannot be put in a test tube, or placed under the world's finest microscope? Faith steps out into this world and reasons with the invisible God. (Isa. 1:18) Faith launches the believer beyond the human spirit into the Divine spirit's world. The new birth is the launching pad. Prayer must have this launching pad in operation to reach beyond oneself for meaningful prayer.

Then who and what is this intangible God? He revealed Himself in Jesus Christ. What about Him? He is omnipotent; He raised the dead; calmed the sea; all nature obeyed His commands. He is not some mere man decaying in a tomb or a molded image occupying space in some temple. But He is eternal inhabiting every inch of space in this universe, who can create worlds, and galaxies man has yet to discover. He is the One to whom unworthy man lifts voice in prayer. He knows no limit or impossibility.

Who is He? He is the only one that gives victory and assurance in the secret closet. Paul's words to the Roman church were: "There hath no temptation taken you but such as is common to man, but God is faithful, who will not suffer you to be tempted above that which ye are able; but will with the temptation also make a way to escape that ye may be able to bear it." (Rom. 10:13) Did not Job find his heavenly Father sufficient under the most trying circumstances? Does not each one of God's children know the truth of His sufficiency? Who but the Omnipotent God can sustain us when it appears everything is about to crush us? What a firm foundation on which prayer's faith can be based! Two kindred spirits, God and man commune; this intimate linkage brings accountability to the prayer warrior whose limitations need constant scrutinizing. Romans 8:28 takes on new meaning, for His Omnipotent power is always at work in the most devastating circumstance. Satan does not have a chance when the soul is locked into Calvary.

When we pray, it is gratifying to know there is an Omniscient God who knows the number of hairs on your head. He has that detailed knowledge of every human being. There is nothing about His child He doesn't know.

He, the only wise God, knows when and where the enemy will attack. Prayer prepares us through an inward buttress that will sustain our perfect relationship with the Father. If the enemy seeks to entrap us, He always makes a way to escape from anything that would be harmful to us spiritually, and if it is something like a dreaded disease, it is "Thy will be done."

Satan must work with limited knowledge and power. His armies are the great host of demons that sided with him when he rebelled against God and was cast out of heaven. He is not God, this places him in the limitations of angels, therefore, he cannot be every place at once. Because of his limitations, he must depend on his many demons to carry out his ungodly goals that labor under their flawed restrictions. Any being that is not God is subject to mistakes and failures. We can rejoice that Satan is diminished in power, but he still has angelic capacity. However, these constraints do not reduce the demons' passions to fill hell's pits with their conquests. Their fervor is fired by the consuming hatred against righteousness and everything for which the God of heaven stands.

Prayer is God's power against evil's limited forces that are still greater than man's power within himself. The difference between natural man and the believer filled with the Holy Spirit is, natural man's depravity relates to evil because his nature is evil and attracted to evil leaving the original conscience quickly conditioned for further pollution. While the believer who is filled with the Holy Spirit has had that carnal nature cleansed by the Holy Spirit, thus the believer seeks righteousness over against unrighteousness. This cleansed nature does not mean that it will remain so without an hour-by-hour vigil. That is what Paul was talking about when he said, "pray without ceasing." That is what prayer is all about, keeping the prayer channel open for the Omniscient God to correct, search out questions, and teach. Willful sin is that which disconnects man from God. Satan's arrogance challenged God, wanting to be God and he fell; Adam disobeyed God and fell. Each had a choice. Prayer does not question God's right to demand obedience, but prayer is submitting in obedience. Submissive prayer recognizes God's rights over personal rights. Prayer further understands God's righteousness stands without blemish.

When we pray, it is imperative to realize Satan operates under limitations. He is not omnipresent. It is impossible for him to be everywhere at once. This again, necessitates depending upon his demon hosts, which diminishes his effectiveness. However, these demons can attack like a swarm of killer bees.

Satan's whole success rests upon man's corrupt depravity that is continually bent toward evil. Inwardly natural man finds it easy to do evil, and difficult to be moral in the Biblical sense, because of being susceptible, even pulled to his natural evil tendency. Satan knows he has fertile ground available in which he can plant his sinister seeds. He pounces on man's self-centeredness, because here is where man's demands are. It is in this self-centered nature that the sins of the Spirit are harbored and accumulate.

If prayer is to be effective, there is no room for a power struggle. There must be a singleness of purpose, a purity of motive, and a prayerful approach to our Father with the simplicity of little children. It is God's child reaching out with a need, or praise of appreciation. Such a humble access permits attention. Every blood washed believer has the privilege of an audience with an Omnipotent, Omnipresent personal caring heavenly Father. Why and how? All because of Calvary, prayer is the means of attack, and the power to demand the enemy to release the captive. Now each believer has his own sanctuary, which cannot be invaded without his personal consent. The Father has provided the security, but He has left the keys in mankind's hands. God the Father will not force man against his personal will. To stay in that sanctuary of security, it must be, not MY will, but THY will be done through me.

For those who are praying for the willful soul, prayer targets that willfulness through the power of the Holy Spirit. Jesus reminds us that the prayer of importunity can break through stubborn obstinacy. Rebellious wills can be crushed by circumstances, when they come to their wits' end and desperation sets in. Our only weapon is the daily surrender that adds visible force to our prayer. The Holy Spirit knows the area in which to move, and prayer penetrates that area.

Our God pursues fallen man today as He did Adam and Eve who experienced His relentless pursuit that even in their fallen estate they could not deny. Man's fall did not, nor could it, destroy God's image instilled in His eternal creation. Even the devil cannot alienate the human being from God's image.

Common grace is given to all men to make it possible to respond to God's question to Adam. "Where art thou?" Within this question lies the hope of the most defiled and corrupt soul. Prayer pierces the walls of the inner structures of fallen man as nothing else can do. There is a reality of doubt that keeps appearing in the mind, when continual prayer for years has not broken through the will of that loved one. The song, speaking of heaven, "If You Could See Now," keeps running through my mind. The imagination can not begin to allow an adequate scene of the exquisite glory of that land beyond the sunset; but what if our God would pull back the veil of the gulf that separates heaven and hell, and the picture of the lost crying "Now You Can See Me, let this scene freeze itself into the mind all your earthly days." Would that change our concern and prayer life??? Would that scene put a passion in the soul that would make a more critical approach to the battle that needs to go on in the prayer closet? The will can't be forced, but God's child can be delivered from prayerlessness and prayer's absolute necessity, when gripped by the weeping and wailing of the tormented. Rise up O men of God, the hounds of heaven, and moans of hell, are reminders the prayer closet is our only weapon our limitations can use to slay the enemy, and release immortal souls from sin's death hold.

Does God's people need to pray? There is a war raging for the minds of our people, especially our precious children. In this country, we have never before encountered such hostilities against righteousness. The insidious invasion is stealing the minds of the spiritually blind. Our tax dollars are being used by the treacherous depraved in our educational system who have betrayed their trust and replaced Christianity with their humanistic religion, dumping it into innocent minds before the students are mature enough to evaluate it. Once the mind is captured, it will not be long before the heart is conquered.

How can we possibly defeat such a sweeping foe? How about having a prayer fortress that bombards heaven, who alone has the weaponry to uproot the enemy and defeat him at his own game? This prayer urgency cannot wait. The liberal humanists control now what seems to be all segments of our society? It started with the motto, "better red, than dead." It was recently reported there are thousands of atheistic Marxists holding professorships in our colleges and universities indoctrinating young pliable minds, hiding behind their Ph.D.'s. This degree can intimidate any opposing thought. They hold the welfare of the student in their hands.

A young lady came from a Christian home that unwittingly sent her to a state university. Now she tells her parents she is an atheist. She is teaching in the public school. The atheistic ideology won; now her parents live with the bitter regret of trusting the university with their precious daughter. Ungodly betrayal is on hands of all those who had a part in this brainwashing. How many thousands of Christian parents can relate a similar story. Where were the parents when the decision was made about where they were going to send their child for an education that they were paying for?

Who is responsible for these tragedies that these universities have placed on the Christian's doorstep? It would not be realistic to point the guilty finger only at the educational system, but much of this travesty must be the culpability of the church and particularly the pulpits. If the pulpits of America had been true to proclaiming God's Word under the anointing of the Holy Spirit most of what has morally happened would have been annihilated before it got a foothold. But when prayer meetings are no longer needed, the spiritual life seeps away, and the church becomes no more than a meeting place where socializing becomes the main reason for the church to exist. The prayer meeting has long since departed. A pastor said: "I abandoned my prayer meeting long ago." "How did your church officers like that?" "Oh, they did not find out for more than a year." (Church Business)

PRAYER IS THE ONLY EFFECTIVE WEAPON THE CHRISTIAN HAS!

Action without prayer power behind the action leaves only small waves that fade quickly. God anointed prayer creates a lasting stamp on any proceeding. Yet, our greatest ammunition against our spiritual enemy is useless because of prayerlessness.

There is a war raging that we cannot avoid which has engulfed the minds of our society. In our nation, we have never before encountered such hostilities against Righteousness. The humanist's insidious invasion is stealing the minds, thus the hearts of our children. These captives are brain washed victims entrapped in their innocent years, when unable to evaluate truth.

This is secular totalitarianism, which demands by force indoctrination, if necessary, which includes casting aside vital Christian Faith, and any moral obligation to God. Which means, becoming subordinate to their political correct agenda. Anything less will bring the heavy hammer of the intellectual elite down on the misfit. This type of secular humanism attempts to make history without God. They first must revamp our forefather's history that is the foundation of our great nation.

The war will continue as long as there is a remnant of God loving souls who fear nothing but God's wrath. In Dietrich Bonhoeffer's book, The Cost of Discipleship, he said: "When Christ calls a man, he bids him come and die." Only the Lord Himself knows how many or few faithful followers there are that are willing to hear His call to "come and die." Can it be imagined, these "called ones" would be found among the prayerless? Prayer demands the "come and die" to complete dedication. A Cross must be at the heart of prayer. The half-hearted will not be found in the inner sanctum pleading the father's cause, or naming the lost hopeless souls that need to be rescued.

This spiritual war meets the enemy in the prayer closet. The spiritual undergirding received in that closet will be needed to combat the humanistic political correctness that is in the real world, such as: many influential pulpits of our old line denominations, the morally promiscuous values of the NEA, or the likes of ACLU advocating the alienation of any sense of the living God in our social structure. Are the Christians helpless, without adequate funds, lacking influential power to turn the tide around, and buried under a liberal media that uses its dominance and intensity to brainwash the average person's mind? As society's situation is evaluated from God's point of view, without material weapons, are we hopeless, without any certainty to match the real world which we are forced to inhabit? Is God going to rain fire from heaven and liberate us from all the bleeding in this world, or has the Lord given us the tool to master the outrageous iniquity that is shoveled in our path? What about the prayer that moves mountains! O, but there is a cross that has splinters, it draws blood, and hatred, and that may lead to unknown areas that are infested with untouchables. Prayer is our only ammunition that will be sufficient to meet anything the devil's gang can envision. The impact depends upon whether fasting and praying emanates from the prayer closet. Our God gives the weapon needed, and everything is banking on how it is used, how often, and whether it is well oiled, or whether for the lack of use, rust has gathered. Or is prayer's power questioned and there is no expectation because it has become no more than a routine, without scriptural possibilities?

A prayerful life gives courage to stand for Righteousness and to be silent when words would not have our Father's approval. Prayer establishes the divinely driven conscience, and liberates from the fear of man. Our adversity fears the prayers of the Saint, but delights in the prayerlessness of the professors of Christianity. Holy Spirit anointed prayer is the power behind single-minded obedience, and reassures self-confidence. Prayer places God given value on life that declares boldness not found in human limitations. Prayer dares to pray for those who despitefully use you, or to go the extra mile, or gracefully turn the other cheek.

Dietreck Bonhoeffer, a German pastor, whose was hung by Hitler because of his outspoken opposition to his cold-blooded villainous acts against humanity said: (I copied the words and not the source, but I think these words are worthy for each one to meditate), "First, they came after the Jews. I didn't raise my voice. Second, they came after the Professors, and others who refused to join their camp. I didn't dissent. Third, they came after the Catholics. Again, I didn't protest. Fourth, they came after me, and there was no one left to object." He was left to stand alone in the face of certain death.

No angel swept out of the sky to rescue him, therefore, it would have been much easier to recant His faith's risk, that had a price. The cost was his life. It is necessary to have something far greater than anything in this life on which to cling in order to find that inner rest needed in those critical days of waiting for the inevitable. His poems reveal his hours of prayer. Prayer is the sustainer, the keeper, the provider, the nourisher in life's darkest hours. The fiber of the soul is ripped open, naked, and the real man is unfolded. The living communication with the living God is the catalyst that takes man beyond himself to be God's suffering servant.

The hopeless and prayerlessness are much easier to conquer, for they are anchored to this world, and this world has very little to offer when a suffering cross comes knocking at the door. There is no painless Biblical Christianity. In God's holy walk, there is no escape from a personal cross, to maintain that walk will require fasting and prayer. Man made ideology will not meet the demands of a restless heart, especially in life's devastating hours.

A fearful church has taken its seat in the grandstand–observing combatants in the arena. The church refuses to dirty its hands in the real world, while the few "wholly committed" struggle against overwhelming odds. In fact, the grandstanders can enjoy these "extremists" being mugged by unbelievers, and their lukewarm liberal allies. Because of prayerlessness, the church seeks a comfort zone that avoids conflict. The modern church has no desire to have a confrontation with the devil's massive might. Why? Too many of its obstructionists and outright adversaries are members, and too often are the controlling factor in the church. If the pulpit would have the anointing of the Holy Spirit, this anointed preaching would uncover the snake pit. This scriptural preaching needs to be circumvented if war is to be evaded, and false peace is retained. But most pulpits fear man more than God.

Again why, does the church reveal this yellow streak and want no part of the price that must be paid to defy "the Goliaths" that attack the Lord's army? Spiritual effectiveness is locked in the prayer closet. Convincing reality rests in the spiritual condition of the average church, and the overwhelming mayhem that has invaded our families and culture. The average church would rather be "organizers" rather than " agonizers." The "organizers" have little opposition, and demand little self-denial. While the "agonizers" feel the weight of the lost and the burden of the praying cross.

Fasting and praying takes time, and sacrifice, which includes energy.

Where are the Daniels that already know the results of their prayer before it happens? Too many are terrified with the thought of the hungry man-eating lions coming dashing out of their cages, eager to rip into shreds the closest victim. These lions are man-eaters. Did Daniel seek a way to escape? His God implanted convictions that refused to wither. From where did that type of conviction come? Can anyone deny that his faithful prayer life was his cornerstone of strength and assurance?

The home is bombarded with a sickening and relentless attack with godless ideology that is imbedded in the mind, which is unbearable for those who are spiritually weak and unable to ward off the daily attack of evil forces. For those who pray so little and without passion are sapped of strength, and fall prey to the abusive onslaught, leaving mental and emotional scars that can hinder life long spiritual growth. Too many professing Christians have surrendered their Godly responsibility because they are overwhelmed by the continual hassle. Life has become exhausting. The wear and tear on the already shattered nerves makes it easier to concede the spiritual area of their lives to try and lessen the contention in other areas. But the demands keep increasing when spiritual authority is abandoned. What was thought to alleviate this intense stress only enhanced the frustration! The burden progressively inflates and proliferates a bloated twisted perspective that will backfire in all other areas of personal responsibilities.

Only the Lord knows the number of Christians that struggle under this miserable relationship with the Lord. The best effort soon withers and shrivels into another spiritual defeat. The answer is not to be mired in regretful despair, but to enter the secret closet and stay there until heaven breaks in upon the barren soul. This answer may demand a prayerful waiting that involves deep soul searching as to the contract that needs to be made with the Lord. Somewhere along the line backsliding or willful sin has broken the vows that were taken when He became the needed Savior!

Is it possible to find one situation where the problem was solved by running away from it? Yet this is an everyday experience in all too many people's lives. There is the marriage problem that has magnified and now is a source of heated contention. Getting away from the problem isn't too difficult, just get a divorce, or someone else may feel the problem can be resolved by packing a few clothes and walking out the door without returning. But the marriage covenant is broken. Becoming an escapee didn't save the marriage, hearts are broken, children's lives are decimated and scars will be carried into their marriage. What a difference it would have been, if the people involved would have dropped to their knees and asked the Lord to give wisdom and grace to find the God-approved answer. Heated tempers and unwillingness to forgive cannot have prayer in the equation; no prayerless heart has any resolve. Prayer is the spiritual salve that will heal the deepest wounds.

The chaos in the home breeds contempt in the child, which results in an antisocial behavior. This conduct is carried with the child when attending school, in the home, on the streets, venting his antiauthority venom until some power has to bring that animosity under control. If that child at an early age was taught that ultimate authority rests with his Heavenly Father at the family's family altar where study and prayer were openly declared, would the anger and rebellion have grown to be open hostility against honoring father and mother? It is very difficult to be disobedient to dad and mother who just prayed for him, and for whom the child prayed. Few realize how prayer can change the atmosphere of the home. Look at what has happened to our schools since prayer has been removed. Prayer recognizes God to be the God of final authority.

The Christian home too often reeks with discontentment. The Apostle Paul talks about being content in whatever place the Lord places His child. But the younger generation wants to have everything now, the same things mother and dad have after fifty years of marriage, and a lifetime of working and saving. In order to have those material things, the young people will see it, want it, and get it, without thought of how the new home, cars, furniture, insurance expenses are going to fit into their budget. Then, serious financial problems become a source of dissension. Bill collectors are calling, knocking on the door, and threats of repossession charge the home's atmosphere. Neither prayer nor God was taken into the decision process, just what self wants.

While working in a camp meeting in northeastern New York State, newspaper headlines told the bitter account of great numbers of young married couples who were declaring bankruptcy. Their homes were listed in the hundreds of thousands; big cars and elaborate furnishings were returned to the banks. It was impossible to make the payments in a slowed down economy. Effort and money had been poured into a bottomless pit, and the self-centered shame and reproach will linger in their lives, and in the lives of their children. Could this embarrassment have been eliminated if the prayer closet would have been visited daily? Would the Lord have directed their lifestyle to be more frugal, and to live within their means? Would prayer have brought a sense of economical reality? Has not our Heavenly Father given us direction when prayerfully sought? A Godly prayerful heart does not need to appear to be something more than we can afford, but will give contentment with debtless living. . . Christians' discontentment is caught in the clutches of society's measuring stick for success, not the Biblical standards, but rather calculated by the neighborhood standards, the make of the cars in the driveway, the size of the lot and its location, and by the magnificent home. Success depends upon winning the war of self-gratification, but in Godly contentment that prayerfully takes a modest, unpretentious house whose payments are affordable on the present income, and allows time for family to interact with one another.

How can that self-gratification ego become that humble reasonable self-respected soul whose self-esteem does not need the appeasement and the affluent appearance to be impressive? By knowing his worth that is found in the Lord Jesus and His redemption which is enhanced by a constant prayer life that has an intimate relationship with God the Father that enriches life and gives quality of life to the person. Prayerful contentment makes life have purposeful meaning. This resolved needs to be in the center of God's will, but this cannot become reality without a vital prayer life.

ELIJAH DEFINES THE CHALLENGE!

Elijah, a lowly man, his haunts were no more than temporary resident, isolated, unaffected by society, God oriented and God driven, without prestige prosperity or status. Without fear, he confronts kings. Israel's three and half years' drought was coming to its climatic end and Mount Carmel has been chosen to be the place where the battle between God and Baal defy one another. Ahab has been looking for Elijah, "the troubler of Israel" for these years. Elijah notifies Ahab where he could be found, and requests him to bring all of Baal's priests.

The scene in 1 Kings, the 18th chapter is so familiar, its description has been played over and over in the minds of most Christians. The sacrifices are ready to be consumed by the fire from heaven, Baal's prophets are pleading, cutting themselves for hours, but no fire. Elijah repairs the altar, has them soak the wood and sacrifice with water three times. The faith of Elijah is without measure, and with pure confidence. Most of us would have chosen dry wood for a quick fire. But the setting is to consider the difference between God and Baal, and if Elijah's prayer of faith will bring heaven's fire down to consume the sacrifice. Just sixty-four words, no polished or elegant words: "Lord God of Abraham, Isaac, and of Israel, let it be known this day that thou art God in Israel, and that I am thy servant, and that I have done all these things at thy word. Hear me, O Lord, hear me, that this people may know that thou art the Lord God, and that thou has turned their heart back again." (1 Kings 18:36&37) AND THE FIRE CAME! Why long prayers, when short faith believing prayers do the job?

Is there even a glimmer of fear of failure? What Elijah is praying, " I have done all these things at thy word." He didn't set the stage to show what he could do, but what God would do through the prayer of a faithful servant who wants God to have the glory. He was not praying in some secret closet, multitudes were looking on. He has placed his head on the block.

This brings us back to our prayer life. Wow! Where is the Elijah of today, who will face the Humanist, homosexual, the ACLU, the power structure of our society, the intelligentsia, the Hollywood perverseness, the American Way, which are seeking to replace our God with their gods, and doing it. Will our prayer life "turn their heart back again?" Elijah prayer brought the fire down and the people said: "the Lord, He is God, the Lord, He is God." (1 Kings 18:39) Under Ahab and Jezebel, Israel was buried in every kind of corruption imaginable. The past administration has taken America down that same road. We wallow in our cesspools of iniquity. Faithful prayer can bring America back again, but where do we find those who will pay that kind of price by putting their lives on the line?

Since we cannot match the financial power structure, nor the media's ability to saturate society with its socialized one world propaganda, our only claim to adequate victory is the channel Calvary gave, holy anointed prayer. God's enemy has mandated territory that should belong to God. The prayer warrior claims that which is his Father's.

God's ownership needs to include the pulpits, the family, and especially our children and what is influencing them. Our schools are God's territory and if need be, we must conduct a people's march around our schools, placing a prayer circle about them, giving a shout that assures victory. He is the same God that crumbled Jericho's walls.

Will coming generations rise up at the judgment, pointing their fingers in our faces with the charge, all spiritual and Biblical standards were gone when they arrived. There was no spiritual foundation on which to build. The indictment will be against God's people's prayerlessness. The incrimination will reveal a weak spiritual prayer depth that would have restricted the assault.

Not only did Satan successfully deceive Adam and Eve, but also the review of history will reveal how his deception has made shambles of kings and kingdoms. This night of desperation was settled when God personally came through Mary, the virgin. By this time Satan's confidence had grown to the extent that he dared to tempt God. It was Jesus, the very God, who opened the gentile's door, so all humanity would know the way that would crush Satan's insidious onslaught. Our Lord spent forty days fasting and praying. His physical nature needed what prayer can give. Why, because He knew what would sustain His human nature. Fasting and prayer was an absolute necessity if He was to lay His life on the line for Truth and open the door to rescue lost mankind. His example was to establish a pattern for living a life of personal spiritual victory. What was the preparation, prayer and fasting? Prayer and fasting is our basic weapon for successful conquest, yet it is so seldom used. The average prayer will be five minutes or less, while fasting is probably denying a sweet. Such lack of spiritual discernment and willful purpose leaves the spiritual condition at a place where it will self-destruct.

If it were necessary for our Lord to spend forty days fasting and praying, how much more is our praying needed to glorify God, if the enemy of the soul is going to be defeated daily? How many spiritual battles will be lost before the weapon (fasting and prayer) God has given will be used to be the means for triumphal victory?

Think of our children; will we ever have another opportunity to engage in the fasting and prayer, the decider, the neglect will prevent our children's spiritual maturity while we busy ourselves with lesser matters. Who can imagine the wails that will shatter the walls of the eternally doomed?

It is frightening but can be rewarding to know that one day we will face our prayer record. Our God knows no defeats. He wants His children to experience that same victory. Calvary was His way of assuring personal victory over sin, death and hell.

Paul said: "I am crucified with Christ nevertheless I live; yet not I, but Christ liveth in me; and the life, which I now live in the flesh, I live by the faith of the Son of God, who loved me, and gave Himself for me." (Gal. 2:20)

Meaningful prayer carries with it the willingness to permit self to be crucified. Prayer's Life is living in Christ. Christ inhabits the crucified soul that is dead to the flesh, and its appetites. Prayer is the Divine life that is my life, the soul of my soul. Prayer breathes the atmosphere of God; inspires lofty ideals; is representative of my assurance to a title to my home that my heavenly Father has deeded to my continual obedience. Prayer grapples with the impossible; seeks to model the Divine; is all in all to those who live the crucified life. Meaningful prayer is allowing the Lord God to live and work through the channel of the inner being; asking the Father to conduct His Grace through the pure inner passageway He has given, in whatever avenue He chooses.

Striving prayer is feeling-acquiring Grace needed for personal spiritual victory and blessings belonging to personal persistent to complete and full surrender that allows God to do what needs to be done. This striving praying stresses personal effort, personal struggle, diligent driving, extra exertion, laborious duty, or whatever the cost. Is not striving prayer what much of our praying is when the burden is to heavy to carry? All God wants is a clean conduit through which His Grace can flow without sin's interruption to do what needs to be done.

If there is any wrestling to be done, it needs to be in combat with the powers of darkness, not with the Helper who wants the enemy defeated more than those who seek to get the Lord to act on the situation. Too much wrestling with God comes from the lack of willingness to submit to God's will. Prayer can become a crusade to get God to see things self's way. God's whole plan is always projected with eternity in mind, while our foresight rest in the immediate.

A. W. Tozer says: "Prayer is no substitute for obedience." (*Of God and Men*, p. 50) How much of our striving in prayer has been substituting prayer for obedience? To avoid obedience and inject words of self-interest is an insult to the very God to which we appeal. Many pray for revival or some loved one, knowing they are not living the surrendered crucified life, and then wonder why the self willed prayer is amiss.

Hopefully this rather lengthy quote from Geraldine Taylor's book, *The Biography of Hudson Taylor*, published by Moody Press, will give insight to a struggling prayer life.

"The last month or so has been, perhaps, the happiest period of my life: and I long to tell you a little about what the Lord has done for my soul. I do not know how far I may be able to make myself intelligible about it, for there is nothing new or strange or wonderful, and yet, all is new!"

"Perhaps to make myself clear I should go back a little. Well, my mind has been greatly exercised for six or eight months past, feeling the need personally, and for our Mission, of more holiness, life, power in our souls. But personal need stood first and was the greatest. I felt the ingratitude, the danger, and the sin, of not living nearer to God. I prayed, agonized, fasted, strove, made resolutions, read the Word more diligently, sought more time for retirement and meditation, but all was without effect. Every day, almost every hour, the consciousness of sin oppressed me.

I began the with prayer, determined not to take my eyes away from the Lord for a moment; but pressure of duties, sometimes very trying, and constant interruptions apt to be so wearing, often caused me to forget him. Then one's nerves get so fretted in this climate that temptations to irritability, hard thoughts, and sometimes-unkind words are all the more difficult to control. Each day brought its register of sin and failure, of lack of power.

I hated myself. I hated my sin, and yet gained no strength against it. I felt I was a child of God; his Spirit in my heart would cry, in spite of all, Abba, Father; but to rise to my privileges as his child was utterly powerless. I thought that holiness, practical holiness, was to be attained gradually by a diligent use of the means of Grace. It seemed there was nothing so much to be desired in this world, nothing so much needed. But so far from in any measure attaining it, the more I pursued and strove after it the more it eluded my grasp; and I began to think that, perhaps to make heaven the sweeter, God would not give it down here.

I do not think I was striving to attain it in my own strength. I knew I was powerless and told the Lord so, asking him to give me help and strength; and sometimes I almost believed he would keep and uphold me. Do not get the impression that this was the daily experience of all those long months. But it was a too frequent state of soul, that toward which I was tending and which almost ended in despair. And yet, never did Christ seem more precious, a Savior who could and would save such a sinner! Sometimes there were seasons not only of peace but also of joy in the Lord. But they were transitory.

I felt assured that there was in Christ all I needed, but the practical question was how to get it out. He was rich, truly, but I was poor; he was strong, but I weak. I knew full well that there was in the root, the stem, an abundant fatness; but how to get it into my puny little branch was the question. I saw that faith was the only prerequisite, was the hand to lay hold on Christ's fullness and make it my own.

But I had not this faith. I strove for it, but it would not come; tried to exercise it, but in vain. Unbelief was felt, the damning sin of the world, yet I indulged in it. I prayed for faith, but it came not. What was I to do? When my agony of soul was at its height, a sentence in a letter from John McCarthy (in Hangehow) was used to remove the scales from my eyes, and the Spirit of God revealed the truth of our oneness with Jesus as I had never known before. McCarthy, who had been much exercised by the same sense of failure, but saw the light before I did, wrote: " But how to get faith strengthened? Not by striving after faith, but by resting in the Faithful One."

Reading those words, I saw it all! "If we believe not, he abideth faithful." I looked to Jesus and saw (and oh, how joy flowed!) that he had said, " I will never leave you." "Ah, there is rest!" I thought, "I have striven in vain to rest in him, I strive no more. For has he not promised to abide with me, never to leave, never to fail me!"

"But this was not all he showed, nor one-half. As I thought of the vine and the branches, what light the blessed Spirit poured directly into my soul! How great seemed my mistake in having wished to get the sap, the fullness out of Him? It was evident not only that Jesus would never leave me, but also that I was a member of his body his flesh and his bones. The vine is not the root merely, but all root, stem, branches, twigs, leaves, flowers, and fruit. And Jesus is not only that, he is soil and sunshine, air and showers, and ten thousand times more than we have ever dreamed wished for or needed. Oh, the joy of seeing this truth!

The sweetest part, if one may speak of one part being sweeter than another, is the rest which full identification with Christ brings. No longer is there need to be anxious about anything; for he, I know, is able to carry out his will, and his will is mine. It makes no matter where he places me, for in the easiest positions he must give me his Grace, and in the most difficult his Grace is sufficient.

So if God places me in great perplexity, must he not give me much guidance; in positions of great difficulty, much Grace; in circumstances of great pressure and trial, much strength? No fear that his resources will be unequal to the emergency! And his resources are mine, for he is mine, and is with me and dwells in me. All this springs from the believer's oneness with Christ. And since Christ has thus dwelt in my heart by faith, how happy I have been! If only I could tell you, instead of writing about it.

I am no better than before (may I not say that in a sense I do not wish to be, nor am I striving to be); but I am dead and buried with Christ, and risen too and ascended; and now Christ lives in me, and "the life which I now live in the flesh I live by the faith of the Son of God, who loved me, and gave himself for me." I now believe I am dead to sin. God reckons me so, and tells me to reckon myself so. He knows best. All past experience may have shown that it was not so; but I dare not say it is not so now, when he says it is, and that old things have passed away.

I am as capable of sinning as ever, but Christ is realized as present as never before. And further walking more in the light, my conscience has been more tender. Sin has been instantly seen, confessed, pardoned; and peace and joy (with humility) instantly restored; with one exception, when for several hours peace and joy did not return from want, as I had to learn, of full confession, and from some attempt to justify self.

Faith, I now see, is "the substance of things hoped for," and not mere shadow. It is not less than sight, but more. Sight only shows the outward forms of things; faith gives the substance. You can rest on substance, feed on substance. Christ dwelling in the heart by faith (That is, his word of promise credited) is power indeed, is life indeed.

May God give you to lay hold on these blessed truths! We should not look upon this experience, these truths, as for the few. They are the birthright of every child of God, and no one can dispense with them without dishonor to our Lord. The only power for deliverance from sin or for true service is Christ.

Only the Lord knows the multitude of Christians who have, or are now struggling under personal striving rather than resting in the Crucified life. I would dare to say, too many linger in the struggle of self effort. I have been there and now see the folly of straining, by trying to be more holy. There is no such thing as being more holy. The scripture says; "Be ye holy." Prayer will never make the soul more holy, nor will fasting. It is only being crucified with Christ, where there is a complete sell out, utter and whole surrender to His will, where the Lord is absolute Lord of all of life, and resting upon that daily Truth. Paul said it: "I die daily." It is a moment-by-moment, surrounding self and its constant confronting personal self will.

Certainly prayer and fasting has a large portion in the crucified life, which fights futility when the rest found in the crucified is ignored, and considered to be nonsensical.

Does resting the crucified life mean a passive apathetic resigning to what will be, will be? Is the crucified life a dormant docile indifference? How did Paul face the crucified life? 2 Corinthians 11:21-28 he speaks of his suffering stripes from beatings, the stoning, the perils that constantly confronted him. He forced the battle. The never ceasing war was his daily trial. Paul was anything but passive, but through every brutal abuse there was a rest in the crucified life.

The crucified life makes prayer synonymous with the Cross bearer.

PAUL INDUCES THE BELIEVER TO A MORE EXCELLENT WAY!

Purposeful prayer demands to know God's excellence that continually enlarges the soul's capacity allowing individual capacity to engulf all that is possible of God's fullness. Paul gives the affirmative to covet God's gifts (1 Cor. 12:31). Then to what does this type of covetousness lead? What happens when we long for, or aspire after more understanding of God's depth? This craving for God's excellence becomes an ache, a hunger and thirst for God's best. There is a seeking that which deepens by the day until it will become an obsession, a fixed soul preoccupied with a pursuit that will mandate exploring all God is, and a prayer that manifests an agony that uncovers a self will that must die the horrible death of self being crucified. Thus requiring an ultimatum to the personal will to surrender unconditionally to God's will. This earnest passionate prayer will be rewarded.

Personal surrender carries a daily reminder that God's best gift mandates a thorough examination if the prayer channel is to remain vigorous and effective. Keeping the prayer artery clear takes willful dedication. There are no short cuts. Just as an athlete that wants to succeed must search out every weakness and deal with it if he is determined to be the best. Whatever may obstruct an effective prayer life must be defeated by a submissive will and the cleansing power of the Holy Spirit if the spiritual war is to be won.

A Chinese doctor was translating for a missionary. The doctor was a large woman with a big heart of love. In the midst of the message, the Holy Spirit brought conviction to the doctor's heart. The doctor stopped the missionary and confessed to the nurses who worked under her supervision, the sin of frequently losing her temper. The doctor had love but had not controlled of her temper.

It is certain, a competent prayer life cannot have these inner barriers that may be unknown to others, such as, bitterness, jealousy, unforgiveness, rebellion, or revenge (the sins of the spirit). These are blockers that prayer cannot get over or through (Psa. 66:18-20).

Since we are made in the image of God, the soul demands excellence and that source is only found in the Godhead. Prayer is our connection, and this connection stipulates a holy heart and life.

A mother's crushed and fractured heart has the contents that move the heavenly Father's love and concern to action. Hannah's prayer opened the grievous fountain that was exploding within. Allow her words to speak of her disquiet spirit: "and she was in bitterness of soul, and prayed unto the Lord and wept sore." (I Sam. 1:10) These piercing words carry a suffocating dying spirit that refused to die spiritually. She had come to the temple to bring her complaint before the Lord. It was more than an appeal, but uncovered remorse that the soul could no longer contain. She carried a disgrace that was not of her choosing. In the age in which she lived, the humiliation and shame of infertility was unbearable. Her society would not accept an infertile, unproductive woman whose major responsibility was to produce children.

This burden increased by the year. Hannah was held in contempt, especially by the other women. Her sorrow and battered spirit brought her to utter surrender to God's entire will. The perfect position our God so desires. Serious intention demands attention. Her position in that culture was at best, dishonorable.

It was in this state of wretchedness, that Hannah vowed a vow with Almighty God. In fact, her agony was so distressful that Eli accused her of being drunk. Her response was: "I have poured out my soul before the Lord." (1 Sam. 1:15) The words, "poured out," stare at the reader. It is the emptying out of all the content within. It is what Jesus did on the Cross, He drained himself of His lifeblood. If when God "pours out" His wrath; meaning to shedding of the blood of the Saints; or the good Samaritan pouring oil into the wounds of the one who was beaten and robbed; or the "pouring out" of the Holy Spirit on the day of Pentecost. Hannah was "pouring out" all that unworthiness that had built up across the years. This is prayer at its best as far as God is concerned. Prayer is emptying all, so our God can fill all with His will and purpose. Prayer must be united with Deity, and Deity cannot question this type of submission and faith.

There appears to be more to this prayer than just wanting to remove the shame that infertility incurred. For years she had prayed and agonized over this defaming handicap. Could it be that all those years, and all those prayers, that she wanted this child just to eliminate this unfruitful stigma, but that now she had come with an utterly crushed and repentant heart and mind, completely submitted to God's whole will. Her prayer was now equated with everything in the light of God's purpose, and not her will. Her vow was so comprehensive and thorough that when the child was weaned, she personally took him from her arms to the temple never expecting him to return to the home permanently. His dedication was more than just laying hands on him, but was a lifelong commitment. This surrendered son walked before kings, confronting their sins; blessings their obedience, using all achievements to glorify his Lord. The Prayer of this dedicated mother has come down through history to be a pattern for all mothers.

God honoring prayer terminates all self-will and willful ambitions that could be dissipating the moral fiber of the soul. There are multitudes of reasons these circumstances cause prayers to remain unanswered. The rationale will vary with each individual. One person has a problem with willfulness, which leads to disobedience that defies the light that the Lord gives. Another harbors a secret sin that refuses to give the Lord His rightful place. Another cause can be plain indifferences, making God's will a trifling matter. But the most common of all causes is the sin of omission. But whatever the source, the results will always remain, asking and receiving not as long as the purpose is to exert personal will against God's will.

ANSWERED PRAYER IS TO GLORIFY GOD.

Jeremiah 28:13 clearly explains the course prayer needs to take: "And ye shall seek me, and find me, when ye shall search for me with all your heart." Anything less than the surrender of the whole heart, will enhance greater spiritual disappointment. James 4:3 says it this way: "ye ask and receive not, because ye ask amiss that ye may consume it upon your lusts."

After honest personal searching and a pure motive is found, the heart will be free, and then the prayerful seeker will find the delight of our God's attentive ear. It is necessary to study the content of our prayers. Are these prayers self-centered? Are these prayers so designed to make us look better in the eyes of other Believers? Is the intent to glorify our Lord?

A lady prays for her husband's salvation, but her motive could be that he would treat her more kindly, and go to church with her like some of the other women's husbands do. The motive was not that he was lost and would be forever if he did not come to Christ. Should not her prayers visualize her dear husband walking consistently with God, casting Godly influence on all the lives he touches?

Many pray for their children not because they are lost, and need the Savior to transform them into new creatures in Christ, but because the children or the individual child is giving the parents too much trouble. The prayer concern is focused on stopping the fighting; ending the rebellion; and bringing some peace to the home. There is nothing wrong with that, but their prayers have avoided the root problem; the child's needs to know personally the Savior. The parents have centered on what they want and not on the basic need, which is imperative if the home's problem is to be solved.

Asking amiss is at the heart of unanswered prayer. There are things that are important and then there things that are imperative. Would God consider the imperative before the important? Our problem is, we make our problems mandatory, while God's purpose and will for all mankind is downgraded to another level. With the pressure of the moment, it is so easy to get everything in reverse.

Prayer makes clear the direction of the soul's intent. Righteous, truthful prayer guides the soul into heavenly portals and opens the Father's heart. Abraham stood before the Lord revealing the concern of his heart and said: "...wilt Thou also destroy the righteous with the wicked. Shall the judge of all the earth do right?" (Gen. 18:23) Because of the filthy moral stench that saturated Sodom and Gomorrah, the Lord God could no longer condone its depth of iniquity. It appeared God saw no sign of them repenting, and rebellion had taken them down the road of no return. There comes a time when the long suffering of God will end. That time had come and the decision was to utterly destroy all the people and everything in cities. When God's decision was made known to Abraham, terror struck his heart that would include Lot and his family. He must intercede in their behalf. The horrible shock that Lot's whole family would be annihilated made Abraham approach God with his proposition. If are fifty righteous, would a righteous God destroy all the inhabitants? Did he think that Lot's family, which had married into the city's gentility and idols, would have at least fifty who had not been sucked into that vile culture? But when his proposition gets down to five, there were not five, only four and God's angels had to pull them out. God listened to Abraham's plea, but iniquity so abounded that God would not withhold judgment. The scripture says: "the Lord went His way." (Gen. 18:33) and "Abraham returned to his place." Sodom and Gomorrah had sealed their fate for eternity.

How is Sodom and Gomorrah related to prayer? Did Abraham get concerned too late? If he had interceded early, would that tragedy have taken place? Are personal loved ones living in Sodom and Gomorrah now? How much prayer is bombarding heaven, knowing unless delivered from that hell, it is but a step into eternal hell, which can approach quickly and without warning, as in Lot's case. Who can afford to allow their concerned prayers to arrive too late? Is the prayer closet unoccupied while loved ones are bound and chained to today's infamy culture? Imagine what the meeting will be like at the judgment. What can justify the empty prayer closet, when facing loved ones at the judgment and their horrifying stares meet ours? The day of Grace had passed. Who can grasp the depth of being lost forever!

Sarah laughed at the suggestion that she would bear a child in her old age. It must have made God wonder about who she thought God was, so He said to Abraham: "is there anything too hard for the Lord?" (Gen. 18:14) Does that laugh reveal Sarah's true faith? What kind of Deity is she worshiping? Does the mention of the inconceivable and thought of the impossible uncover the type of Deity worshiped? Is the reason most believers pray so little, because their God is so small there is no logical purpose to take prayer seriously? Have not many professing Christians done quite well without praying too much? Do not their assets prove it?

What does our concept have to do with prayer? Everything! The basic ingredient of prayer is faith. A small god, results in ineffectual faith; an Omnipotent God permits faith to be larger than human capacity, and a faith to grasp God's endless resources to accomplish the impossible. The prayer of pure faith claims who God is, and how His unlimitedness reveals His true self. Is it not imperative that each believer seriously considers who he or she is worshiping? If God is not personal, that indwelling Being that longs to drive every motive, then life's motives are compelled by personal ambitions, and man becomes his own god.

If faith entertains a limited god, prayer will definitely be diminished likewise, and will have little affect on every day living. How many professing Christians have solemnly considered the God they worship and His tremendous dimensions of proficiency? He fills this universe with His presence, no matter how far away, the furthermost star, His presence is there. In a moment, He could make all the waters of the earth disappear; in that moment, at His choosing He could shut down the thermostat on the sun and freeze everything or turn the thermostat up and burn the earth into a crisp ball.

The prayer of faith contains an Infinite God who has no limits, and can remove mountains that multitude of Christians face daily. Allow the pondering mind to fully grapple with the kind of capacity our eternal God has and the prayer life will respond to the unachieveable as far as human potential, believing all things are possible through the price paid on the Cross. Prayer can channel the heart, mind and soul into that kind of Omnipotence. Too often, like Sarah, it is easy to laugh when God suggests the impossible, and when that is the case, the limitations of prayerful faith are revealed.

" Is anything too hard for the Lord?" Prayer will be meaningless if our faith limits God. Prayer can only expect what faith allows.

PRAYER APPROVES AND ACKNOWLEDGES GOD'S HOLINESS.

Holiness is the foundation of all piety and character. Since God is holy, can He be satisfied with anything less than a holy people? Can any other consideration be acceptable if He calls His people to be like Himself? Elijah's power and character were of such a nature, that he could contact the Father of righteousness and holiness and get immediate results. Elijah's simple prayer was a total faith venture beyond human reason. Did his prayer put God on the spot, and did God view this man's will as an affront to His majesty? Here was a mere mortal daring to challenge Omnipotence. Was this situation God's will or wasn't it? Would God act beyond His will just to satisfy this man that boasted about what God would do precisely what he had asked? Did he wonder if God would present Himself as the only true God? Or was faith so certain, that these questions never crossed his mind?

How often has God's child been placed in a situation where faith had to take prayer beyond the reasonable? Prayer and faith must always work together if the cost is to be paid. However, both must be under the Holy Spirit's discipline, and daily living must match holy obedience. Prayer requires utter surrender to God's perfect will that has one purpose, that whatever happens the dilemma must glorify the only true God. God and redeemed man are welded together for one determination to exalt, praise and honor man's Creator. Everything about God's child's prayer life, is not about himself, but about emulating the Christ who steps out of glory to become the willing and only sacrifice to rescue lost man.

Prayer must have a resolve that engulfs the whole heart, mind, will and soul. Man's approach to God in the midst of life's spiritual battle is rooted and grounded in a heart and will that would gladly take the consequences of the results. Jonathan Edwards said, "I resolved never to do anything which I would be afraid to do if it were the last hour of my life." So I, like Daniel, am so resolved. Can prayer be expected to be answered otherwise? Do I then have to face the reality of this test, certainly? Our God has no favorites.

THE VEIL OF MOTIVE SECRECY THAT COVERS THE REAL PERSON, WILL RESTRICT THE RESULTS OF PRAYER AND ITS POTENTIAL.

Too many professing Christians' prayers are used to get, rather than the will to give and be obedient to His will. Paul called this type of living a concealment that seeks to cover the existent of an inner contradiction that is an embarrassment to God and self. Paul talks about this veil that obscures the spiritual reality by saying: "but their minds were blinded; for unto this day remains the same veil untaken away in the reading of the Old Testament; which veil is done away in Christ." But even unto this day when Moses is read, the veil is upon their hearts. (2 Cor. 3:4&5)

The blindness soundlessly exists because the veil is still cleverly being used to cover the secrets buried in an impenetrable cover of the inner life. That which is hidden so resourcefully, fondled and treasured, and the trap that continues to cheapen and disconnect the prayer line. Multitudes of weak powerless Christians are trying to pray over or around that garbage, seeking to be satisfied with a show of spirituality. Honest prayer dismantles the sham that the veil attempts to camouflage. Spiritual blindness leads to the lack of spiritual perception. Lack of spiritual perception has a progression that diminishes the business of weighty prayer time, because prayer is avoiding the problem that is hindering prayer.

It is easy to blame or be caught up in a culture that proliferates itself on self concern, weaving its way into the Christian family, there increasing its daily intimidating influence. Vanity and self-indulgence becomes a way of life, which can be shielded and not appear openly to a great degree. But this idol causes prayer to be useless.

Paul called this pompous attitude a veil that isolates, disconnects, parts, and disassociates the individual from proper contact with our Intercessor. Paul is saying, the veil is over the contamination in the heart, and spiritual perception has been lost in the climate of the age; making prayer's spiritual effectiveness a mere superficial effort. Regardless of personal effort, spiritual soundness has silently vanished. When Christians find themselves off God's course and refuse to have the veil removed by continuing on their self-made path, spiritual tragedy awaits just around the corner. The problem is, the blindness has gone so long that it has become a way of life, and the veil is not recognized.

When the idol that is tucked away in the heart for years it will harden the conscience, deaden the spiritual sensitivity, make excessive and inordinate increase in the affections for that which the idol attracts self satisfaction sets in, and vanity and arrogance will feed off the idol worship. Only those who have this hidden idol will know what the idol is. But one thing is sure; there is no way to pray over it.

The hope is, that honest, searching prayer will recognize that a veil has been erected. The prayer that seeks first the Lord God will reveal the disdain that has produced the futile effort that has bound the soul to the contemptible idol and how vanity has gloried in its power. Robert L. Stevenson said: "vanity dies hard; in some obstinate cases it out lives Man." The Psalmist wants to know, "how long will ye love vanity." (Psa. 4:2) Could this be answered by saying, as long as the veil veils the heart?

John Newton revealed a veil that sought to place a partition in his life: "many vain intruders tease me most at such seasons as I most desire to be freed from them; they follow me into the pulpit, and meet me at the Lord's table. I hope I do not love them or wish to lodge them! Often in my prayers some idle fancy buzzed about me and made me forget where I was and what I was doing."

With nothing between our soul and the Savior, is our intensity in prayer of such consecration that no veil dare separate us from God's best? When all veils are honestly and wholly removed, God's endless resources are at our deposal. Prayer's hope and reality lies here.

It is astounding how God answers prayer no matter how difficult the predicament or how it developed. God had honored Jehoshaphat as he "waxed great exceedingly," and had much business. (2 Chron. 12&13) But that did not mean the success made him grow wiser. How is that known? He "joined affinity with Ahab." (2 Chron. 18:1) This was not his only unbelievable decision; he permitted his son to marry into a family known for its animosity toward the living God, besides being idol worshipers. Imagine Jezebel being your mother in-law.

There are many speculations as to why he would allow himself to be drawn into this kind of relationship, but there are none that could excuse him. Christians becomes victims of faulty judgment continually. Our limitations prevent pure decision making, regardless of how pure the motive, and only our Lord knows the real motive.

Jehoshaphat had things going well and didn't want that peace to be disturbed. When friction increases, peace is always desired, many times at all costs. Does this sound familiar? The school board is stacked with secular humanists. They have championed the cause to eliminate the Christian social structure and its influence in our educational system, replacing the founding fathers base faith structure with their humanistic religion. For some decades they have been cramming this secular humanistic religion into the minds of our children day after day. But to move the church into the slush and sewage of today's culture should mean war. But the church has lost its holy fire, and is paralyzed, while each generation is being indoctrinated in humanistic religion. It is the church that has allowed this sinister movement to wipe out Christian standards, following in the footsteps of Hitler and Stalin. It is necessary to get rid of God and His people if you are going to gain full power. Chamberlain had the liberal church behind him when he proposed to have peace at all costs. History reveals this tragedy, as well as the persuasive Biblical account that uncovers

Jehoshaphat's disastrous blunder. Possibly these decisions were made with good intentions, but with fatal results. Biblical Christianity has retreated to the comfortable sanctuary. Peace at all costs is running rampant in the one world agenda.

Jehoshaphat reaped what was sown, as did Ahab, as America will. Jehoshaphat allowed himself to be caught in Ahab's overwhelming welcome. The banquet was on, sheep and oxen were killed in abundance. The congenial act move quickly to the dinning area when Ahab set the hook by saying, in so many words, you know Jehoshaphat I've been having some trouble with a bunch of egotistical fellows at Ramoth Gilead, with your forces we could whip these fellows, how about it?

Jehoshaphat's reply was, don't you think we should inquire of the Lord first. Ahab said, we can do that, giving the order and four hundred false prophets arrived. These "yes men" were eager to please the king. When given the question whether he should go war with the enemy, in one voice they said, go up, the Lord will deliver them into your hands. Some how Jehoshaphat had enough spiritual discernment to know that was something was missing. He asked, "isn't there a prophet of the Lord here that we could enquire of him?" (2 Chron. 18:1-6)

Ahab reluctantly replied, there is one prophet, I hate him, and he is always prophesying evil upon me. This prophet was no yes man. He was God's man at any cost. Micah was brought before the two kings; being before hand told what the other four hundred prophets had prophesied and that he was to give his approval as well. After agreeing with the false prophets. Of course his sarcastic answer caused Ahab to snappily warn the right wing prophet, "that he was to speak the truth." (18:7)

Then Micah warned the kings they should not go to war, and that the false prophets had lied. With that statement he was struck in the face and sent to prison to have a diet of bread and water.

Reviewing the situation, it was four hundred to one, and the one was a right wing fanatic that never spoke well about those who wallowed in sin.

The battle is on. The charge is closing in on Jehoshaphat with their chariots and horsemen and he "cried out, and the Lord helped him; and God moved them to depart from him." (2 Chron. 18:31)

But how does this account link to prayer that can be helpful? Can we learn about God understanding us and answering prayer even after we have messed up? Are there questions that can give insight when we are led mistakenly into a forbidden situation? Where does the Father look when sincere prayer arrives? Does He look at the situation or the motive? Always the motive. A human limitation involves faulty judgment, and lack of foreknowledge that can reveal a deep stupidity that places us in ill-advised positions without the act being willful.

Can God answer prayer in the midst of brainless decisions? Is weakness ever considered by the Lord not to be willful? It appears that because Jehoshaphat was naive and human limitations were a factor, in spite of this, the Lord intervened immediately. The cry, Lord I was a fool to fall into this trap, my stupidity needs deliverance and forgiveness, and in repentance I cry.

God hears the cry in the midst of every crisis when light comes and the cry has surrender and obedience in its plea.

But our Lord will not excuse empty-headed decisions without giving light needed for future decisions. Jehu greets his king with these words: "shouldest thou help the ungodly and love them that hate the Lord? Therefore is wrath upon thee from before the Lord." (2 Chron.19: 2).

A prayer base is imperative for the unknown that is hidden along the king's highway. We are keenly aware how the terrorist works havoc. The enemy is conscious of how prepared our heart is before he attacks. If prayer is an indifferent activity, expect unlimited aggressive assaults at unforeseen times. The day started with earnest prayer will be a fortress.

Prayer's fervency has much to do with the victories or defeats each day, and the results will be life's spiritual gauge.

INTENSE PRAYER SHATTERS PHARISAIC RELIGION.

This Pharisaic religion infects the average Bible believing church. The artificial front is exposed when adversity's ugly head appears. Prayer confronts overwhelming circumstances whether it is social, personal or spiritual. Prayer focuses on the action and the inaction bowing the heart to His will. This surrender dare not be just a passive attitude that carries an apathetic prayer concern. If the soul does not burn with the present day situation, there is something radically wrong with the spiritual understanding of what God's child's accountability is. Luke writes: "shall not God avenge His own elect, which cry day and night with Him, though He bear long with them? I tell you He will avenge them speedily." (Lk. 18:7&8)

The Lord infers that the cry should be day and night unto Him. This is not part-time work, or whenever you think it may be necessary. It takes time to be Holy, and prayer is a large part of being Holy in thought, word, and deed. But when our pulpits propagate a cheap faith that knows little about carrying a rugged cross, and is handing out sleeping potions with soothing words that embrace political correctness which reassures his people to be at ease in Zion, is there any wonder that there is little passion for prayer? A cold heart carries no burden, nor does its passion wish for one.

John Wesley bluntly attacks this widespread shallowness: "How terrible is this! When the ambassadors of God turn agents for the devil! When they who are commissioned to teach men the way to heaven, do in fact teach the way to hell!" Wesley continued: " If ever asked, why does this?" I answered, "Ten thousand wise and honorable men, even all those, of whatever denomination, who encourage the proud, the trifler, the passionate, the lover of the world, the man of pleasure, the unjust or unkind, the easy, careless, harmless, useless creature, the man who suffers no persecution for righteousness sake, to imagine he is in the way to heaven."

Until this type of strangle hold is released and crucified, the church of the living God will continue to die a slow but certain death of spiritual suffocation. Only when the God loving people seek a prayer burden, as John Knox cried: "Give me Scotland or I die." Only when the soul dies to self and self is crucified, will the Pharisaic religion be revealed for what it is. But it will never come to be a reality until there is a "cry day and night" for the souls of good church going people who will miss heaven. Who will shoulder this responsibility? Who of us can afford to refuse this accountability? Vital prayer is the key that will unlock what Satan feels that he already has, your family and church locked up. This type of prayer will not come easy. We must learn what prayer sacrifice is, and its cost.

PRAYER ALLOWS GOD'S SPIRIT TO FLOW UNHINDERED!

Thus, there must be a covenant if this prayer flow has any power. Joshua brought the people together to make a covenant with the Lord. Their covenant was a vow to put away strange gods, to only serve the Lord, and to obey His voice. (Jos. 24:23 & 24) There was not to be anything that would obstruct God's Spirit from continually abiding and controlling every area of their lives.

Peter wrote about having an "unfeigned love" for the brethren. The prayer life of multitudes are restrained and frustrated by their relationship with other people. Hidden bitterness can smolder for years and impede any prayer power. Hidden resentment can fester and infect all areas of life by grieving the Holy Spirit, spreading a disease that will bring reproach on everything that the Lord wills to accomplish through His people. What a contrast about which Peter speaks: "seeing ye have purified your souls in obeying the truth through the Spirit unto the unfeigned love of the brethren see that ye love one another with a pure heart fervently." (1 Peter 1:22)

Prayer power is bathed in total love for God and man. This love is not a counterfeit that pretends, but is rooted in the depth of an abiding covenant with the Lord God. It never presumes on God's grace.

John has our Lord saying: " I have declared unto them Thy name, and will declare it; that the love where with Thou hast loved me may be in them, and I in them." (John 17:26) Prayerful love gives birth to communion. Is not communion with the Lord prayer? Does not God's Spirit impart Divine relationship through a clean and pure heart? Has He not opened the Holy of Holy to the blood bought? Then does not this surrendered soul have the same mind, goals, vision, concern, love and compassion that He has? He, the Holy Spirit, flows through the obedient heart that has no pretense, spilling into seeking lives that God's manna was created particularly for and into their hungry hearts. Prayer has hungry dreams that refuse to die with time; holding forth unfeigned love where the prayer closet has given birth.

COVENANT PRAYER PUTS ALL DESIRES AND DECISIONS IN GOD'S HANDS .

Who knows more about my needs than my heavenly Father? With the Holy Spirit in me, working through me, being the directive force in my life; would not I be wise to trust that type of love? Prayer communion gives an abiding assurance that soars above the most heart wrenching experience that can be placed on our threshold. It is in these times when there is a bonding that reaches beyond the ordinary, affirming the truth of God's word and the outreach of God's people. Suddenly oneness in Christ Jesus is real and personal. The praying church is fulfilling its mission to God and man.

Masses of people are searching for security, some have sought a guarantee that whatever happens their security is not threatened. When something is purchased, what type of warranty does it have? But there is more to a warranty than the warranty itself. A warranty is worthless if the person or company is not trustworthy. Sears sells Craftsman tools that have a life-time guarantee. If anything happens to a wrench, take it back to the store and they will replace it with a new one, no questions asked. There is a sense of security in buying Sears' tools.

Prayer is based on God's Word, which is trustworthy in every phase of life. This is the anchor in which the believer can safely invest, God's Word is His warranty. Now it comes down the Person guaranteeing the warranty. This prayer has the warranty of Almighty God behind every word in His Book. All rightness, all purity, perfect justice, and more, is completed in the attributes of God. He can not change. When the believer's prayer is anchored here, his assurance is attached to certain stability. That which was lost, is found, only in Him. The warranty of His Word is dependable, everlasting, and transcends human wisdom. God places who He is on the line and dares the skeptic to believe His Word and take up His cross and permit His cross to become his cross, and see what that prayer will do in a skeptic's life.

Prayer has a softener in it. Prayer mellows the spirit; sweetens the attitudes; humbles the pretentious; enlightens the haughty; quiets the fears; controls the passions; gives rest and hope to the weary; strengthens the weak; casts the burden upon Him; and lifts the fallen. Prayer allows His love to be expressed through self-affirmation, verifying the factual truth that Divine Grace has been shared in many immeasurable ways.

Knowing is a fulfillment, but spiritual knowledge can only be known by personal spiritual experience. The scriptural writers keep saying: "I know." Prayer is that vital part of the soul that actually knows Him to whom the prayer is expressed. This fellowship is on a moment-by-moment affinity, allowing the image of God in us to response to our personal Redeemer, which delights both God and mankind.

PRAYER IS OUR PRIVILEGE TO COMMUNICATE WITH THE TRINITY.

The Father, Son, and Holy Spirit is the object of our love. Self-love has nothing to give to the one who wants to be loved. There is no real love unless genuine love is returned. Prayer, true prayer returns the love already given.

Prayer has an everlasting effect and prepares the heart for the unexpected as well as the fulfillment of God's will through His promises. There is God's will and then there is man's will. Unless these two wills are totally united, prayer will be ineffective. Man's will in itself cannot benefit God personally. Our God has no need for man's input, outside the fact, He covenanted man's love. Calvary was about God's love, but also, opening the door for man's love, to be returned to Him. It is our God who works in man's behalf. God has already laid all the groundwork needed for any one to live a daily victorious Spiritual life.

Whatever the situation, at any time, God has a plan already in operation for His obedient child's good. Did He not say: "all things work together for good to them that love God, to them who are called according to His purpose." (Rom. 8:28) His plan is never stagnant, for stagnation breeds filth and disease; leaving spiritual contamination that renders prayer effort fruitless.

Calvary's highest purpose was and is to perfectly unite God and man into oneness. When this union is complete; providential care will expose His child to whatever the Father feels is necessary to build the type of character that will fit the pilgrim for life's journey and eventually his heavenly place in eternity. Does His child always understand the way He has chosen? Does he ever ask, "why this rugged road with all its pot holes?" Is not His foresight adequate for His child's trust? Can prayer be filled with question marks and be sufficient to allow the soul to rest in peace?

It is said that an Eastern Monarch once charged his wise men to invent him a sentence to be ever in view that should be true and appropriate at all times, and in all situations. They presented him with the words: "and this too, shall pass away."

The storm may pass away, but what happened to the believer while in the storm. It is while in the storm that it exposes who and what we are. Many believers come out of life's storms with mental and emotional injuries that linger after the storm has long since passed. The storm appeared unjust, a bitterness that questioned God's right to take that loving child; or the storm has revealed malice toward another that has been buried, and the storm uncovered its ugly head. Could it have been the reason for the storm?

The storm was to be for the believer's good. What has been taught! How can prayer help, if the Light the storm has given has been refused? The storm was given for the believer's good. Why? Many times it is difficult to see the good. But again, the believer surrenders to God's will that he may not understand, allowing his faith to lift him above what he does not fathom. Only when all conditions are met, will prayer be restored to its rightful place.

PRAYER MUST BE SOUGHT AS A SOLDIER SEEKS VICTORY IN BATTLE.

When Satan sets claim on something or someone, he will not yield that territory without a destructive combat. Some high profile Christian allows temptation to present itself by repeated confrontations, and in a few minutes can yield, and bring shame and reproach on everything holy. This person falls because of the position in which he allowed himself to be placed. A lifetime of influence is destroyed.

Why? Satan won temptation's battle that raged in the tempted soul. Regret will not undo. Excuses will never be adequate to repair a lifetime. How can this happen? Only when the prayer closet is neglected.

Somewhere God's voice was refused to be heard, and conscience was hardened. How susceptible are we? What is the best defense for these subtle temptations? How about earnest daily prayer and the diligent study of God's Word, and not the five minute variety. It takes time to be holy. It is at this time in His presence when God speaks and reveals the way of escape from the enemy attacks. How else would we be aware of this devious antagonist. Just as we must have proper food to build the immune system to defeat disease, so the spiritual being must have the necessary daily spiritual food if the spiritual immune system is going to be sufficient to overpower temptation. There is nothing cheap about a victorious Christian life. The cost is everything.

If the occupation with important matters is imperative, there will be little time for prayer to address the spiritual issues. When material success may be attracting the attention, spiritual matters are forfeited. Satan has won the battle, you and the family have lost and it could be for eternity. The enemy's deceptive message of anti-god, anti-righteousness, anti-holy, anti-family, anti-decency has defeated you in the midst of material success and a tragic social climate.

Horrible accounts of spiritual casualties are scattered all along life's highway who thought they could ignore the time for prevailing prayer and the study of God's Word. It would be amiss if the multitudes who are crying from the hell's pits were not mentioned, who like the rich man, didn't have time to tend to the beggars' sores. He was busy building larger barns.

In this warfare, there is no other course to be taken for complete victory except the burdensome Cross. Our Lord has already been down that road, but He too faced this warfare. Matthew has written: "then was Jesus led by the Spirit into the wilderness to be tempted of the devil." (Matt. 4:1) What a nauseating experience for God to allow His arch enemy to tempt Him! But how else would His humanity know the subtlety that tests mankind? These tests we cannot escape, but prayer transfers the overwhelming burden from man to the Almighty God.

Most believers see how fast they can run from the battle, especially if position is involved, or the church boss puts his foot down, or if reputation is to be saved, or there could be a division. Fear within is the greatest enemy. The solution is not usually found in the advice of others. That is not as wearing as the prayer closet, that is where the answer is found. But that means taking on the pain and anguish that our Lord experienced in Gethsemane. Most Christians contend that is beyond the call of duty. If Satan is continually claiming new territory that involves God's people and their freedom; loved ones who are caught in the subculture; a society that has replaced righteous morality with a Gnostic humanistic religion that would put Sodom and Gomorrah to shame; if these circumstances do not drive praying people to the prayer closet, there is no hope. Why insist on peace when war is devouring us.

By the size of the prayer meetings, it is apparent the prayer struggle has ceased. If the enemy refuses to quit, how shall we escape if we neglect the accountability of prayer, and prayer is an accountability that God's record will reveal.

PRAYER REVEALS TO THE BELIEVER THE TRUTH OF DIVINE TRUTH.

Divine Truth is forged on the pages of God's Book, because the Lord God has bound Himself to His Word. Its authenticity, its fidelity, has been put through the fires kindled by skeptics and God haters down through the centuries. The martyrs' dying testimonies still speak to the unbelieving heart, giving validation to the truth of His word. Prayer continually activates truth; truth shatters self-reliance; self-reliance must yield to surrender; surrender generates obedience that produces martyrs.

But when man chooses to claim personal rights over God's proven principles, then life will affirm a totally different result. The Israelites were discontented with the food the Lord was supplying. Manna had become distasteful. They wanted food of their own choosing. This set up discontentment that developed into a mass of malcontents.

A disgruntled, miserable Israelite people demands their rights to demand from God " a lusted demand." Manna was no longer wanted, they gave an order for flesh. The Psalmist spoke of their request: "and He gave them their requests; but sent leanness into their hearts." How many praying people live in leanness of soul because their prayers have become, " this is what I want, the present situation is not sufficient for the taste I have developed." God is to comfort and to enhance the propensity for the more refined. The Cross is not a refined instrument that is easy to carry daily.

It is impossible to build a mountain moving prayer life on an emaciated faith that views God as "the on-call servant." A prayer that has a lean heart, is no prayer at all. A self-centered heart will end in spiritual disaster. Reread the account of the Israelites. But did God's people learn by what is so vividly declared by the scriptures?

Prayer must be encased in God's truth, with human will wholly submitted to God's will and purpose. It comes down to, does God know best. Who knows what the multitude of blessings Israelites would have gained if they had not put personal wants over against what God had given. Beware of pushing a personal agenda, rather than allowing God's will to overrule personal considerations.

FAITHFUL PRAYER DEVELOPS HOLY COMPASSION!

Compassion about which the scripture speaks must rise above an ordinary feeling of concern. Compassionate meaning is fully exemplified in the Godhead. It was compassion that moved our Lord through the act of power to deliver the Israelites out of Egypt. By this act of compassion, there was not only the feeling of mercy, but to have any depth, the actual act had to be fulfilled. The good Samaritan is God's compassion carried out through man. Prayer takes man beyond natural concern that is basic in common Grace. It is in those prayer hours that God mellows, strikes at the heart of the ego; prayer rounds off the sharp tongue; it permits tenderness to grow; it moves kindness to the center of life; it entertains gentle grace in the inner man; always revealing the beauty of holiness.

There is no way to separate compassionate love and effective prayer. An occasional prayer is cold and casual, only moved for a moment, but seldom moved beyond self-interest.

Compassionate prayer advances into the area of the unlovable. Here where the dirt and filth will rub off on God's servant. M. D. Babcock said it this way: "If Jesus Christ is everything to me, I know He can be everything to any man; and because I know it, then woe is me if I do not do all that is in my power to let every man who does not know Jesus Christ, if I am loyal to Him and keep His commandments, I am in touch with everybody to the ends of the earth who need Him, and I cannot wash my hands and say that you must excuse me from this matter."

Without Divine driven compassion, there is no sense of Divine mission or understanding. Is that not what Calvary was all about? This devotion cannot be whipped up in some meeting and last, if not bathe in prayer. It is in the prayer closet where the battle is won, and Grace is supplied to go into the streets, dumps, and alleys to find the depth of mankind's need.

Some one says, " I must have burning desire, where will I find it?" Not by reading books on " How to;" not in a pump-up scene; not in the church, these people are not there; not in committees, but by fasting and prayer. Carnal man's capacity can not possibly reach the compassionate pinnacle that the Spirit filled prayer warrior can, whose soul has been flooded with empowerment beyond normal capabilities. Prayer takes us into the arena of the impossible. Each of us must ask ourselves if our faith is up to the requirement.

PRAYER OPENS THE FULL MEASURE OF OUR LORD'S DEVOTION TO OBEDIENCE.

Job's world was the symbol of God's abundant grace and blessing. Satan challenged God by suggesting it would be easy to serve God, if this was the kind of reward to be received. Satan continues to suggest that if all of the good things would be taken from Job, he would curse God for his plight. God replied in so many words, evidently you believe Job's faith and his obedient walk is nothing more than a charade. God ALLOWS Satan to take everything but Job's life. To us this is unthinkable.

But behind Satan's plan, does God have a greater and better plan? Satan's plan is open and destructive, while God's plan is hidden, and always for the believer's good.

Then what is God's hidden plan? Will not this devastation move Job's prayer life into a depth not known before? Is it not easier to appreciate what was, when it isn't any more? Isn't it in these times when we find out how real our faith is? If prayer and faith are never tested, how do we evaluate their worth, and whether they can be trusted in the future when new storms will strike just as suddenly.

How many times has it happened, when overwhelming events have appeared in such force, it materialized so quickly there was no time to prepare. It leaves its hurts and open wounds bleeding without any awareness that God is even near, let alone being in the midst of the situation. Now, where is the prayer spirit? Has prayer been left among the bleeding wounds? How difficult would it be to pray what Job prayed: "the Lord giveth and the Lord taketh away?" Most of the time when the unbelievable has happened, words find the vocal cords not functioning. The grief is so heart breaking that there can only come a deep sigh, or a groan. In the midst of God's teaching, are these utterances praying? Does not our Lord hear these who are the most sincere and earnest of all human prayers. Does not God see through all the unintelligible utterances and get to the motive behind the cry?

It is in times like these, words cannot be expressed, when the full measure of grace assures the soul by the still small voice whispering: "I will never leave you or forsake you." Groans are heard, and the bitter blows do not hurt so much. Prayer can now find words that still may be bathed in sorrow and grief, but still emerge in confidence.

Only those who have prayerfully plowed through this kind of tragedy can appreciate the devotion and blessing that sustains and keeps the obedient heart in the time when the tempest would threaten the very foundation of faith.

PRAYER RETAINS DIGNITY WITH HOLY INTEGRITY.

The soul cannot be defeated, crushed, defamed and slandered by false prophets. Those who stand for the inspiration of the Scriptures will feel these bitter barbs, but the savage attacks will never lessen the holy resolve. The liberal considers such a position as anti-intellectual, even to the extent of being ignorant. Paul writes to the Corinthians from the Amplified version these words : " When we are slandered and defamed, we (try to) answer softly and bring comfort. We have been made and are now the rubbish and filth of the world, the off scouring of all things, the scum of the earth." (1 Cor. 4:13)

But prayer replaces talent with Grace. Prayer will replace intellectualism with holy living; eloquence will be supplanted with Holy zeal; oratory is restored with piety; social science is replenished with Biblical application; a holy heart relinquishes position to become a servant of His choosing. Prayer puts the soul in the position to be used by the Lord regardless of the cost to the servant.

In earlier years, there was an attempt by the Bible believing conservative to become respectable to the liberal hierarchy by being intellectually competitive; or by zeal beyond theirs; and by a determination to match (at least) the average oratory skills. The hours spent to raise acceptability were not in vain. But prayer is the force behind the enlarging of capacity. Limitations are recognized, but prayer will present these limitations to the God of the impossible and fully expect His power to overcome the hindering obstacle.

But trying to be acceptable can be a spiritual trap. Because the worldly desire for respectability places the effort on pleasing man rather than on the laborious study of God's word and the hours wrestling in prayer that will please God. The point of compromise is dangerously close. But prayer and Bible study can keep the proper focus to where the cost personally no longer matters.

The liberal wants God's man to bend, but the liberal will refuse to compromise his position, making the Bible believer the bigot, who is narrow-minded and cannot see anything beyond the Biblical standard, which the liberal believes takes very little intellectual qualifications. The inspired Word of God is openly rejected in the marketplace of ideas.

When the soul falters under the pressure to be acceptable by the world's standards, expect the Biblical standards to vacillate and spiritual decay to continue.

How many ministers have entered the harvest field with their hearts aflame, but then pressures began to accumulate, and gradually the flame went out, but they have gained acceptability. But at what cost, to themselves, their influence, and to the people God had called them to serve. This is not only in the area of the ministry, but institutions founded by Godly people who have sold their founding heritage to fit in with the present daily subculture.

These are words Rowland Hill said of Wesley's tribe: " He and his lay lubbers go forth to prison the minds of men, his ragged legion of reaching tinkers, scavengers, dray-men and chimney sweepers." They were the rubbish and filth of this world, the scum of the earth, but at the heart of the revival that swept across England.

What a long way we have come from the founding fathers of Methodism.

Our respectability is well known. The gospel is dressed up to suit what society liberal humanism demands. We eagerly accept the honorable station that has been carefully abolished by the liberal hierarchy, which has left our souls lean and unworthy of calling ourselves the followers of "the Way."

How different from the New Testament Christianity where life itself was at stake. Read carefully Peter's words: "we ought to obey God rather than men." (Acts 5:29) There is no fear, no wish for acceptance, no panic concerning the labels that were attached to their faith.

I say, how dare you put God's Biblical standards on the bargaining table. This reproach will follow anyone who compromises God's truth for position, acceptance, or any other reason and they will receive God's judgment.

Regardless of the many pressures or adversities, I have yet to see a person or an institution fall to the betrayal level of this magnitude, that is a committed prayer warrior, or an institution that has a board filled with prayer warriors. When speaking of warriors, the meaning is, those who go to war with the demons of hell day in and day out, and pray through to victory.

The praying soul, that continually places God first in all of life, will be given Grace that will NOT compromise His Word. This cannot be accomplished by a five- or ten-minute prayer session, or by a few words from some devotional book. Prayer that counts is labor which too many find ways to avoid.

PRAYER ELEVATES MEEKNESS TO THE STATION OF GODLINESS AND ABHORS EGOTISM.

But how differently the world considers meekness. The worldviews meekness as spinelessness, weak-kneed, in many cases cowardly, fearful of anything that may encounter a rough confrontation. If this be true, then Jesus' words in Matthew 5:5 "Blessed are the meek: for they shall inherit the earth" is approving this weak-will type of Christianity.

But the scriptural meaning of meekness has a far deeper significance, reaching far beyond outward behavior, but necessary to capture the right relationship with God and man. Meekness is the temper of the soul that emulates its spirit chiefly towards God. It is the willingness to walk the low road, so that you may be able to walk the high road of holiness. Our Lord is appealing to the condition of the mind and the heart, which are perfectly submitted to the whole-will of God. It is a virtue found in the heart of the Christian. Meekness is the integrity and righteousness that must be established in the faithful prayer. Meekness is inwrought grace of the soul.

Meekness is what the Father seeks, if so, then it must be implanted within and flow through the prayer life. It is a fruit of the spirit; essential to absorb holy instruction; yielding for Divine direction; humble enough to be gentle in spirit and action.

Holy prayer elevates the meek soul into the Father's presence. God showers His rich blessings He longs to bestow on the tenderhearted Spirit filled saints that delight Him. The Amplified version opens the fountain of our Lord's with these words: " blessed happy, blithesome, joyous, spiritually prosperous that is, with life-joy and satisfaction in God's favor and salvation, regardless of their outward conditions, are the meek (the mild, patient, long-suffering), for they shall inherit the earth."

Self-centered egotism is totally contrary to meekness, leaving the prayers of self-serving to end up in God's waste basket. It is the redeemed refined spirit that meekness brings to the prayer closet that initiates joy in our heavenly Father's heart.

PRAYER IS THE MOST SERIOUS WORK OF THE DAY.

The prayers of the saints are more precious than time. Jonathan Edwards wrote in 1742 the significance of consequential of prayer: " I have often said it would be a thing very desirable and very likely to be followed with a great blessing, if there could be some contrivance, that there should be an agreement of all God's people in America that are well affected to this work, to keep a day of Fasting and Prayer to God, wherein we should unite of the same. It seems to me, it would mightily encourage and animate God's saints, in humbly and earnestly seeking God, for such blessings which concern them all." John the Revelator wrote: "And when he had before the book, the four beasts and four and twenty elders fell down before the Lamb, having everyone of them harps and golden vials full of odors, WHICH ARE THE PRAYERS OF SAINTS." (Rev. 5:8)

The prayers of the saints are God's treasure, and what God treasures, God keeps. O how priceless are the weak fumbling words of a pure heart. These are the prayers that remove the dark valleys that stand in the way of God's purpose, calm the wild sea with a word, close the lions' mouths, take the heat out of the fiery furnace, or make the viper's sting harmless and will demolish a jail without injury to its occupants.

What our God cherishes, He has attached this treasured privileged to the modest workaday activities of the most insufficient obedient human beings. Without doubt, he whose prayers must put daily bread on the table will weep over his need and use the sleepless night hours to plead his case. While those who have no idea what it is to pray food on the table, thoughtlessly accept life's blessings without thought to thank the Giver of all blessings. Which one is the closest to God's heart? Dare the time be taken again, to say, it takes TIME to be HOLY. "The golden vials full of odors, which are prayers of the saints."

Only the blood washed has prayers' entitlement. Only God's child will take the time to meditate and pray, for who can fully describe or measure the richness of soul that develops in these blessed hours? To claim this birthright, demands time that too few think they can give, allowing a spiritual leanness to take over. Only the pure in heart shall see God, this is true whether time is taken or not. The pure heart willingly takes up the prayer cross, and gives the time required to carry that cross.

PRAYER ENGAGES AND SATISFIES THE SOUL'S SPIRITUAL HUNGER.

Who has not read about Hannah's desire to have a son? The scripture speaks of her " adversary who provoked her sore." Whether this was Satan taunting her faith, or the women who were in her company, the scripture does not say. But the account does reveal the hunger in her soul to the extent of the loss of appetite for food; her spirit was sorrowful; her soul was in bitterness; she wept; she fretted before the Lord; her prayers were filled with tears for she craved a child. Her want for fullness, much as any other woman, was not necessarily a selfish request, because she vowed a vow with the Lord that as soon as the child is weaned she would take him to become the Lord's servant.

The assurance came as she struggled before the Lord in the temple. The burden was lifted and "her countenance was no more sad." Who of God's children has not known the deep peace when the committed soul prays through? The spiritual hunger is satisfied.

The cry of the spiritual hunger comes from an eighteen-year-old in India: "I am 18 years old, a college student. One day I chanced to read a little book, THE HEART OF THAMBY. It seemed to me there was a great similarity between Thamby's heart and mine. "Since I read this, streams a new light into my mind. When a teacher used to talk about the great Christ, I used to think, 'O that I could see Him directly!' Then I began to wonder if Christ really lived...

"Buddha says the reason for man's sorrow is sin. That is very true. I can't get deliverance from sin. Is it true that the great Christ sits on the right hand of God and will come to this earth one day? I wish I could see Him then.

"When they pray in the Church in the morning, I used to stand outside and listen and enjoy the music. The heavenly music still follows me."

Multitudes live in this type of spiritual hunger, never tasting the heavenly manna; standing outside listening; the music creates a greater hunger; but never knowing personally that the ravenous appetite can be satisfied. How willing the Lord is to receive a prayer that has a hungry longing to have that hunger fulfilled. Everything depends upon how hungry your soul is. Hannah laid everything on the altar for God's will to be done. Hannah experienced the reality of her prayer being answered: "For this child I prayed; and the Lord hath given me my petition which I asked of Him." (1 Sam. 1:27)

PRAYER OPENS THE DOOR FOR THE HOLY SPIRIT TO OPERATE FREELY.

The one hundred and twenty in the Upper Room spent their days in prayer after our Lord's ascension, and then Pentecostal power filled those praying believers. The Holy Spirit opened the floodgates of heaven. This power moved in any direction that would glorify Deity. His anointing presence was evident that this display of power was not self-manufactured. These were unlettered people who were turning the whole area into a God conscious arena.

History has left a conclusive trail made by men who prayed and waited before God until the anointing of the Holy Spirit saturated their being with purifying cleansing and power. One writer notes that George Fox was so burdened about his sin and prayerlessness that he went to a priest and said:

"What should I do?"
The answer: "You ought to get married."
Another said: "You ought to join the Army."
Still another advised: "You ought to try tobacco and hymns."

George Fox went alone. For 14 days he fasted and prayed, and the power of God's anointing came upon him and he was never the same.

George Whitefield and John Wesley, along with some sixty other preachers gathered to pray through the night. Around 3:00 a. m. John Wesley said; "There came to me the blessing of God, and for the first time I know what it is to be filled with the Holy Spirit." The outcome was a Wesleyan revival that swept across the land to spare England from the bloody revolution that France experienced. An ocean could stop the overflow of God's Spirit. The Spirit of the gospel came blasting its way through the wildernesses of our beloved land. Those who craved a homestead in those remote areas could expect a knock on the cabinet door by a circuit-riding preacher in any kind of weather.

These Spirit filled men caught the fire that Peter and the rest of the disciples experienced on Pentecost. The threats, unfavorable events or bodily affliction could not stop the Spirit filled hearts. Our spiritual legacy started in a prayer meeting that kindled the holy fire.

" And they were all filled with the Holy Ghost." (Acts 2:4) This power is that which operated miraculously under and in all kinds of adversity.

One thing is certain, there is no need for more religion. The world is filled with religion, the same that infested the earth when our Lord walked its dusty paths. Everything religiously will stay the same, until God's people will saturate the prayer room with the holy desire and will continue to do so until the cleansing fire falls. Unless there a deep passion for dedicated obedience, plan on just being religious with no power, thus, no miracles in the making.

Is it not sad there are a great number of professing Christians, good people who do want to pay the price to enjoy this God given imparted power and the lifestyle that goes with it?

PRAYER DEVELOPS STRONG AND EFFECTIVE WITNESSING.

There is a developing process that goes with its preparation. Jeremiah and his heavenly Father were communicating about witnessing, but Jeremiah was resisting, giving excuse after excuse about his limitations that would interfere with what the Lord wanted him to do.

His heavenly Father gives him reassurance by saying: "I sanctified thee" when you came out of your mother's womb. In so many words the Lord was saying, you were prepared for this mission before you arrived. What a tremendous thought. God's plan for each person is already conceived in His mind from the very beginning. How did Jeremiah know about God's plan? He knew through prayer; and personal dialog with God as He gave him direction. The concept is tenderly reassuring; "Be not afraid of their faces. I am with thee to deliver thee." Isn't this just like a loving father would do to his child that is fearful to step into a new adventure? This is the heavenly Father speaking to the young Jeremiah. What a bonding that reveals when he is speaking to his Father about personal fears and limitations for the task given!

The young Jeremiah was supposed to deliver God's message to the old hard headed, stiff necked people who had forsaken God, and formed their own idea of religion. These rebellious people were going to show this young prophet that their present religion suited them. (Is not this up to date?) This is the message Jeremiah was sent to give: "stand ye in the ways, and see, and ask for the old paths, where is the good way, and walk therein, and ye will find rest for your souls. But they said, we will not walk therein." Whenever the messenger receives this type of disobedience, be assured there will be more prayer discussing the problem of outright unmanageable spiritual insubordination.

Prayer undergirds the hard places where soul is fiber that is built that can lovingly tolerate the: "we will not walk therein."

There are still the Jeremiahs that have chosen the road that may mean certain death.

"Open Doors News Brief reports that brother Edwards, who is choir man of all the Assemblies of God in Iran, has now been asked to become president of the Iranian Council of Protestant church. The last two presidents were murdered.

"Brother Edward's brother, Haik Hoverseian-Mehr, is one of three Iranian Christian leaders martyred in the past months."

How about me? Will my prayer life be adequate for the storms ahead? They are coming. Nor will anyone escape the test when they come and the witness means death. O sweet hour of prayer where strength is renewed for whatever comes.

PRAYER UNLOCKS THE SOUL'S UNDERSTANDING TO BOTH GOD'S AND MAN'S NEEDS.

Prayer is the pipeline that flows from God to man, and then back again. The pipeline is useless if it is plugged with self-will and willful sin.

The heavenly Father has made a covenant with Israel and it is Malachi's responsibility to remind a wayward people that God is still concerned for His people with these words in 3:7: "return unto me and I will return unto you. If my people will keep the covenant then: prove me now herewith saith the Lord of hosts, if I will not open you the windows of heaven, and pour you out a blessing, that there shall not be room enough to receive it."

All answers to prayer depend on His people keeping the covenant, which is a coming together in an agreement; to fulfill an obligation; to determine to balance an agreement. Covenant meaning runs deeper than an agreement. It is a vow that binds the agreement.

God's covenant-breakers have dealt treacherously, but not without knowingly transgressing the covenant; but still continue to pray. The pipe line is filled with hatred, an unforgiving nature, anger, dissatisfaction and bitterness, which are all covenant breakers; which stops the flow. The covenant breaker is determined to pursue a personal agenda, whether it fits into God's will or not. Dealing treacherously with a covenant made with God opens the opportunity for more treachery, deceit and betrayal to

God's call to holiness. But still there is an attempt to pray and expect God to respond. When there is an effort to pray from an unrepentant heart, prayer mocks everything God stands for. Shame and honesty have won no championships in the Lord's eyes.

If the pipeline is to have a free flowing communication, the prayer must come from a pure motive and a clean heart. Otherwise, prayer will only be words with no relationship with the redeeming God.

Prayer with an uncontaminated channel is that which fires the soul to claim God's territory. Prayer can place the integrity of the God of all creation on the line. Before the multitude Elijah cries: "hear me, O Lord, hear me." Could he have taken that bold position if he had willful sin in his heart? I think not! He continues his prayer by stating the purpose of his prayer: "that thou hast turned their heart back again." The petition was for the souls of his people. They had chosen the way of Baal. Ahab and Jezebel had led the people into a sinister lifestyle. Elijah, God's prophet had to confront Satan's insidious plot that had secured and imprisoned the minds and hearts of God's people.

It is one thing to challenge the hierarchy with a well-equipped army. It is another thing to defy a spirit filled prophet who has access to Omnipotent power. Prayer brought that power into play on that mountain, while human resources and effort failed. The fortitude of the soul is born in the flame of adversity.

Prayer always is focused on good against evil. Whether the adversaries are armies, Kings or standing alone in front of false religious fanatics, prayer stands in God's anointing no matter who or what the troubler is. Prayer is the reinforcement that fortifies the prophet who is threatened to stop preaching this death and doom religious fanaticism and fall in line with the present culture and the trouble would stop. The liberal and the secular humanist make an art out of making the good guy the bad guy. How difficult was it for the prophet to have the grace to always take the unpopular position? The prophet needs to assure the elite that he is not the troubler, but that those who have no absolutes, no right or wrong and act on what feels good at the moment are the source of the trouble. Does our God just hand out this anointed grace? Or is there a price to pay daily in a Godly walk and a prayer life that has purpose, and is spirit directed that has access to heaven's resources? The point is God's man will eventfully win the battle. Now can we who call ourselves Christian not learn the personal application of this example? Prayer brings the fire down, and the victory comes with it. Spiritual victory always has a background of faithful obedience. Vital prayers has hell bound souls in mind, impossible situations, suffering and hurting people, the missionaries, the governmental leaders, and more. Prayer gives the believers access to grace needed to wage the ever present spiritual war.

PRAYER BATHES THE SOUL IN HUMILITY AND HOLY RESPECT.

What a contrast the scripture draws between the Pharisee and the publican. The Pharisee makes sure all see him in prayer. His prayer revealed a soul filled with religious arrogance that trumpeted how he thanked God he was not like that lowly publican. His conceit and self-importance permitted and privileged God to hear from one so noble and righteous. That prayer did not go any higher than his head inspite of all the multiplied adjectives he used to describe his self-righteous life.

How different was the publican's approach to God when he prayed. He did not seek attention; but stood afar off; would not lift his eyes toward heaven; smote his breast as if to lower himself lower than he was. His self-abasement and unworthiness were as weights on his soul. His sin and his daily life were beyond his capacity to handle. His sinfulness and shame caused him to seek a secluded place where only his God could hear his plea for mercy. His prayer was as if he would dishonor God by daring to utter it. His undeserving weakness in heart and soul gave his prayer no merit and without favor. He wanted God to hear how much his soul needed divine attention and not some lascivious praise to satisfy his ego. If he had any ego it was already pulverized in approach to God.

This humble publican realized what so many do not understand that our Lord said that without Him we can do nothing. The publican realized if he was to be grafted into the vine, he must surrender all or wither and die. Life and eternity were too big for him to master. He needed to empty himself of all the inward baggage that had become so burdensome.

The prayer of the humble and lowly unloads all the sinful weight at Jesus feet. Only the Divine Redeemer can and will meet this need, while the self-righteous Pharisee cloaks himself in disdain and self glory. Oh, Lord God bathe my soul in holy humility that I may enjoy the assurance of the Father's listening ear.

PRAYER REVEALS AND MELTS ENVY INTO AN APPEAL FOR ITS CLEANSING.

Prayer needs to contain the awareness of how subtle Satan can slip envy into the main stream of thought and be the demon that drives life's motivations. This first murder in the human race was the result of envy. Cain was overpowered by envy when God accepted Abel's sacrifice and not his and his envy drove him to slay his brother. If the depth of this insidious spirit can inject such evil into the motives, then this hidden agenda must alert the believer to its malevolence. Where can vigilant awareness be found? Only in faithful study of God's Word and prayer that will arouse the danger signal that the spirit of envy is seeking entrance into a particular area of life. It cannot be observed outwardly necessarily, it works like a cancer, that even the possessor is not conscious of its presence unless vigilance is taken into the prayer closet and its search for what is happening in the motive life. After all, vital prayer is to seek and search.

The Philistines became envious of Isaac because his material blessings far exceeded theirs. The envy grows to such portions that the people pressured the King to ask him to leave. This spirit of envy has plagued mankind ever since the fall. All through the scriptures it has left its stream of tragedy. Joseph's brothers allowed envy to saturate their lives to the extent that they sold him as slave; the men of Ephraim who were not called when the Israelites invaded the Midianites, demanded a share of the spoils that the victory achieved. Envy is found close to home, when the friend receives a promotion when it was clear the husband was more capable; or when sitting in the Sunday School class with the mind rehearsing "I could do better." Envy is a vicious malignancy that eats at the spiritual vitality of every person who harbors it. It can only be mastered by the consistent labor in the prayer closet.

Thomas Dreier has this advice to give to those who live in the world of envy: " One of the most contented men we know is never envious of the possessions or achievements of others. What I have is what I need to fill my place in the world,' he says, and what is in their possession is what they probably need for their work. If what they have belonged to me, I would have it. The fact that I do not possess it is evidence enough for me that it does not belong to me. All that concerns me is how I can become more useful. When I learn how to do more, the things needed for the carrying out of my ideas will be made available to me. That is what has happened to me in the past, and I see no reason why it would not continue to happen to me. It is what I think about that matters, not the things I claim to possess."

PRAYER THE GUARDIAN OF THE SOUL!

Prayer is the needed guardian of the soul because there is an invasive enemy seeking to invade a shallow prayer life, frustrating the carrying out of God's plan for the believer's life.

Matthew wrote: "for he (Pilate) knew that for envy they had delivered Him." (Matt. 27; 18) Envy motivated our Lord's crucifixion. Is this not a serious warning to God's people as to the depth that this evil obsession will cause religious people to go to accomplish its end, what is?

The Holy Spirit gives prayer depth and guidance. Paul writing to the Roman church said: " likewise the Spirit also helps our infirmities; for we know not what we should pray for as we ought; but the Spirit itself makes intercession for us with groanings which can not be uttered. And He that searches the hearts knows what is the mind of the Spirit, because He makes intercession for the saints according to the will of God." (Rom. 8:26&27)

Prayer anointed by the Holy Spirit will turn heaven's searchlight on each one's inner personal life. Salvation is more than the initial experience. It is walking in the light given, which means a daily careful check to see if obedience is constant, and how temptation is being handled. This probe dare not be minimized, for such carelessness will allow self-made goals to invade the areas where the Father wants His purpose to be fulfilled.

The self-life can quickly occupy the areas that change both the countenance and presence of who and what is on the throne of all personal motivations. If prayer is genuine there will be utter surrender to the leadership of the Holy Spirit that does the investigating. The Holy Spirit will not spare personal feelings or wishes. In fact, He exposes those things, such as the need for restitution, or mending broken relationships that were supposed to be taken care but put off until later. He sees all delay tactics. The Holy Spirit as a teacher explains what must be done if praying ground is to be retained. Since He is aware of the coming judgment, He will urge immediate action, and remind the believer that today is the day of salvation. There is no assurance of tomorrow.

When self is the major factor in what happens in the personal prayer life, self has no security, no peace, only fear, leaving only unrest behind. There cannot be this amount of turmoil and conflict causing chaos in the soul and have spiritual victory in the prayer life. The prayer cannot rise any higher than what self will allow the spiritual life to be.

Honest prayer uncovers what and who we are, and where the present choices will lead. Our Father will not disregard a straightforward candid prayer. But expect the inspector to be just and honest, refusing to allow the corners to be cut or the questionable to be accepted. Expect the Holy Spirit to be your guide in the prayer closet, and giving new light; otherwise, He would not be the teacher and director we know Him to be. He is not willing that any would perish. His responsibility is to lead us into all Truth.

PRAYER IS THE SAINT MAKER.

Prayer readies the soul for each circumstance in life. It is seen in Daniel's case. The King's decree had been signed. No other god could be worshiped and no one dare ask any petition of god or man for thirty days save of the King, if anyone breaks the decree, he shall be cast into the den of lions.

Jealous men schemed and plotted a conspiracy against Daniel, of which the King was unaware. They had studied the man, Daniel, who walked before God and men with such godly integrity that there was no occasion that could be used against him. There was only one thing the conspirators found that would prevent Daniel from keeping the decree. If he continued to do what he always had done, he would step into their trap. Their surveillance revealed that day after day, three times a day he would open his window facing Jerusalem and pray.

Daniel knew the decree had been signed. Apparently there was no battle raging in his soul as to whether he would be faithful in his praying three times a day, or risk being torn apart by hungry lions. It appears there was no hesitation as he opens the window to pray. Their scheme had worked and in the morning their menace would be history. With speed they delivered their message to the King. Daniel had violated the King's decree.

When I told this account to my little daughter before she was old enough to go to school, I would ask the question: "why were the lions' mouths closed?" She would come back with: "because he believed God."

Daniel laid his faith on the line. His faith was more than mere words. Only a soul that is totally committed to God would do that. His prayer life had made him ready for the day when his faith would have the ultimate test. Willingly Daniel walked into the jaws of death, rather than compromise his prayer hour. Does the picture of a saint present itself to a questioning world?

Living in God's presence through which prayer opens the door to such inter-locking of soul with the Holy Infinite God, should grip the heart of every believer. My heart is humbly crushed to think of how insufficient my prayer life has been when it comes to building sainthood. O yes, my prayer list is long and continues to grow but the inadequacy of sufficient change in surrounding circumstances has not changed to the point of loved ones being redeemed. At this crucial point, the need is to dig deeper. Daniel's faithfulness changed a nation. Mine, must be to see lost loved ones won to Christ.

It is not that we aspire to duplicate Daniel for we are not in his position. But we can desire to duplicate his prayer life. Too many believers get serious about praying only when a crisis arises. But the lasting impact is not in the crisis but in the consistency that has been build with time. There is no way that mediating upon Daniel's prayer can enhance the personal prayer life. It must be practiced day in and day out then when the climactic moment comes at that unexpected hour, the prayer foundation kicks in. That prayer strength now saturates every decision that must be quickly made. The stature of the soul is fortified and measured by prayer's faith. Thus, sainthood arrives without the saint knowing it.

PRAYER IS THE CHRISTIAN'S MOST POWERFUL WEAPON.

Multitudes are trapped in circumstances beyond their control. A web of impossibilities presents unbearable conditions that leave the soul exhausted; emotions are shattered; nerves are stretched to the breaking point; effort is futile; worry is saturating the mind; all to no avail. All has been tried, but the circumstances stand unsolvable. There is concern as to just how long the grip can hold on to the end of the rope.

Isn't it strange how people will try everything else but the Lord who promised to make their burdens light? A simple prayer of repentance can contact the God of all power. Power for every situation is available. This power is obtainable to each believer when the Father's conditions are met.

The early church was under persecution. Herod killed James and saw how it pleased the Jews, who considered the Christians to be no more than scum. The tyrant decided to delight the Jews farther by putting Peter in prison for the night in order to consider what should be done with him. It could mean another execution the next day. But a small group of believers realized the seriousness of Peter's fate, and began to pray. The occasion needed the miraculous power of God do what they could not do. Their God was always available and adequate: always able to deal with the unyielding when personal weakness feeds on His strength. In the night hour our Lord responded to their prayers by sending an angel to unlock the chains and the gate, leading Peter to the house where the prayer meeting was in progress. The next morning he was on the streets proclaiming God's salvation. What power God's people have at their disposal when sought in obedience!

Prayer is the simplest of all duties, but neglected the most, or restricted to a few minutes because of the rush of the day. Prayer, the believer's greatest weapon, left unused and unappreciated.

Possibly this is the reason the believer is constantly running into the endless unmanageable conditions. Are not these untimely situations necessary to remind the believer of his personal powerlessness?

The early Christians learned quickly that there were forces at work that were relentless in their effort to destroy everything righteous. Evidently today's Christian has not learned that lesson. But the early church found that prayer could produce the unbelievable, for the scripture would remind the fainting heart that when "prayer was made without ceasing of the church unto God for him," the impossible became possible. See the locked chains and locked gates unlocked by His Omnipotent hand! The weapon is ours if untarnished faith will use it.

PRAYER IS AN APPEAL FOR THE GOD MAN TO BECOME INVOLVED IN PERSONAL AND NATIONAL AFFAIRS.

Redeemed man is the instrument our Lord has planned to use to instruct, and conduct worship that will glorify Him. Why does our Lord want His created beings to worship and glorify Him? Is He some neurotic, with whip in hand and judgment hanging overhead insisting mankind wallow at His feet? (These are some of the questions the skeptics would present.) But is this what we know about God? God is our Maker, with out Him life's purpose would not exist; nor would we have eternal life. Love is not love without the freedom of choice. These days we are very interested in the freedom of choice. Each one has this choice, but now accountability kicks in. The privilege is personal, to believe God or not to believe, to try to slip by or be fully committed. But the completely surrendered believer will have such a thankful heart for being delivered for the guilt of sin, that there will be no problem falling at His feet, and becoming a love slave to glorify Him. Moses and Aaron fell on their faces and "the glory of the Lord appeared unto them." (Num. 20:6)

The wonderful majesty of God is viewed in all of nature. Behold the glory of the heavens; the grandeur of the mountains; the splendor of the glistening glacier stream; the sublimity of the calm peaceful sea; the awesome waves of a raging ocean; the dignity of the stability of the universe that reveals an Omnipotent Mind in control. Just to stand amazed in the presence of an Omnipresent God, is to prayerfully worship the Master of all things. The prayer that glorifies God brings all this majesty into focus. Prayer allows the soul to revel in His dazzling magnificence that makes the despondency caused by unchaste people to appear minute.

The stars were the illuminating beams glistening on the snow crunching under my canvas boots while delivering papers in the northern Indiana winters. The winter's short days made night time a regular part of my fifteen-mile route for thirty-one cents a day. The memory of those cold clear nights made my heart leap within my breast. The scene was magical, beyond description; the cold wind seemed to be minimized, I was seeing the handiwork of my Infinite God. My soul seemed to sing what words could not utter. I walked in the presence of God's handiwork with heart lifted heavenward.

The glory of His majesty is one thing, but troubling circumstances affect the state of mind that can take the praying soul down into a valley of despair where the glorified scenes are not present, only memories. Here, there is no view in sight that could set the soul leaping for joy. The depth of darkness demands that prayer break through with some hope. Is our prayer life going to be adequate to bring the gloom of the hour and the heavenly Father together? Are these valley experiences the only time found to seek God with all there is in the soul? Now the situation says, there is a recognition of who God is, a desire to worship and even glorify Him in the midst of hopelessness. Can our God bring the song of praise to the soul in this sad hour? If prayer has built a solid prayer foundation across the years, prayer will pray through to the dawn of a new day regardless of how dark the night is. The God who gives the praise and joy will restore it in the midst of tragedy.

Prayer permits the splendor and magnificence of God to break through to the obedient heart. With that breakthrough, comes responsive worship that mounts to glorifying the God of all gods. The soul is filled with His presence. So many times the scripture uses the word "filled" when referring to the glory of God, "the glory of God filled the house." The intangible glory fills. This filling comes with prayer touching God, which is glory beyond measure, and places praise, worship and its glory at the summit of God living in the soul.

PRAYER SEEKS AND ACKNOWLEDGES GOD'S HOLINESS AND ITS DEMANDS FOR MANKIND TO BE HOLY.

Good people can be biased, show favoritism and destroy confidence. But God, the Bible declares, is always pure and unstainable, profoundly virtuous who knows no injustice. While there are others who play god and use others for their own benefit; not so with the sinless Savior whose motive is always for our good, and will profit us for eternity. There is nothing half-hearted about His loving care, for His moral excellence and goodness will prevent impropriety. His honor can never be dishonored; His integrity is unquestioned; His benevolence is incomprehensible; His mercy is immeasurable; His generosity and righteousness are without bounds; His purpose is undefiled.

Because of who He is, justifies every decision He makes in our behalf. This makes praying not just a personal agenda, but allows the Lord to work through prayer to accomplish His will, and His will only. Would not the believer rather have his personal life in the capable and caring hands of God the Father rather than his own imperfect knowledge and short sightedness of the future?

It comes down to the fact, who should be trusted with our lives? Personal limitations and restricted abilities are well known to us, or should trust be placed in the righteous holy God who knows the beginning from the end? His judgment is always right, while our minds are subject to error. His character stands in complete completeness, while ours know the scars of depravity from the fall.

The personal prayer will be the key to deciding what road each one will take. The effectiveness of prayer and will, demand what the personal spiritual victory will be.

The prayer life cannot be elevated above what the personal surrender is. As prayer allows the soul to abandon personal will, to that measure will spiritual victory be achieved.

PRAYER IS THE BRANCH THAT KEEPS THE SOUL AND FAMILY GRAFTED INTO THE TRUE VINE, CHRIST JESUS.

The scripture says: "If ye abide." Abide means remain, to endure, to dwell; while abiding gives this understanding: lasting, unending, steadfast, immutable, and unshakable. If prayer takes this position, it has God's blessing. Prayer keeps us abiding in Christ, allowing His power to awaken the soul to fulfill His purpose in the believer's life. Abiding is always in proportion to personal surrender, giving all mankind the privilege of implantation into Divinity.

Prayerfully abiding in Christ has daily refreshment. There is nothing stale in the Godhead. What does an established soul need more than the invigorating touch that only our God can give the human soul?

This abiding has the promise of the fullness of joy, the richness of Divine love, and God's multiplied blessings.

Abiding is God saying, stay where I have placed you, with spiritual strength minister to the weak. Abiding in Christ is the source needed to have victory over temptation, while His Word will give definite instructions.

Are there added reasons to be continually abiding in Christ? God is the giver of His personal sacrifice, the granter of pure love; bestower of the Comforter; the resting place; the inexhaustible seed that continually replenishes all of creation. Prayer is our hook up.

Are there problems if there is the choice not to remain, not to abide? The results are all around us. The spiritual power lost is without measure. This loss of power has settled into homes, into every area of our society, making a spiritual blackout that only the Infinite God can fix. Man's efforts will be worthless, and our godless culture will bury us in the ruins with all other nations who have committed spiritual suicide.

Who would dare to pray in the name of Jesus that does not live daily in that name? Prayer ends when inward convictions confront the real motive that has become a fruitless branch that has been cut off. Prayer's condition depends upon whether the heart is fully abiding in the center of God's will. Adam Clark said: "God can do without man, but man cannot do without God." Nor can prayer be successful without fully abiding in Him.

Prayer allows the believer's spirit to evaluate. Natural man's fallen nature is blinded to his being dead in trespasses and sin. This was the condition of the religious Jews as Jesus weeps as He prays over Jerusalem. Their spiritual imperceptiveness so grieved the Master that tears came as He thought of the multitudes that would perish in their religious arrogance. His heart goes out to those He wanted to save. His consistent living, the numerous miracles were all a daily obvious fact, but they rebelliously rejected Him as their Messiah. What would it take? He left the riches of glory, became a servant but His thankless mission was rebuffed by those who wanted no part in a faith that demanded a pure lifestyle.

Jesus drew a picture of a hen who has the care of her chicks. She sees an enemy, such as a hawk, circling overhead, immediately she gives the danger call and the chicks run to the mother hen as she gathers them under her wings, protecting them with her life.

Many religious people are unable to evaluate their spiritual darkness over against the Light of the world who came to rescue them from that darkness. How utterly blind religion can be without Christ to make an appraisal of holiness and the unholy!

Prayer gives the ability to make the distinction between a pure heart and unclean heart; it gives the wisdom to sift the wheat from the chaff. Prayer gives the proficiency to choose between basic moral values and desires of the flesh.

Prayer allows us to sees the lost as Jesus saw them. We live in a sad day when the non-Christian can see little difference between themselves and the Christian. This is one of the main reasons prayer and Bible study are imperative. Without this preparation, confusion will leave the mind and heart without a foundation on which to build a Godly life.

PRAYER MAKES US AWARE OF THE REAL ENEMY.

Prayer gives an alert conscience an awareness of the enemy's subtle advance and will set off the alarm. Our prayer life is a thermometer of how deep our spirituality is. Is the personal spiritual life only talk without the honest walk? Prayer discloses all our weaknesses that need vital attention, and makes us concerned for good church people who are no more than that. Prayerlessness is the greatest curse in many religious people's lives.

Prayer is the key to resist resentment that life's crushing events have dealt. Caring, loving people can only do so much, because the hurt goes far deeper than human caring can reach. The battle with the loss is within where human words cannot reach. The bereavement refuses to vanish, but causes time to linger over the tragic event.

Prayer must bring the soul to the state of humbleness and submission to the will of Divine will. The subdued spirit will acts on scriptural truth that is repeated over and over again, and the might of Almighty God, the constant reminder, "I am the Lord God Almighty." This mighty power is demonstrated in the deliverance of the Israelites out of Egypt, the wilderness experience, and will enter into personal bereavement, as well. No matter what type of distress arises, it only needs His spoken word for liberation and an inner peace.

Prayer's greatest challenge is casting all anxiety on the Almighty God. There is no true humility until this load is placed on Him, and it becomes God's battle. David had committed his life into God's hand as he faced the Philistine giant. Does not the scripture entreat us to commit our way unto the Lord? This vow is more than mere words, this vow must be placed into action. That action is the proof.

There are those who place their fearful worry into God's hands, but Satan knows the weak place in the armor and will attack at that hurting spot. And before the believer is aware of what has happened, he or she is back in the midst of anxiety's turmoil. Once again the stress builds up and the issue wallows in defeat. Praying through to absolute victory is the only answer.

A prayerful Christian carries serenity of God into the daily life. Jesus talks about this spiritual victory in the sixth chapter of Matthew. He declares there is no need for vain repetition for the heavenly Father already knows your need before the petition is made. Jesus appeals to the anxious heart with the assurance that there should not be any thought about what you will eat, or drink, or whether you will have raiment. To give more assurance, he mentions the fowl of the air, they do not sow nor reap, but the Father gives them their necessities. Then He asks his audience to consider the lilies. They toil not, nor do they spin, but does the heavenly Father who made them not care for them?

In personal hardship, circumstances beyond human control, and where these cruel situations have produced a crop of resentment, prayer is needed as never before to give victory in resentment's storm. Paul suffered reproach, in stripes above measure, five times forty stripes save one, three times beaten with rods, once stoned and left for dead, shipwreck, perils in the wilderness, perils in the city, perils in the sea, perils among false brethren, weariness, the cold and nakedness. Is there reason for resentment? But hear him, I count all things loss, that I may win Christ. I press on toward the prize. (2 Cor. 11, Phil. 3)

Will our God allow life to make us or break us? Is He not the Encourager? Prayer mends that which is broken, heals the wounds, cleanses the fear, and cures the torment that resentment's pain inflicts. I prayed with a young husband who was completely crushed. His wife was unfaithful, broke the marriage bonds. Words are inadequate at this time. Only as he surrenders this tragic experience to the caring God will he find the power to forgive and restore the broken relationship. Prayer is the key to all human relationships, when every thing is cast upon Him, even resentment's cancer.

Prayer gives a Godly tone to life, a firm assurance to meet the challenge of the day. Prayer is the harmony that abides in spite of present circumstances, and prayerful cadence will quicken the weary step. It presents a pleasant overtone to what has been disagreeable. Prayer allows us to place the proper accent on life's vexed situations. At times the problem needs a soft moderate approach, while there may be times when there should be a flash of holy wrath as our Lord displayed when He chased the money-changers out of the temple.

Each individual has a spirit that has a tone, which is reflected in attitude, motive and sound quality. Prayer gives these notes a heavenly ring and sets the music in motion, which creates the atmosphere for the individual as well as all that may be in the area.

Paul's words to the Philippians have a musical ring as he suggests: "in everything by prayer and supplication with thanksgiving." (Phil. 4:3) The tones of "thanksgiving" encompass heaven, and the saints are broadcasting on heaven's wavelength. Thanksgiving rings with praise that comes from hearts that received His grace when thrust into soul wrenching conditions; while others center their thanksgiving on how He has miraculously supplied life's blessings that appeared to be unattainable; others praise Him for His watchful care over love ones who are separated by miles; others rejoice the acclaiming of the Holy Spirit conviction of lost love ones and friends bringing them to the saving knowledge in Christ Jesus; multitudes extol Him for who and what He is; others have found Him alone to be worthy of worship and willing to become His life long love slave; others proclaim Him for the privileges Calvary brings to the redeemed soul.

Life is fractured in so many ways. Only a solely committed faith prayer can breach the chasm that contains the threatening obstacles. When prayer tunes the soul to heaven's listening ear, then heaven's melodies will encircle the whole situation in life's darkest hour. Paul would say it this way: "be careful for nothing; but in everything by prayer and supplication with thanksgiving let your requests be known unto God." (Phil. 4:3)

James speaks of a prayer that: "ye ask, and receive not, because ye ask amiss, that ye may consume it upon your lust." (James 4:3) This could rightfully be called the worthless prayer. Does a prayer like that have a consequence? Who can tell the depth of the hidden hypocrisy that thinks he can cheat on God by using prayer as his concealed weapon? Regardless of how passionate the prayer, willful sin stops prayer before it gets above your head. God hates sin. This so few seem to understand.

The Psalmist said: " If I regard iniquity in my heart, the Lord will not hear me." (Ps. 66:13) How can he dare to deceive his own heart? Many professing Christians are caught in the trap of their own making. They are still attempting to cover the superficial witness, concealing unlawful appetites, harboring appeasements, having a contemptuous spirit, and a disrespectful abhorrence towards holiness.

Solomon speaks about the worthless prayer: "he that turns away his ear from hearing the law, even his prayer shall be an abomination." (Prov. 28:9) Each heart determines and sets up conditions acceptable or not acceptable that qualify or disqualify the legitimacy of the prayer. God's standards are fixed, and man's prayers must meet those standards. Jesus reminded the one that came to the altar to pray and to give a gift, and the Spirit reveals that there is a brother that you have ought against him, no need to pray further or give the gift, go get that straightened out with the brother and then come. The Father will never go against His standards, and personal willfulness is against His standards. Jesus loved the rich young ruler, saw all the potential, but his wealth was his god. Wrapped in his self-will, he walked away from his eternal opportunity.

Imagine that young man having a sick child. He would completely ignore the decision that placed his wealth before the Lord, would get on his knees and earnestly plead for the child's healing and expect God to rush to his rescue. There is absolutely no way prayer will be effective when another god is harbored in the heart.

PRAYER IS THE BELIEVER'S IMPREGNATED FORCE, ESPECIALLY IF THERE HAVE BEEN YEARS OF PRAYER PREPARATION BEFORE THE CRUCIAL CRISIS HAS OCCURRED.

If prayer and faith have little purpose and followed a hit and miss prayer life across the years, what kind of faith would be available at the time the crisis came?

When the invincible stone is rolled in front of our door, have our years of preparation built the foundation needed, where faith and prayer have to do what human wisdom can not do? When the uncontrollable is placed in helpless hands, then what? The event is real. It is not happening to someone else, but for this hour, heaven and the Almighty God's grace is imperative. But this kind of faith and prayer are like foreign aliens. The shame of prayerlessness and a faith that has had little use in the past, stands paralyzed in personal judgment. The prayer life is irrevocable.

Daniel's prayer life had formed a faith in his God daily. He was not in that lion's den alone, an angel was closing the lions' mouths, and eliminating the beasts' appetite. His prayer of Faith over shadowed the tragedy that had befallen him, and wicked men's plans were defeated. His godly and prayerful life received God's promise for faithfulness at a crucial time in his life.

If prayer is not cultivated and developed, the expectations will be negligible when cruel fate drops in unexpected. Why? The groundwork has been neglected, by a procrastinating prayer life. Prayer takes time and work day after day. To minimize the need to enhance and advance the personal prayer life, is to be weighed in the balance and found wanting. We dare not fool with the sacredness of our heavenly communication privileges.

One day the uninvited, (place your crisis here), will appear and be very real, where human capacities will be helpless and Divine access will be the only hope. A faithful prayer understructure will be more important than the gods that stole your prayer time. Daniel's prayer life prepared him for that hour.

PRAYER ALLOWS US TO BREATHE HEAVEN'S AIR.

Would it not be possible to feel prayer opens the perchance that mingles with the heavenly host? Is it not said that man can walk with God? Then does not man breathe the same breath God breathes?

Heaven's atmosphere can be anywhere, especially in the believer's soul, for the Holy Spirit has part in heaven's atmosphere. Because He (the Holy Spirit) is God and has all the same motives and attributes the Godhead has, the believer relishes to absorb His word; wills to walk with Him where He chooses; desires to embrace His mind; yearns for more of His wisdom; and hungers and thirsts after His righteousness, which creates heaven's atmosphere in the soul. Our Mediator sent the Holy Spirit for that purpose.

Nehemiah Adams chimes in with his note of "certain joyful, though humble, confidence becomes us when we pray in the Mediator's name. 'It is due to Him; when we pray in His name should be without wavering. Remember His merits, and how prevalent they must be. Let us come boldly to the throne of grace.' When we do we claim heaven's atmosphere for ourselves."

This ambience can evolve from a like-minded group. Paul wrote to the Ephesians: "and has raised us up together, and made us set in heavenly places in Christ Jesus." They had the same mind, had the same dedication and the devotion. This unwavering reverence raises the prayer's expectation; displaying a fervor that enhances holiness; develops a loving passion that compliments godliness; intensifies a love that glorifies His love; develops a loyalty that disregards the questionable life; sets a piety that rests entirely on scriptural pronouncements.

But this atmosphere is not something that can be worked up, or manipulated for self-enjoyment, but the soul must be bathed in incessant prayer. The price is wrapped up in what comes out of the secret closet. Talk will not do it, organization is inadequate, religious activities are feeble attempts, all without heavenly results. The work of faithful prayer alone is the contact that ushers in the heavenly atmosphere that creates the breath God breathes.

PRAYER PUTS THE PRESENCES OF GOD
IN OUR WITNESS.

The only way anyone can tell if the witness is authentic is being aware the Holy Spirit is using the human vessel as His witness. Witnessing is no more than mere words if the Holy Spirit does not verify its truth. The observer may not agree with the witness, but he cannot escape the Holy Spirit's presence verifying the Truth.

The veracity of the witness is always measured in or by the presence and conviction of the Holy Spirit. Otherwise, the seed falls on stony ground. The enemy can make a deceitful witness appear real and attractive, but the Holy Spirit reveals truth, as He did in Acts 5:1, when Ananias and Sapphira pretended they had given all, but the Holy Spirit unveiled their lie to Peter and the consequence was tragic. When the Holy Spirit controls the witness, it will never be in vain.

But what is the ingredient that insures the presence of the Holy Spirit in the witness? Does it not start with a pure heart in the prayer closet, where the believer is open to the searchlight of the Spirit? This is a daily inspection. All extra baggage is scrutinize as to its worth in the light of eternity, holy honesty will allow the believer to walk in the Light the Spirit gives.

What true believer would dare to bring reproach and shame upon the cause of Christ? The prevention is the daily prayer closet that sets the tone for the day. The Proverb writer makes it clear: "a true witness delivers souls but a deceitful witness speaks lies." (Prov. 14:25)

PRAYER FILLS THE SOUL WITH GOD'S GRACE
AND PEACE.

Grace and peace are used together in many places in the scripture. It is difficult to separate one from the other. It is evident you cannot have one without the other. Both are God given, bestowed because of favorable regard. The kindly act reveals a caring disposition involving Divine favor. The prayer seeking soul covets God's pleasure and delights in that harmonized relationship between God and man.

Paul in his battle with the "thorn in the flesh" received God's answer in these words: "and He said unto me, my grace is sufficient for thee; for thy strength is made perfect in weakness. Most gladly therefore will I rather glory in my infirmities, that the power of Christ may rest upon me." (II Cor. 12:9) Because of grace received, he had peace with God's solution. There is no evidence of Paul protesting God's reply, but he is content with God's will for his life. If he were to suffer let it be for the glory of God.

The believer who comes out of the prayer closet in full confidence that the suffering will not be more than his spiritual strength can bear, will be filled with both grace and peace; which are the superstructure of the inner life. Both will carry our weaknesses into the storms ahead, becoming our viability that fortifies against the terrors of fear. When prayer brings stout-heartedness to the inner being that has grace and peace there will be stability and confidence of victory. For what can separate us from God's grace and love? Only ourselves!

Jesus left the light at the end of tunnel with these words: "peace I leave with you, my peace I give unto you; not as the world gives, give I unto you. Let not your heart be troubled, neither let it be afraid." (John 14:27) Without a vital prayer life this assurance is impossible. Prayer takes us through the valleys of infirmities, grief, harassment, and instabilities.

Prayer allows us to face up to the realities of life. Prayer reminds me I am not the supplier, only the willing vessel. How many have entered the prayer closet battered by life, beaten, grasping for spiritual breath, and have emerged filled with triumphant grace and peace? Where else can anyone find a renewed spirit and a revived purpose?

PRAYER DEFINES CONVICTION
THAT PRODUCES ACTION.

It is not difficult to feel defeated when praying for family and loved ones, when it appears nothing is happening spiritually. Years fly by, with little or no desire to seek the Lord, addicted to a culture that is bound with its many personal appetites, enslaved with peer pressure, dominated by what the humanist philosophy called success, delighted with personal comforts, finding contentment in the pension plan and the size of the bank account, but negligent about seeking God, shortsighted in not considering personal accountability to the Giver of possessions possessed, trifling about the influence and its effect on time and place. But influence does not stop there, what about its impression on others for time and eternity. How miserable it is to be wrapped in your self-world! A vibrant prayer life will not allow that to happen.

There is a temptation to say, is it worth the time to continue to pray for those so lost in their world of plans and activity that life is only seen in the here and now? After years, the thought comes to questioning the depth of the believer's faith. This can be good or bad; good if the Spirit is searching the heart; bad if doubt has an effect on faith, which will automatically have a negative consequence on the prayer life.

When prayer weariness sets in, the prayer warrior must realize he has an accountability to be faithful in prayer regardless of what the appearance of indifferences may be. Prayer indifference will appear with him at the judgment. There will be no excuse.

It is God's will that none will perish, therefore the battle is against the powers of evil, and as long as that evil power is controlling the lost soul, and if there is no will that wants to be released, there will be no movement towards the Lord. Our Lord will not force the human will to make a choice that his will does not will to make. Until the human will wills to serve God, then results will be apparent and accountability rests on choice.

There is always the possibility that the person praying wants their will and not God's will. Then there is the problem of self-will from within. The Lord may want to put the individual in a particular place, but the one praying has other plans.

There is the possibility that the one praying has not captured the horror of being lost for all eternity. If so, prayer will never reach its full potential because the prayer is fallible as a result of lack of concern and deficiency of Biblical knowledge of what it means to be lost forever.

This consciousness of being lost must be taken into the prayer closet. How can intercessory prayer have the necessary conviction unless the soul is captured by the certainty of Biblical lostness? Can the human mind fathom fully how fixed eternal punishment is? Only prayer can take the believer to the depth of human capacity to comprehend at least in some measure, the Biblical perspective of a human soul that perishes forever. Faithful prayer will cry out in their behalf while the opportunity is still alive.

PRAYER THAT IS EFFECTUAL HAS THE IDENTIFICATION OF THE HOLY SPIRIT'S LEADERSHIP MOMENT BY MOMENT.

R.G. Le Tourneau said: " when young people ask me how they can know God's will for their lives, I sometimes answer them that they don't need to know that. If you have a guide whom you can trust, you don't need to know the destination to follow Him. So, I say the way to know God's will for your life is to follow Him today, do His will in the present moment because that is the only life you have any promise of."

Is not Mr. Le Tourneau saying, if daily the believer is in the center of God's will and fully committed to Him, then that is God's will for him for that day. To commit is to practice. Practice what, commitment to do, to give over, to render service, to continual to commit. Commitment signifies reliance, to agree to be trustworthy. It is to give over your title deed with full confidence it will bring full assurance to your spiritual life that it may be fulfilled in Him. Commitment to service cannot be complete without full commitment to the prayer closet.

Commitment is a pledge to the Godhead that everything that comes the believer's way is signed over to Him. Which means, there will be times when there will not be any way to see where your foot will land. In the creek bed there were stones, which were called the stepping-stones, where those who knew where they were could cross the creek without getting too wet. If it was dark, crossing the creek was necessary, but it was a faith walk. If the stone was missed, it meant getting soaked. Commitment is walking with God and taking the next step, even though the rock cannot be seen; there is a trust He will plant your foot on the rock. That is trust so few Christians have.

Many professing Christians' commitment is so shallow they will only operate where they can see, or give if it won't hurt their bank account too much. Regular attendance at the Sunday morning service, a few short sentence prayers before jumping in bed, a few lines read from some devotional book are insufficient commitments. This is not hand the title and deed over to the Lord and say, time, effort, planning to put God first is all in the title and whatever else the Father would like to add.

Very few will understand what wholeness is because there is little comprehension what holiness is. Since the Holy Spirit is our best teacher, there is a daily need to have classroom sessions, which are held in the prayer closet. It is in these sessions where the Holy Spirit teaches the seeking believer. But that means hours of prayer labor.

From the prayer closet comes the spiritual productivity where kind word or deed is done; the hospital call, praying with hurting, daily smoothing the troubled waters, being unashamed of Biblical truth, honest in work ethics, even making restitution by restoring stolen property.

Prayer is a daily commitment that does not end until man takes his last breath. I do not know if prayer will be a continual process in heaven, but praise will.

PRAYER IS THE DIVINE DIRECTIVE ON WHICH SPIRITUAL VICTORY RESTS.

Prayer keeps the focus on the journey leading to the promised land. But past lessons shall not be forgotten. It is the proven past that gives wisdom for future progress. God gave Israel a charge, " thou shalt remember." The past was to keep them on the straight and narrow in the future. What were they to remember? Remember how the Lord led them through impossible situations in the wilderness; remember how that experience humbled them; remember how it proved to them; remember how they found out what was in their hearts; remember they were to keep the commandments by choice. (De. 8:2) This was an assurance they needed to guarantee victory in the promised land. Unbelief would be the cause for defeat; distrust cannot follow God's directive; they were to consider the folly of doubt.

Victory has the way to arouse pride. But if the Israelites would remember what happened to them in the wilderness when arrogance caused rebellion, it would humble them and cause them to maintain steadfastness in God's leadership. Without the hard knocks and God's wrath poured upon them for their disobedience, this would made them aware of their limitations and not allow conceit to have a seedbed for spiritual problems to grow. Humbleness has God's blessing, while ungodly pride is the enemy.

Is God just to prove His people? How else could His people see the real motive and drive of their heart? It took forty years of testing, and a generation to die off to get the right stock needed to enter the promised land.

The rebellious ones did not enter in. Their remains were buried in the desert sands. God will be God.

Are we not children of the wilderness, just traveling through with the promised land just ahead? How similar are our points of God's directives. The same dangers confront His people today. Then how can we expect less? The same standards are ours to keep all along the journey.

All these experiences of the Israelites are tied into our daily lives. The answers are answered in the prayer closet. We do not have a Moses, we have the Holy Spirit as our director. The orders are given in those prayer hours. No prayer, no director; no prayer to hold the line, no heaven; rebellion, dying in this world's wilderness; prayerlessness bears the fruits of lostness.

Who would dare to consider the cost of prayerlessness for all eternity? We are called to fight the battles in the wilderness now to gain the promised land later, and prayer and Bible study are our greatest weapons. The choice was given to the Israelites then, but now it is our choice.

PRAYER IS THE MAJOR FACTOR THAT UNITES THE HUMAN WITH THE DIVINE.

Ezra returns to Jerusalem, and is devastated with the deplorable conditions. The poorer class that was not taken into captivity had dropped into a deeply depraved state by intermarrying into a heathen society. The heathen gods had degraded and sapped what spiritual life they had. They were trapped in the loss of will to achieve. When this happens, accomplishment is on the bottom round of the ladder. Disgrace and shame had lost its meaning. What a picture of today!

Ezra prays "O my God, I am ashamed and blush to lift up my face to Thee, my God; for our iniquities are increased over our head and our trespass is grown up unto the heavens." (Ezra 9:6) Prayer pushes action. First on the long list was separation. There had to be clear-cut separation from heathen marriages. Which meant the drastic decision to break up the families that had married into the godless culture. What desperate measures must be taken to undo what sin has done. From where does this kind of strength and power come? What a man! He had to be God's man, and that godliness had to capture the people in order to unleash such heart wrenching demands.

Prayer cannot effectively demand, but that prayer can be the God given empowerment and the potency needed to stand up to the situation.

How many of America's pulpits demand God's order for His people to be separated from ungodly sin! The calling has lost its manhood, and surrendered to the religion of secular humanism and its godless demands for a society without any mention of the living God. Now we find ourselves wallowing in the cesspools of iniquity. When the pulpits are apprehended from the floundering pulpiteers that gripped Ezra's soul, there will be a spiritual awaken that America has never experienced. But it will never happen as long as prayerless is practice, and vital prayer is the forgotten cause.

When prayer ties the human and the Divine together, miracles of all miracles will be resurrected, the spiritually dead soul will become alive vibrating with Divine energy. Human helplessness creates an environment that connects with Omnipotence. Every Spirit filled soul wants that kind spiritual bonding.

Ezra found prayer to be the lifeline that can heal the shame and anguish of a fallen people. Israel's devastation was not too great for Ezra's God. God had handled degrading disgrace before, and saw their sin defeated by a surrendered, separated people. When God's people pray, marvelous things will open endless possibilities.

PRAYER WRESTLED IN THE SPIRIT HAS OUR FATHER'S ATTENTION.

Wrestling in the Spirit is a spiritual conflict: a battle with evil, including demonic principalities that would seek to shape the destiny of the soul. Wrestling in prayer saps spiritual energy, many times taking the soul into the pits of anguish because the burden is so enormous that its weight threatens the weakened condition caused by the spiritual struggle. The conflict is rescued in the prayer closet.

Jacob found himself engaged in the prayer tussle with the angel. Jacob was soon to face an angry Esau over whom he had used questionable means to gain his birth-right. He now sought Divine intervention to quiet the storm he was about to confront. Evidently, he was not getting the assurance that God would intervene. All through the night his prayer fought back the enemy, refusing to lose the battle that was going on in his soul. He could not go any further without God's blessing.

What is life without God's blessing? It is no real life at all. Many professing Christians want God's blessing but will not pay prayer's price, which means, praying until they pray through and receive the blessing. The attitudes all too many times are, Lord, I need this assurance, and this need must have a quick answer, and then I'll be on my way. Prayer assurance costs the prayee. The Lord is not a waiting servant that jumps on the demands of some lukewarm Beings He created.

All too often, like Jacob, if trickery and deceit are covered, it will take a pure and surrendered heart if God's blessing is going to be given. It is at this point when the battle rages in the soul that has concealed deception must face its confrontation; admitting the wrong; daring to be confronted for its sinfulness; pride and self-will that have raised their ugly heads; realizing how low and corrupt the soul is, is not an easy recognition to anyone who has built life on deception. Jacob, for many years had avoided who he was in his soul. Now was time to come clean, but there was no way he could circumvent sin and get God's blessing. So it is with all mankind, want the blessing, the cost of complete and entirely surrender is the price. There may be a war, but lay down your arms and admit defeat, and then the victory blessing will be given.

These combatants, good and evil, God's heavenly hosts against the demons from hell, will continue this battle for the souls of mankind until the end of the age. There will be a winner and a loser, and I am glad I have chosen to be on the victor's side. But no one can escape clashes with the enemy that are certain to come, but with a cleansed heart all decisions can become victories.

These battles will be contended in the prayer closet or under the starlit heavens as Jacob's was. Here is Jacob's cry: "and Jacob was left ALONE; and there wrestled a man with him until the breaking of the day . . .and he said: I will NOT let thee go, except thou bless me." (Gen. 32:24&26) Notice, these spiritual battles are alone. This is a triangle between physical man, the invisible hosts of heaven, and the demons from hell. Some one may be helpful, but the sole decision is in each individual's hands, alone. Jacob's determination is fixed: "I will not let thee go, except thou bless me." Is he not saying, whatever it takes, I will not let go until the blessing is given? Does this not teach a great lesson in prayer and its warfare? Does not this act of will reveal strength of mind and purpose of will to settle with nothing less than total victory? Which is the basic foundation for prayer.

PRAYER PLACES GOD AT THE VERY CENTER OF LIFE.

This takes planning, it just does not happen otherwise. Paul must have had this in mind when he instructed the Thessalonians to: "pray without ceasing." (1 Thess. 5:17) Prayer is not only an act, but also an attitude. When prayer places God in the center of life, the whole life revolves around a day that has been prepared, organized, and has the mind-set to put God first. If the day does not start with this in mind it will not be likely to end that way. A prayerful attitude has to be a desire, and desire's purpose is to execute God's intention.

How many are like the lady who was embittered by her inability to handle her overwhelming situation. She said: "I have been overweight for six years. It has affected my marriage. I no longer have any pep and bounce like I once had. I want to serve the Lord, but the drive is gone. It is easier for me to plop in front of the T.V. than do any thing for Jesus."

Life and its purpose and meaning is gone for this lady, there is no control over the will to be what God wants her to be. God centeredness has been replaced with self-centeredness. There is nothing more controlling than a self-absorbing complacent mind-set. An essential part of vital prayer will purge and refocus energy into God's rationale. There is no way the mind can be picked up and repositioned by human will. Yes, the human will can reposition into deeper depravity. But human will within itself, cannot cleanse the mind and heart to be God centered. Without the Holy Spirit doing the cleansing, there is no possible way the mind can be in a position to please God. If this cleansing does not take place, the mind is under the control of a depraved nature, coercing acts that are distasteful and destructive, because God has not been placed at the center of life, controlling its activities.

Paul admonishes us by saying: "But I keep under my body, and bring it into subjection lest that by any means, when I have preached to others, I myself be a castaway." (1 Cor. 9:27) If the mind and heart are not cleansed by the Holy Spirit it will be impossible to place the whole being in complete subjection to the Holy Spirit. Praying through to victory will place the soul and body under the Biblical standards for the Master's utilization and place it in the proper situation for Godly use. Prayer will give the verification that the Holy Spirit has conquered the enemy.

PRAYER ARRANGES LIFE'S PRIORITIES.

Prayer takes priorities' stumbling blocks out of the way and replaces them with godly perspectives. Prayer places a spiritual hungry man's priority and dreams are the key to the purpose and thrust to life.

Priority does not mean second place, but the top ranking dignity to the Godhead. It is the push of effort to place all activities in their proper order, and the discipline to carry them out through the day. This is a daily task that must have a willing mind and soul. Godly priority always adds up to choice. Choice is critical because there is always a huge temptation to take the route of least resisting barriers and obstacles that are threatening. Jesus spoke of this choice, one is the straight and narrow way that to lead to heaven; the other is the broad way, the going with the flow, which is the way to an eternity of lostness. It is one or the other. There is no in-between.

What are these choices? Usually for the Christian, it is the choice between the best and the excellent. It can be between going to church or watching the ball game. There is nothing necessarily wrong with watching a ball game, but the more excellent way, the top priority is taking the family and going to church. Our choices speak for themselves, climbing higher on the spiritual ladder or going lower on that same ladder. Extra effort and planning are needed if the priority is to keep our Lord in first place. My daughter would say to the young people, " you have to have a plan." Life is far more than hit or miss, it is God's purpose for the day.

Our daughter would come to my meetings on the weekend and bring her school work. Sometimes I would work with her on Saturday night and when the clock struck 12 o'clock she would say: "we need to stop." She never studied on Sunday. If her school work was not completed, she would get up at 4 o'clock Monday morning to get it done before she went to school. It is true, we choose what we want to do, and what we will to do.

Out of choices come fruits, which can be good or bad. Christians are known by their spiritual fruits, which are: love, joy, peace, longsuffering, gentleness, goodness, faith, meekness, and temperance. (Gal. 4:22&23) These are the priorities for each day. All people have every right to expect these fruits, and even pick some to enhance their personal lives.

How does prayer enter into these priorities? Prayer always gives proper consideration to what is vital for personal spiritual advancement and for others' needs that are known. In our family devotional time, if our daughter was to have a test that day, that test had a definite place in the family's prayer time. Prayer reaches out to have God's blessing upon all that He already knows will happen that day, and prepares the soul for its happening. If the crisis comes, the ground-work has already been laid. The prayerful soul does not need to call for God to make known His presence, for He is already there.

Praying people evaluate their spiritual priorities daily, which are never neutralized by what other professing Christians do. Actions reflect the fruits and the character. Prayer will have an enormous impact on sorting out the proper priority for the day. Prayer is the prime mover that refuses to allow the soul to consider anything less than excellence.

PRAYER BINDS THE SECRET OF THE FATHER'S UNREVEALED PRESENCES.

Only the Lord knows the countless times God's angel of mercy delivered us from tragedy by an unseen automobile, a slip on the roof, the miss of an unknown object, or a flat tire that stopped you from becoming a part of a pile-up just ahead.

Some would write that mercy off as being lucky. But God's people do not live by luck; they move and have their being in the hands of Almighty God. Nothing can happen that He does not first allow to happen. God permitted Satan to test Job otherwise Satan could not have touched him. God's people have the privilege of Divine mercy's care. Does that mean we will never have any adversities? No! God knows best what we need individually. But what good would steel be for a battleship if it had never been placed in the fire so it could be tempered? We must know ourselves, and life's fires are the only way the true self will be exposed, and made ready for use.

Prayer concentrates on more than this life, it takes the soul into the heavenlies and allows our hope to rest in the full will of God. Personal pleasure and rich joy originate from the throne room with its endless enrichments for the everlasting soul. What in this world can give that enriching ingredient?

Prayer that moves the Father's heart is issued from a pure heart that has the motive that God be glorified regardless of the circumstances in which we find ourselves. Professional praying chills the heart of God. It is like a wintry blast that leaves the soul shivering with its self-generated callousness. Such praying is spiritually suffocating, choking all the life out of any substance that gives prayer life and vitality.

God's child is confident his prayers engender an intensity from holy motive that warms the Father's heart, which gives passion that fires fresh faith. The assurance encourages faith to risk the unknown. The expectation of earnest prayer brings new boldness to claim greater territory in Jesus' name. Prayer keeps our private line open for any emergency call that we may not see or know, but He always knows where and when the emergencies will be. " The angel of the Lord encamps round about then that fear Him, and delivers them." (Ps. 34:7)

PRAYER IS MEDITATION UPON GOD BEING GOD, WHO HE IS AND WHAT HE IS.

Prayer sweeps us into the heavenly fulfilling the soul's desired aspirations. The Psalmist envisioned our Creator as "the searcher," the all knowing One, knowing our downsitting, and taking note of our uprising, understands our thoughts and motives, compasses our path, and acquainted with all my ways, not one word that drops from my lips that He does not hear. He knows the behind and the before as He places His hand on me. His knowledge is too wonderful and high for me to grasp its full significance. Where can we go that He is not already there? The Psalmist said: "if I ascend up into heaven, thou art there; if I make my bed in hell, behold thou art there." The Psalmist spreads his vision further, "if I take the wings of the morning, and dwell in the uttermost parts of the sea, even there shall Thy hand lead me and Thy right hand shall hold me, darkness cannot cover me, for He is light, and in Him is no darkness."

What an astounding view for the human mind to complicate and embrace. Beholding the Infinite God in all His majesty. Even what little man can comprehend, is minute, but still staggers the human intellect. Then think what man does not know, and what is beyond that. God's wonders startle the imagination, overwhelming man's limitations, which leads to the quest to reach into His awesome world to ponder the unthinkable splendor that the human mind longs to explore. The incredible wonderment urges the believer to seize every opportunity to snatch even the slightest knowledge that would give new insight into His amazing Truth, and His Infinite capacity. The spiritually hungry heart grapples to reach beyond himself. Because wherever the eager soul reaches, He is there; never to hinder this yearning to relish His goodness and mercy. Sharing His endless blessings, which are at the center of the Father's heart. The shout from the soul, Oh Father don't allow the eternal soul, God given to wallow in the trivial, but energize this mind through the Holy Spirit to comprehend with the heavenly; to search truth's beauty; to walk with the holy.

Prayer is the usher that takes us into the awesome majesty of His thought world. To have an audience with the God who planned the universe and all its contents is a privilege Calvary has given the believer! For the believer to hunger for less, is to deprive the soul of the opportunity Christ's sacrifice cost.

Prayer will reveal more and more of the benefit this birth-right has opened through our Lord. Prayer is the avenue that our Father has chosen to communicate man's deepest desires to know more of the God of gods.

PRAYER'S IMPORTUNITY AROUSES GOD'S HEART.

The importune prayer has a shameless persistence and an insistence that will not give up. This nature of prayer is like a pit bull that is tenacious, holding on with locked jaws until the foe is totally submitted.

The Amplified version of Luke 11:9 gives prayer an inexorable plea: " So I say to you, ask and keep on asking, and it shall be given you, seek and keep on seeking, and you shall find; knock and keep on knocking, and the door shall be opened to you." Does not our Lord sanction, even encourage a steadfast, without wavering immovability for prayer to have more than the usual praying power? This type of prayer embraces faith even when it appears all hope is gone. An unshakable faith has its roots in Biblical truth. Evidently the Father sees a persuasive faith in unceasing prayer that He cannot avoid.

Is there not a test in the prayer of importunity?

Does it not appear the Lord is asking, just how determined are you? Can you take the perpetual agony that goes with continuous praying? If this type of praying lingers, is there a fear that the Lord may point you in a direction you would not want to go? The enemy will make sure, the longer the situation persists will mean deeper distress, thus, a greater test of the will. Will the soul be exhausted before the answer comes? How many times have praying Christians given up just before the Father opens the door?

Importunity is patience and waiting, but not just waiting but waiting in anticipation and expectancy. The longer the wait, the more Faith is examined and tested. The waiting period may uncover some baggage that needs to be cleaned out that has contaminated effectual faith. This revelation cannot be ignored.

A good question for all of us is, has our importunity faltered and does unanswered prayer now lie at our doorstep because we could not endure the rigors of the hours demanded to meet the resolve needed.

PRAYER IS THE FOOTSTEP THAT LEADS THE SOUL INTO HIS PEACEFUL REST.

This is the promise of our Lord; " I will give you rest." (Matt. 4:28) rest, peace, but where? The world and our nation are in turmoil. Terr strap explosives around their waists and commit unthinkable acts; prisons are needed for young and old; godless educators have washed our young people and now these people are in the places sion making in every segment of our lives. Everywhere greedy, selfish, power hungry, envious people are ready to settle for temptible religious humanism where there are no rights or wrongs. All this has seeped into every profession, industry, and legislative area–local, state and national. Liberal judges who are not elected are controlling our country, not the elected officers; perverted sex is acceptable. You say, "look at that mess and tell me prayer is the footstep that leads the soul to rest? I am so concerned for my child, the drugs, pornography is in my child's face at every turn; the hated rap is accessible everywhere. Please tell me, how can I expect to find peace and rest in this chaos?"

A little over thirty years after our Lord said: "I will give you rest," the Apostle Paul writes from his dungeon in Rome: "and the peace of God, which passes all understanding, shall keep your hearts and through Christ Jesus." Is not Paul saying, it does not matter what evolves around you, but it does matter what is going on inside of you? There can be all kinds of tumult and uproar all about you, but prayer can bring peace and rest even in dysfunctional homes where there are hurtful agitations continually.

Self-effort falls short, but God's grace can take defeat out of any situation. From the filth found in a dungeon Paul writes: "rejoice in the Lord always, nd again I say rejoice." Then he rises to new heights by saying, "be care-
¹ for nothing; but in everything by prayer and supplication with thanks-
'ng let your requests be made known unto God."

ᶜor the broken hearts that are caught in unbelievable circumstances.
be a caring word for you to find a place where you can get alone
'ord. Then pray until you find His rest and peace. He promised,
ᵻnot do otherwise.

LLOWS THE OUTFLOW, THE SWEETNESS OF
VEN TO EMPOWER AND CONTROL.

Ah,
rists
more
brain-
f deci-
hostile,
he con-

ᵻer: "the conduit through which the power of heaven is

ᵻs us a glimpse of our Lord's prayer life. Mark in
ᵻg, rising up a great while before day, he went out
ᵻy place, and there prayed." Mark again writes in
nt them away, he departed into a mountain to
ᵻd it came to pass in those days, that he went
ᵻd continued all night in prayer to God."

Why was God praying to God? Because a part of Jesus was human, and He, God took on the physical identity of man. His humanity was entirely human, which had the same demands we as human beings have. Therefore, the human part of His Deity could not be satisfied without the contact with Deity outside Himself. His contact was prayer, the same as ours. His humanity had definite needs, and prayer fulfilled that need. If our Lord's humanity needed to get in touch with the Father, how much more does His created beings' humanity necessitate personal communion with the Father.

Why would our Lord pray so much, and about what? Have we forgotten His purpose in coming? Was it not to seek and save that which is lost? Then can we not expect the greater part of His prayer was for the lost? Was this not His blood being shed on the Cross, all about redeeming the lost? The prayer burden on His heart was for the lost.

Does our Lord's approach to prayer have anything to say to His followers? His "called out ones" can do no less than to fit schedules into the praying mold of our Lord. The spirit of man demands an audience with his Maker. Anything less leaves the soul like a missile that has lost its laser guidance system.

THE BURDEN OF THE BELIEVER'S PRAYER MUST FOCUS ON THE LOST.

There is no way the human mind can fully comprehend what it means to be lost forever, but Jesus does open a glimpse of its reality in the account of the rich man in hell and Lazarus, the beggar in Abraham's bosom. If the scripture and Calvary does not grip the heart, then lukewarmness will. The Lord said He would spew that kind of religious indifference out His mouth.

How does our Lord's approach to prayer line up with our prayer list? Where and how is ninety per cent of our emphasis spent in prayer, for what?

There is the believer that can measure his prayer life around himself and his family's personal needs. Prayer seldom goes beyond his or her self-centered advance. Thus, neglecting God's central purpose for prayer. It is easier to substitute religious activities for prayer and call it adequate.

How does this praying concern come close to the flow of heaven's empowerment and control? This kind of saturated prayer breathes in the fruits of the Spirit. This spirit is heaven's empowerment flowing continually in the life of God's prayer warriors

E.M. Bounds in his book *Purpose in Prayer*, speaks of Stonewall Jackson as a man of prayer. He relates Mr. Jackson's quote: "I have so fixed the habit of prayer in my mind that I never raise a glass of water to my lips without asking God's blessing, never seal a letter without putting a word of prayer under the seal, never take a letter from the post without a brief sending of my thoughts heavenward, never change my classes in the lecture room without a minute petition for the cadets who go out and for those who come in."

It was said of James Gilmour, the pioneer missionary to Mongolia, that he never used a blotter in writing. He used the time to pray while the ink was drying on the page he had written.

Will not this type of consecrated prayer mellow the heart, sweeten the spirit, and clothe the character with godly control and care?

Obedient prayer will place the Lord in His rightful place, first place. It is strange that we understand what the word "first" means in every phase of life. There are hours of practice and study to seek to be "first" in every area of life, but "first" loses its meaning when it comes to placing God first.

We encourage our children to contend for first place in scholarship, becoming on the first team in athletics, pushing and planning for first place in the workplace with the best job, pushing to come out in first place in any activity in which they compete. Most people want to be chosen first, first in line is important. It is a lesson in human nature to sit back and watch people shove and push their way into a better position.

Do these same people plan to place the Lord God in first place in their everyday lives? When the Lord says to seek God first, suddenly first means wherever He fits in. Evidently to most professing Christians, God's place in every day life has little importance, only if there is a crisis.

Does the average Christian teach their child to place God first by his or her personal example? Matthew 6:33 drives the point home: "but seek ye

FIRST the kingdom of God and His righteousness and all these things will be added unto you." This is a command that our Lord has given to each believer.

Putting God first will never happen without a daily vital prayer life. Prayer must have depth and meaning to keep the Lord in His proper place, but it cannot be done without an imperative prayer life.

PRAYER EXPOSES SELF-INDULGENCES.

Prayer allows the Holy Spirit to be the guardian of the soul. How easy it is to pamper the flesh. The advertisement ends with, "you deserve it." In other words, "pamper yourself." Self-serving can reach beyond the spiritual safety zone and decisions can be questionable. Self-righteousness can substitute religion for personal spirituality. Self-satisfaction will diminish the spiritual appetite and leave the soul empty. Self-approval allows vanity and pride to destroy humility and pluck meekness from the motive. Self-centeredness plunges the soul into self-seeking pursuits that inflate self-importance.

Self-seeking is the most destructive part of the human being. This enemy drives the sins of spirit into uncontrollable situations, such as, covetousness, greed, jealousy, anger, and unforgiveness. Where does a brash spirit fit into spiritual modesty? A yielding prayerful spirit is obedient to the light the Holy Spirit reveals whether the sin of self-indulgence is evident to others or not.

Isaiah 59:1&2 points out the problem the Lord has with those who seek to avoid the sins of the spirit: "behold the Lord's arm is not shortened, that it cannot save; neither His ear heavy, that it cannot hear: BUT your iniquities have separated between you and your God, and your sins have hid His face from you, that He will NOT hear."

The self-life may not be apparent to the average person, but it will separate anyone from the Father who knows the intent of the heart. Multitudes of professing Christians have all but given up on praying because the heavens are like brass. Their prayers are barren and their faith shattered by unanswered prayers. Prayer becomes useless and doubt has questioned the trustworthiness of praying. The rehearsing of religious platitudes and the routine church going will not veil iniquity. The Psalmist suggested in a direct way, "if I regard iniquity in my heart, the Lord will not hear me." (66:18) Fruitful prayer requires clean hands and a pure heart.

Self-indulgence has a loosening, relaxing effect on restraint; a defiant liberating freedom that moves without restrictions. Self-indulgence renders a relief from scriptural demands that self-gratifies the flesh.

EFFECTUAL PRAYER PERMITS THE BELIEVER TO EVALUATE THE DIFFERENCES BETWEEN EXCELLENCE AND THE BEST.

Prayer reveals the tendency for an undisciplined lifestyle in any area. Prayer reveals self's aggressiveness.

Some things may be admissible, which could be considered the best, but then, there is the excellence which is still higher. Our God calls us to the more excellent way. Paul reveals the intangibles to be the excellence to which the believer is called. "Whatsoever things are true, whatsoever things are honest, whatsoever things are just, whatsoever things are pure, whatsoever things are lovely, whatsoever things are of good report; if there be any virtue, and if there be any praise, think on these things." (Phil. 4:8) Paul places before the believer those things of eternal value, which will not pass away.

Prayer is the invisible that motivates a spiritual relationship with the intangibles, the most powerful elements in the universe, outside of the Godhead, which is still the intangible. What is true rests entirely in almighty God. Therein is knowledge complete, authentic dependability, unquestionable truth, and unexplainable and yet so very real. It is only in this world of intangibles that the believer can have access to the only complete honesty, and true justice. It is only here where unblemished purity is found, where nothing is contaminated or defiled, the absolutes are unadulterated, and impartially is gone.

Prayer pervades the loveliness of the heavenly. Prayer pierces through the depravity of a fallen world; authorizing the believer to choose excellence, and to think and mediate on the choices that enrich the inner being. What priceless privileges the believer has! What endless benefits are to be enjoyed now and forever! What measureless riches He, the very God of all has to give to the prayer warrior who dares to invade and partake of the intangible excellence as their power!

A PRAYERFUL BELIEVER WILL FORBID THE TEMPTATION TO ENTERTAIN ANOTHER'S PERSONAL PREJUDICE.

When the non-traditional is introduced, the walls seem to be too high to cross, especially if holiness is threatened. There is no need to go in the direction of the threat to scriptural holiness at this time, but there is a necessity to deal with the prejudgment of those who come from a sin-infected situation, or some ill-clad individual that appears to have few possibilities. Prayer that honestly confronts any discrimination will find victory in God's grace alone. There is no shortcut; predisposition must be dealt with from the inside out. These people must not be ostracized, but particularly the church must teach that the God they have come to worship is holy, purity demands respect, which means our best. God is not cheap, and does not wallow in man's low life that is disrespectful to God for who He is. Respect their person, which evidently, they do not do for themselves, but kindly teach them that the holy God demands a holy people who act and dress according to the meaning of holiness. Every position most churches have taken is "we are so glad they come" and we do not want to offend them in any way, but they do not think how such shabby indecent appearance offends the holy God they came to worship. Evidently the church does not see how that cheapness and carelessness will automatically carry over into their spiritual lives.

Let a child dress sloppily, be uncouth, have no respect and be discourteous and that will transfer to the classroom, the study habits, and any job he may be fortunate enough to have somewhere one would considering hiring a character with this demeanor. Is this prejudice? This is teaching to respect the holy God.

Does such a delicate matter as addressing a scriptural position on the holy approach the church takes to worship our holy God, need prayer? The church must bathe this issue in constant prayer. The church is ordained to lift holy standards and not to lower them to a subculture that decries holiness. One of the first things the fallen Adam and Eve did was to cover their nakedness. Get the message!

For most people, it is difficult to decide whether there is only a dislike, or outright prejudice. It is possible to disapprove and yet not be prejudiced. But how is it possible to know? When prayer allows the Holy Spirit to unravel the entanglement, the real intent of the motive will be made known. Prayer brings new light that is necessary for the growth to spiritual maturity. Bigotry is one of the clever subtleties that can slip into personal motivations. The second chapter of James deals with the evil of favoritism and the damage it does to the individual Christian and God's kingdom as a whole.

PRAYER KEEPS THE SOUL ON WATCH LEST THAT WHICH IS UNHOLY IS TOLERATED.

Prayer will reveal that which should be tolerated, and what is not to be tolerated. Toleration does not mean lowering the Biblical standards to accept the questionable, political correctness or the unholy, which has been done by most of the major denominations. Prayer keeps the believer on purity's radar. Prayer that is prayer, always seeks God's more excellent way, and cannot be content with less. Too often the deception is having just enough religion to be respectable.

There is always the outcast, like the Samaritan woman who needs a drink of the living water. Our prayer should be, Lord do not allow God's people to permit prejudice to keep the sinful and the brokenhearted from the living water.

Luke 4:9." Then said the woman of Samaria unto Him, how is it that thou being a Jew ask drink of me, which am a woman of Samaria? For the Jews have no dealings with the Samaritans."

Productive prayer will allow differences to gospel light. Spiritual light is a known witness to the human being receiving that light. Light is the effusion that persuades the mind to carefully consider what has been revealed. Light makes itself evident to the conscience that it is to be evaluated when accepted, when the conscience receives light. This Light can become impaired by lack of action, or welcomed as new spiritual capacity. Light gives God's judgments, His commandments; guidance to man, witness to truth. It penetrates spiritual darkness, illumining the gospel; guiding by His light that reflects His character. Light unveils His revelation and that which cannot be extinguished.

This is the type of light Agrippa encountered when Paul proclaimed Christ and Agrippa answered: "almost thou persuaded me to become a Christian." As multitudes today, they almost became a Christian. They almost surrender to God completely. The follow through has slipped away without a positive decision, and no decision becomes a negative decision.

Spiritual decisions that are negative create a cloud of indifference that becomes darker by every tick of the clock. Countless people are trying to pray through that massive accumulation of those "almosts" that are still unrepented.

Is there anything known that prayer cannot attack? Can prayer send the type of light that the cold hearted soul needs? It is here where prayer warriors who are at a distance from the one that exhibits the insensitive unconcern, must wage the spiritual battle. Their prayer will be that the indifferent will not be able to withstand the blazing light of the Holy Spirit and repent. Productive prayer rests on the fact that faith believing prayer can do that which is beyond human reason. The Light that the Holy Spirit sheds can penetrate barriers that were once forbidden.

PRAYER ANSWERS THE BRILLIANCE OF HUMAN THOUGHT THAT SEEKS TO REPLACE GOD'S WISDOM.

Religious humanism wishes to annihilate God, and place a godless secularism in His place. Evidently the so-called elites have not learned history's lessons from nations who wiped God out of their social structure. Allow what a world-renowned Russian biochemist, Mr. Dmitre A. Kuznetsov had to say while visiting the Institute for Creation Research in California to discuss ways to combine creationism in their laboratory research in Moscow over against the evolutionary, atheistic Marxist dogma. Dr. Kuznetsov noted the irony that "it seems that scientists have more academic freedom these days in Moscow than they do in California," referring to Bill Honig, California Superintendent of Public Instruction and his effort to close ICR's Graduate School of science because of its creationist viewpoint.

Arrogant man revels in his foolhardy self-image under the disguise of intellectual superiority that has made himself god. Our achievements over the last fifty years have outgrown God, that has made the educators believe there is no need for God. This type of mentality has saturated our educational system leaving its imprint upon the generation now making the nation's critical decisions. Hollywood portrays the victories in their war pictures of World War II as "being lucky." What a slap in God's face and the face of God's people who prayed earnestly for God's guidance in every phrase of the war. God answering prayer is not luck.

Paul in writing to the Corinthians warns about self-deceit in these words: "Let no man deceive himself. If any man among you seems to be wise in this world, let him become a fool, that he may be wise. For the wisdom of this world is foolishness with God. For it is written, He takes the wise in their own craftiness."(1 Cor. 3:18&19)

What has all this to do with prayer? Prayer and Biblical truth will keep the believer out of the cesspool the humanistic atheistic subculture wants to drag him through. If there is not a God given shield protecting the believer's mind, the godless atmosphere will be absorbing its influence daily. If the believer's mind is not saturated with the mind of Christ he is at the mercy of the sinister forces surrounding him.

PRAYER PRESERVES AND MAINTAINS THE HEART AND MIND ON THE HIGHWAY OF HOLINESS.

This brand of praying must reach beyond the ordinary, which means fasting and prayer is needed to keep the soul anchored in Biblical truth. There are too many Bill Hong's out there ready to destroy and mock the simplistic child like faith. The simple gospel must remain so the child can understand, and walk its truth. To make prayer other than this uncomplicated exercise, is to uproot it from its Biblical foundation.

Prayer gives heart to diligence; diligence is untiring and zealously uses prayer to attack whatever the situation is, even when the evidence is overwhelming and impossible. Prayer reaches beyond the natural facts.

A story is told of an experience in the life of Hudson Taylor, missionary to China. In a time of great trouble, he tells about reading God's statement in the Twenty-third Psalm, "my cup runneth over," and he said: "Lord, this is not true of me; my cup is not running over; there is trouble among my helpers."

But the words came back, "my cup runneth over," he said: "Lord, my cup does not run over; we are out of money."

But once more there came back, "my cup runneth over."

Then Mr. Taylor said, "Lord, this Thy declaration of what is true for me, and what Thy desire is for me, and so I now believe it and take it to my soul and count it as true, and I thank Thee."

And he got up and counted that God had made his cup run over. Like Abraham, he believed God and counted the thing that did not exist as though it did exist (Rom. 4:17) and soon his heart did consciously run over!

Can prayer or the simple words from His Word take us to the place where the believer can believe, that which does not exist, does exist? Can this happen when the unmovable mountain filled with insurmountable obstacles stands in the way? Can this happen when the personal burden is crushing all hope? Can this happen when walking into your child's sick room? Can the believer's faithful prayer allow him to see what can't be seen? Can the believer be assured the cup is running over, when it is not?

Prayer that is more than prayer has the ingredients that claim what is not, and has the diligence that will continue to claim what is not. If not, then prayer is a mere shadow of what the intended possibilities are, but the Father has made provisions for prayer to become man's power over circumstances. It is praying and believing when the cup is not running over. This is praying and believing when it appears to be useless. But again, is anything useless in Almighty God's hands?

When God demands excellence that means in faith as well as in motive. As the believer claims God's promises, all faith is couched in His Divine will and a true believer only wants God's will to be done regardless of what the believer feels needs to be done. This is applied especially when it come to serious sickness. Misapplied healing faith can be a destroyer of faith.

PRAYER SHARPENS THE CONSCIENCE TO EVALUATE.

Prayer can be the co-knowledge of oneself; to have the process to distinguish between the known good and the known evil; and making sure the conscience is not lightly dismissed when awakened. The conscience bears witness to who the Christian is. Individual conscience demands immediate attention or there can be a hardening of the conscience in that particular area.

Conscience is one of the God given ingredients that is anchored in the soul forever, and needs constant consideration with the enlightment of the Holy Spirit, that is the inner computer that testifies to God's moral code. Man can adjust the conscience so that which once was a definite conviction on a certain thing, now no longer produces any disturbance in the conscience. Even gloss over sin, when confronted, expresses this phrase, "my conscience does not bother me." Something seriously has happened to the conscience.

Paul writing to Timothy said: "holding faith, and good conscience : which some having put away, concerning faith, have made shipwreck." There is nothing more troubling than a shipwrecked conscience. A good conscience must be active before the fact. If the conscience only speaks in relation to past acts, the believer is in for a defeated spiritual life. This is an indication that the conscience is out of tune with the Holy Spirit. Without a God directed accurate conscience, there is no compass within and the believer will end up on immoral rocks.

The believer's conscience constantly needs to be sharpened. Prayer and Bible study is the whetstone. There is no shortcut. There cannot be a conquest in the spiritual being without vital prayer and the daily consuming of God's holy word. A condemning conscience closes the channel to the Father's ear. A God awakened conscience examines the details of the inner life. The voice of conscience speaks, but varies according to the values the believer has placed in his motives. Conscience has nothing else on which to evaluate but what is most valued by the believer in his everyday life.

Bible faith and conscience work hand in hand, but it is prayer and Bible study that propels conscience to be "the self that knows itself." Conscience cannot be stationary but will grow in holiness and truth, or decline in its value to the redemption of the soul. All depends on what is feeding the conscience.

Paul makes is clear in I Timothy 1:5, "Now the end of the commandment is charity out of a pure heart, and of a good conscience, and of faith unfeigned." Prayer keeps the believer in this mold Paul suggests. When prayer is neglected the conscience is weakened, and the warning bell is silent, blurring the seriousness of the transgression. An alert conscience is continually revived in the prayer closet by obedience responding to the clear connection to the Father.

PRAYER RELEASES THE FATHER'S RESOURCES AS NEEDED .

Yesterday's spiritual resources are never good enough for today. Today has new opportunities, new testing circumstances that require up-to-date understanding. Yesterday can never be changed; all that presents itself is today, with no assurance of tomorrow. Hear the scripture trumpet sounding these words again, "behold NOW is the time." Today will never return to do or to undo. History will always record our yesterdays as days of victory or defeat.

If today is approached spiritually with only the extent of the human mind as the source of spiritual weaponry, expect to be overwhelmed in the battle with demonic forces. The human way and means leaves self-effort at the mercy of Satanic subtleties. Pride and self-determination in themselves will lose today's spiritual battle every time. Pilate waived his power before Jesus with threatening words, that he had the power to crucify Him or release Him, but Jesus corrected him with these innovative words, "thou could have no power at all against me, except it were given thee from above." Human capabilities are an end in themselves; God's Omnipotence has no end. In spite of the impotence of natural man and the carnal Christian; they insist on holding on to a defeated approach to the spiritual warfare.

Prayer releases God's endowment when used for God's glory. Today needs today's spiritual diet that meets today's spiritual menu that will overcome whatever the enemy throws in your path today. O the necessity of daily devotions at the start of the day that are more than a short page from some book. It is imperative that the spiritual food is more than a teaspoonful. It will not take too long to burn that amount of spiritual food up in the first battle of the day. As accountable people, we need to get serious about the depth of our spiritual lives. The devotional time should take the time to devour a full course spiritual meal if today's spiritual warfare is to end in victory.

PRAYER AND BIBLE STUDY FEED THE SOUL.

Prayer renews the spiritual forces for today, not for yesterday's failures, not for tomorrow's victory, but for today. Today is all we have. Until each believer grasps the urgency with which the spiritual part of man demands this daily spiritual food, there will be no way to escape spiritual weakness that will ultimately mean spiritual death. Prayer rekindles, replenishes, regenerates, and nourishes the soul.

Prayer fuels the Spirit's witness, which is far different than natural man's intellectual witness. From the very beginning God breathed into Adam the breath of life. That breath contained the spirit of God's eternity, thus, man became a living soul. The foreknowledge of God foresaw the necessity for a preventive grace, a common grace to be included that would keep fallen man from dropping into complete corruption. It was from this common grace, (which is far different from saving grace), that natural man receives a benevolent attitude, and can become caring and helpful. A desire to worship is placed in every human being. The history of man reveals man worshiping something, a man-made image, nature, some creature, or man himself, or man will worship the living God. Whatever man worships that becomes his god, which is worked into a religion and that can be a religion of his own making. All religions are man-made, except the Christ centered religion, which is not a religion but a personal relationship with the living God.

An intellectual witness is a man-made religion which can be built around religious activities, church going, and church joining, but knowing nothing of God's justifying grace and becoming a new creation in Christ Jesus. This person can fill all the duties of worship and still be spiritually ignorant of the necessary personal relationship with the Savior. Everything spiritual is operated on man-made duty, rather than knowing Christ personally. Usually this person is so active in religion there is very little time left to pray. Serious intercessory prayer is unknown.

Redeemed man's prayer does not find solace only in activity, but knows personal limitations are never adequate, and there is a necessity to reach by faith into the spirit world where communication with God is found. Paul writes in Romans 8:16 "the Spirit itself bears witness with our Spirit." Again in Galatians 4:6 "God has sent forth the Spirit of His Son into your hearts." In First John 3:24 John says, "we know that He abides in us, by the Spirit which He has given us." Only the redeemed have His Spirit, which fuels the witness.

Our witness must be authenticated with His Spirit dwelling in us. Prayer is the fuel that keeps the fire lit. Man has no power to master the personal appetites that appeal to the flesh without the in dwelling Holy Spirit. Our pure Spirit must witness with God's Holy Spirit, and prayer is that vital link. Prayer takes our physical limitations into God's resources to receive what each soul needs for personal victory. When the Spirit is acting upon Spirit, both God and the prayer warrior can witness to that.

"He that believes on the Son of God has the witness in himself, he that believes not God has made Him a liar; because he believes not the record that God gave of His Son." (1 John 5:10)

→ PRAYER IS NOT NECESSARILY TO BE HEARD BY HUMAN EARS.

God the Father is the object of the prayer.

Prayer that has an announcement for man to hear is like the Pharisee who self-righteously attested his virtues in his prayer that did not leave the Temple. His self-appointed importance was his arrogance in disguise; which is one of the most heinous sins of the spirit. Some Pharisaical prayers consider that much speaking gets the Lords attention; other gauge public prayer by a certain tone of the voice; while others think correct vocabulary will invoke God's blessing, and then there are those who are careful to explain how good they have been; for some the blessing they received is because of the genius gift they have been given; others are faithful to promote their good deeds in their public prayers.

This Pharisaical prayer is quite a contrast from the publican's. It was not necessarily the words, but the intent of the heart. Man hears words, God reads motive. Man's purpose is to reach beyond himself for the solution to his sin problem. Words speak what was in the heart, and receive immediate attention from the Father.

Sin burdens the heart when it is acknowledged. Each person is more than a physical being, he is a spiritual being that is accountable for any sin in his life. His reason for being a human vessel is to be impregnated by his Creator to serve and glorify Him. A man's life is holy only because of the Holy Spirit's cleansing power. Thus, man out of the cleansing experience becomes the channel for God's holiness.

Prayer keeps the channel open so that we are in the proper position to be used as the Father wills. Prayer lifts the believer's standards to God's standards. Prayer gets the man's methods out of the way, and allows the Holy Spirit to function as He sees fit. Prayer pierces the darkness, spreads God's light, touches God, shatters any attempt at hypocrisy, anchors the soul in holiness and refuses to allow the believer's priceless soul to be a phony.

PRAYER ENLIGHTENS AND CLARIFIES THE BELIEVER'S THOUGHT PROCESS.

Prayer settles the debate about the source of true wisdom. The source must be the starting point. The answer, the believer starts with God as the source of all true wisdom, while the natural man starts with himself. The dictionary defines wisdom as an "understanding of what is true, right, lasting, common sense, good judgment." Where is this consistent wisdom found? Man with the knowledge that can send himself to the noon and back again. We marvel! But God made the moon and put it in charge of the tides of the seas and cleansing of the oceans. Man's understanding and judgment is faulty; mistakes are made. Not so with God, like Pilate said of Jesus, "I find no fault in Him."

With the choice of man or God before the believer, where should he go for his final source of wisdom? God's wisdom is like a piercing arrow that penetrates, taking the mind into areas of spiritual enlightment that only God can open. There is no end to spiritual illumination. Natural man's source ends with himself.

What most of the human race has not come to realize is the greatest force, other than the Lord that guides the destiny of man, is the intangible. The Lord has allowed man's choice of what intangibles will rule the world.

Man can choose between hate and love, or greed and generosity, or envy and forgiveness. The list can be numerous. These intangibles now rule as intangible hatred fills the whole atmosphere of every continent of this world and is willing to pay any price to win. O that we could gather these ungodly intangibles and throw them into the pits of hell where they will eventually be. But how do you bind that which is invisible? The only alternative is to place the intangible God against the intangible devil. This is spiritual warfare of which the scripture speaks.

Where does the believer fight this spiritual battle that threatens to destroy him and his loved ones? In the prayer closet, here is where the grace is supplied, the spirit is enlightened by the Holy Spirit, the soul is strengthened to deal with the unseen enemy, the mind is enriched by His wisdom, direction is given, doubts are clarified, the unknown is faced without fear, God's will is reaffirmed, the will's purpose is focused, and the resolve to win the battle with God's intervention is settled. God's wisdom is the believer's haven. Has He not said: "if any of you lack wisdom, let him ASK of God, that gives to all men liberally, and upbraides not; and it SHALL BE GIVEN HIM." (James 1:5) True prayer believes that.

HONEST PRAYER PREVENTS THE HEART FROM BEING DECEIVED.

Deception leaves a lasting imprint on the one who planned to deceive. Deception usually involves a perceived plan to be used to arrive at getting something or being something that no one else will notice, using trickery to disguise the real purpose. There would not be a deception unless there was not a feeling that the fraudulent intention would not be discovered.

Satan is written all over deception. His subtleties are so cunning, and the target is so cleverly concealed that a believer that is not prayed up will not catch on to what is happening until it is too late. This is the reason the word, "watch" is repeated in the scripture, but if the believer is not prayerfully trained and spiritually alert, he will not see the trap. If not found out, it will become easier to sow deception again, but the sower must expect to reap the same but in far greater amounts than what was sown. Paul wrote to the Galatian church: "be not deceived; God is not mocked; for whatsoever a man sows, that shall he also reap."

Can a believer be deceived? Look at the perfect man and his wife, Adam and Eve. They had no depraved nature and yet the keen astute enemy deceived them and the whole human race has suffered that act of self-will. Mankind is not dealing with a human being, but a fallen angel that is determined to mislead and delude God's people to shame the God who threw him out of heaven. Can anyone imagine the multitude who have believed and then brought shame and reproach on the Lord who saved them and on His faithful children?

Prayerlessness reaps a life of deception, but he who knows the battle of intercessory prayer knows and has experienced the fruits of victory over a godless enemy. This type of prayer does not consider the hours spent, but relishes the impact of the Holy Spirit upon the inner being. Prayer takes the soul places in the spiritual realm where nothing else can compare. There is no place for any deception in these spiritual realities. Yet lust of deceit can hide in the quick answer. The wiles of error are always at hand to corrupt and beguile. Who of us are strong enough to match wits with the devil without the Holy Spirit controlling our daily lives? This spiritual defense does not come naturally. This is a daily confrontation.

Prayer builds the barriers that fortify the soul from insincerity and deceit. Anything less will be a snare waiting for the careless believer, and leave a trail of regret.

PRAYER WHETS THE TWO EDGED SWORD SO GOD'S WORD CAN PENETRATE EVERY AREA OF THE HUMAN SOUL.

A godly man, who had built a new house, put these words in golden letters: "I must leave it."

Karl Gerock, the celebrated German poet wrote about these words as follows: "write these words above everything you value. Write it upon your house proprietor; upon your bonds; capitalist; upon your jewelry, young lady; upon your stores, business man; write it mother, in the spirit upon the brow of your child; husband, note, it is written above the head of your wife; man, see it is written above this world, with all the beautiful things it contains! How much cause have we to cleave to One Who has said: "I will never leave thee, nor forsake thee!"

Prayer whets the cutting edge of God's Spirit that makes its penetration that divides the soul, shatters the earthliness of materialism and makes the soul evaluate life in its fleeting state. There is nothing lasting in this life, outside the realm of the Spirit. Prayer pleads for the Spirit to pierce and quicken the inner areas that must over come the materialistic bondage. Prayer by God's Spirit hones the soul to a new focus, and reminds the believer all that is accumulated: "I must leave it." There is nothing so gripping, so attractive, so loved, that will not be separated from death's grasp when leaving this world.

Praying in the Spirit gives a discerning review of our spiritual condition. It may be painful to learn about the attachments that are threatening our spiritual lives. But prayer allows us to deal with these threatening attachments that call for personal separation, remembering the questionable must not be a part of our lives, because what we are in soul will be carried with us to the judgment. Only the material things will be left behind, as the poet suggests, "I must leave it."

PRAYER ENLARGES SPIRITUAL CAPACITY.

Oswald Chambers said: "our spiritual capacity is always measured by the promises of God." But does not the measure of spiritual capacity have much to do with prayer, desire and motive, as well? Spiritual capacity will never be enlarged if the personal will is not geared to will God's will with the whole heart and soul daily.

If the believer receives less that what the Father wants him to have, will not he soon distort and slander Him, as a servant would defame his taskmaster? Any believer can place blame on the Master and charge Him with expecting too much by placing supposedly impossible situations in the believer's hands. What does a charge like this make God? Is God unjust in such a demand? Or is the Lord pushing the believer to expand his capacity? Will this not allow the believer to be a greater blessing to God and man?

How many believers have been called to a definite ministry and have felt entirely inadequate? There is feeling that the Father is asking for more skills than the present capacity has. The uncertainty of the future makes the unfamiliar even more frightening. But God's promises have God's character behind every one of them. Believers have been taught to believe these promises, but now they are called upon to act on the promises. It is one thing to believe them and quite another to put them into action. The capacity must become more than mere believing, but actually expecting God to fulfill those promises. What a leap for capacity enlargement! Is prayer the foundation for an enlarged capacity? Prayer is fundamental.

The believer limits his life when he refuses to allow his capacity to reach new heights. To limit capacity is to limit faith, which reaps spiritual unbelief and spiritual failure; with defeat comes despair that hesitates to try again. There will be a temptation to evaluate natural abilities as the highest point of personal capacity without permitting God to work in extending his capacity that will glorify God, and bless the believer to believe for even greater capacity. Paul gives the Roman church this assurance: "being fully persuaded that what He had promised, He was able to deliver also to perform." (Rom. 4:21) All this push for greater capacity develops in the prayer closet. To think otherwise, is to be deceived by faith that has been overcome by personal unbelief. Prayer is the antidote needed to fulfill the Father's purpose for each life. He who wants a greater capacity to serve, and love God must be willing to pay the price in prayer before and while the action is in progress.

PRAYER GIVES DISCERNMENT BETWEEN GOOD AND EVIL.

What is good and what is evil, and how does anyone know the difference? This individual is raised in a home where each child has a different last name, the live-in boy friend is molesting the teenager; the mother is on drugs; profanity is the common language of exchange and the children know they are not wanted. This other family has a unit of a father and mother that places God first in life's affairs; the children are taught to obey and respect authority: the family devotions are central to the family's life style; the children are sent to a Bible believing church, but the mother and father take the children to the weekly services. Which of the children of these two families will have any basic idea of what right and wrong are? Which of two have a greater chance to overcome adversity and become productive citizens?

Since large portions of our society have extended depravity to the lowest level this country has ever experienced, how can the dysfunctional family, the liberal minister that does not believe the scriptures are Divinely inspired; the godless educator; the humanistic judge; the power hungry politician; the greedy banker; the dishonest C.E.O.; the cheating wall street broker; the dishonest cop; the list is endless. How can any society survive wallowing in filth of this magnitude, and exhibit a Biblical answer to what is right from wrong?

The result of this chaotic society is a very large gray area, where there is no right or wrong. It is, whatever feels right is right, regardless of what anyone else may think. A man sat in my living room, and made this statement when confronted about his spiritual life, "that is your opinion and I don't agree." When scripture was quoted, "all a matter of interpretation." His opinion was to relieve him from all accountability. When the judgment was brought into the conversation he replied: "I am ready." There was no grasp of the meaning of what he must do to become a Christian.

The believer is called to live in this world, and to be able to choose what is right and what is wrong. He is to believe that the scripture has laid out God's plan of salvation for lost man, and what God's purpose for that redeemed man's life is. The Scripture is the foundation for the Christian faith.

In the midst of all the confusion the believer must be able to discern what the Bible says, what is good and what is evil. How wretched a soul that does not have Truth to guide him into all Truth! The believer has this Truth, but what is the best way to evaluate this Truth?

Only man has to be clear-sighted in life and death matters, by seeking out He who is all Truth. And how is that to happen, by the Book and the prayer closet? There may be books and people who open possibilities, but the ultimate, is a prayer, guided by God's precious word, that only is trustworthy. When the believer is in tune with heaven, he will personally know what is right or wrong. He will be able to pray through the gray areas and be certain that he has found the way and must walk in it.

PRAYER APPLIES THE FORCE THAT CUTS SIN'S SHACKLES.

Prayer shakes the foundation of prisons, opens locked prison doors, loosing chain's manacles, frees the captives, causing the fear stricken jailer to cry out, "what I do to be saved?" The heathen jailer is redeemed; the miraculous event adds confusion to chaos for the local administration; and the event is stirring the whole community. What were Paul and Silas doing when this miraculous event took place?

Multitudes are not in fetters physically, but are spiritually, the chains bind helpless victims who struggle with what I should do, what not to do, and that which I should not do, that I do. The chains are securely bound to an unforgiving spirit; others are held in the clutches of pornography; while others lust in personal ungodly appetites. Their effort to loose themselves reveals how powerless personal reformation is. The most vulnerable areas grow weaker by each defeat.

Prayer fortifies the weak, faulty area that is exposed to the threats of the impure desire. Prayer is the strongest asset that will immunize and deliver in the dark valley of decision, unifying the soul for the battle to be kept free from the spiritual chains that bind, emancipating the soul from its fetters of depravity that is a craving master, that will not leave the inner being until the bonds are completely unshackled. Prayer takes the soul to where this liberated freedom is found, at the feet of the Savior.

It is in this new found freedom the soul is perfected, imparted righteousness that lifts daily living to a new level that not only pleases the Father but also ends the inner war. The poet writes: "O glorious freedom." The redeemed through the centuries of time have echoed this freedom refrain again and again. Spiritual freedom has a tune that only the "called out ones" can sing.

If the praying heart did not cry out, and receive heaven's response, there would not be any personal relationship with the Father that gives the freed soul rest and peace in Him. Prayer ushers the believer into His refuge when all hope appears to be gone. In the dark hours of the night in that Philippian dungeon, shackled in chains; back bleeding from the whip, immersed in the indignities of a common criminal, singing and praying while others are cursing their plight, Paul and Silas would watch the God of all put a great amen on their prayer service.

PRAYER HAS ETERNAL RESULTS.

Prayer invades the eternal. Genuine prayer is not limited to this world. There is a permanent component in the human soul that engages eternal life making each human being sacred, made in God's image. The Lord put such worth on the soul, that He made it worth more than the whole world. It should not surprise anyone that life's sacredness is precious and worth the fight to preserve its value. But today's humanistic culture has degraded life and its cost to God by creating a social atmosphere that has no right or wrong which allow some angry person to place a gun at someone's head and pull the trigger without a tinge of conscience because he has done something that he does not like; or a doctor in the name of choice, can take an innocent child and place an instrument at the base of the skull and rip its life away; or the terrorist can wrap a bomb around the waist and walk into a crowded bus and push the button, which kills and maims scores of people out of hatred; or those cruel people that can approach an elderly person with a needle injection that will spare society the trouble to deal with a useless piece of humanity. How cheap a human life has become!

Prayer is at the heart of the value of life. Only the prayer of the redeemed can hold in high esteem the treasure that life is, because he is the Temple in which the Holy Spirit abides. Life, (God in him) is revered because the believer prizes his divine purpose, and counts the cost that has given him eternal worth. Prayer is the eternal force in the believer that continually pushes him toward the high calling of God in Christ Jesus. It is prayer that moves heaven and earth.

George Davis, an eye witness to the Welsh revival related the happening: " I have just returned from a two day visit to the storm center of the great Welsh revival which is sweeping over Wales like a cyclone.

"It is sweeping over hundreds of hamlets and cities, emptying saloons, theaters, and dance halls, and filling the churches night after night with praying multitudes.

"The policemen are almost idle; in many cases the magistrates have few trials on hand; debts are being paid; and the character of entire communities is being transformed almost in a day."

This is the type of prayer that has everlasting results, that gets the attention of the Father, and will open the floodgates of heaven, pouring His blessing upon a repenting people. What does our nation need more?

PRAYER HAS A HEARTBREAKING FORCE, CALLED WAITING.

Waiting causes the believer to delay, when there is an urgency to push on. The test of obedience is fixed on a situation that may hit the weak spot in the believer's spiritual armor. Waiting can add to the possibilities of faltering and questioning the wisdom that appears to hinder the waiting progress. Waiting wears on the nerves, hesitates to believe the impossible, harbors suspicions that nothing will be done, take exceptions through frustration, becomes weary in well doing; waiting is one of life's most difficult tasks. Yet, the Psalmist says, "wait on the Lord, be of good courage, and He shall strengthen thine heart; wait I say, on the Lord." (27:14)

Impatience can become a real burden, and the enemy can use that tenseness to annoy, and lose spiritual composure, such as, instead of unruffled spirit, there is a testy attitude; or rather than being restful, a high-strung restlessness crops up. The only waiting that can be bearable is, "waiting on the Lord."

The scripture uses the word "wait" repeatedly. Psalm 25:5 "on Thee do I wait all the day." Proverbs 20:20, "wait on the Lord." Psalm 62:5, wait only on God." Psalm 69:3, "mine eyes fail while I wait." Psalm 130:5, "I wait for the Lord, my soul doth wait."

Is the Lord trying to get a message to His people that He has His own time? God's time is not known to man? To demand action, would mean surpassing God's will. Who can tell what that would mean in the future? What happens to the believer when the Lord says, "wait?"

Does the believer slip into an anxious mode or does he seek the secret closet for lifting the load "waiting" is producing? If the storm is to become a calming peace, it will be found only in the prayer closet. Prayer may come in the midst of discouragement, and be a time of personal examination to inspect the soul for anything that would hinder the "waiting" process. Prayer must take the position that Job took, "though He slay me, yet will I believe." Prayerful waiting will not break faith with Him who has control over all waiting. Waiting does not mean the Father has cut the believer off, but could it not be to establish a deeper and more vital prayer life? Waiting is always for a purpose, because God sees through to eternity and its affect on the present. Since God's character is fixed, always just and holy, His waiting periods are always wrapped in His perfection. Prayerful faith acknowledges God's rights and willingness to wait for prayer to be fulfilled.

In the midst of waiting, is there contentment? Paul writing to Timothy emphasizing the benefits of contentment in I Timothy 6:6 in these words: "but Godliness with contentment is great gain." This is a loaded statement that pertains to the heart of the Christian experience, for true Christianity is the only religion that can put Godliness and contentment together that becomes a reality. There is no way to have contentment without first being Godly. God made all people that way and there will be endless restlessness until Godliness is found.

Then what is this intangible contentment that all mankind seeks? Since all people want, and seek ways to obtain what will content the soul, then what is the substance of contentment? Contentment's substance contains indifference to what one has; denotes independence; has the confidence of being lord of self; primarily signifies sufficiency in the situation; having strength and faith to believe God's grace is adequate regardless of secular's distraction. Herrich would say: "let's live with that small pittance which we have who covets more is ever more a slave."

What waiting contentment is not! Contentment is not being passive but satisfied in the situation where the Lord has placed you; is not being unattached to the reality of the present life, but being relative; is not being worried, but having the ability to adjust. Contentment rests in peace without the needle of irritability. Contentment is the pearl of great price that few have found because the price is to high. The price will demand all you have. There is no discount.

The poet writes:

> "Can you show me the 'Land of Content,'
> Where the struggle with self is done?
> Where the disappointments and vain regrets are gone
> with the evening sun?

Where pride and anger play no part,
Where only truth can live?
Where wrongs are forgotten and blotted out,
And the best in us can live?" (The Gospel Herald)

The poet's heart appeal is the cry of the masses. Where is waiting contentment to be found, in the marts of trade, in the dens of iniquity, in the arena of entertainment, in the values of personal treasurers, no, not outside of godliness? But where is that Godliness maintained, only in the prayer closet. Try as you will, every known area of life and you will come up empty. Binney said: "Every praying Christian will find that there is no Gethsemane without its angel." Every prayer closet that batters heaven's gates is alive with the Spirit that erases life's dissatisfactions. Prayer gives contentment with little, but arouses expectations for more if that would please our heavenly Father. Octavius Winslow writes: "Prayer is the pulse of the renewed soul; and the constancy of its beat is the best test and measure of the spiritual life." Prayer is at the heart of waiting contentment but never content to the extent that the desire dies for the enlargement of spiritual capacity.

There are certain necessities that the secular world contains that help sustain human life, contentment permits the soul to seek these necessities for the physical need but not to allow this seeking to become an envious or a self-centered pursuit. The motto is, "God is first." Prayer keeps the soul focused on this motto. Prayer is the guardian of the soul.

Thomas Dreier has this advice to give when faced with the entanglement when reaching beyond contentment in the place where the Lord has called. "One of the most contented men we know is never envious of others. What I have is what I need to fill my place in the world," he says, "and what is in their possession is what they probably need for their work. If what they have belonged to me, I would have it. The fact that I do not possess it is evidence enough for me that it does not belong to me. All that concerns me is how I can become more useful. When I learn how to do more, the things needed for the carrying out of my ideas will be made available to me. That is what has happened to me in the past, and I see no reason why it would not continue to happen to me. It is what I think about that matters, not things I claim to possess." Contentment in a world of discontentment is found only in God Himself and the communion with Him in the prayer closet.

THE HOLY SPIRIT GIVES PRAYER GUIDANCE DUE TO THE LIMITATIONS OF THE ONE PRAYING.

Then how important is it to know the Holy Spirit personally by allowing our spirit to communicate with His Spirit? Romans 8:26&27 gives further insight: "Likewise the Spirit also helps our infirmities; for we know what we should pray for as we ought: but the Spirit itself makes intercession for us with groanings that cannot be uttered. And He that searches the hearts knows what is the mind of the Spirit, because He makes intercession for the saints according to the will of God."

The Holy Spirit guides prayer "according to the will of God." Prayer has guidelines that must have proper direction. Is it true that those who know not the Holy Spirit cannot expect to receive the prayer guiding direction needed?

Who is this one, called the Holy Spirit that is an imperative for our spiritual lives? The Holy Spirit has the same attributes that Jesus or God has. He is Eternal, Immutable, Omnipotent, Omniscience, Omnipresent, all that the Godhead is. Therefore we are in no lesser care than God Himself. He is the Creator that moved upon the face of the void and darkness of the deep. He is our comforter, our convictor, our guide and our companion. As our Helper He considers our infirmities, our inability to pray properly, for what we should pray, how to be more proficient in prayer, placing prayer in the proper perspective, raising prayer to its highest and its most holy level, giving an acceptable decorum, because we are liable to endless mistakes.

How are we to know the Holy Spirit's presence? His Spirit will witness to our spirit. Therefore, He pleads our prayer, allowing prayer to rise to its highest level, placing prayer where its future will fit into the Father's full purpose for the one praying. Does the Holy Spirit then prepare the answer according the personal request, or to fit the prayer for what is best for all eternity? The most effective prayer could be the one where the words are unutterable. The Holy Spirit does not measure prayer by the fluency of expression, but by heart motive and what is expedient. C. H. Dodd defines prayer as: "Prayer is the Divine in us appealing to the Divine above us." The Divine in us must be yielded to the Divinity of the Holy Spirit for pertinent prayer management. Our best prayer is "not my will be done, but Thy will be done."

Jesus positions the Holy Spirit as God in this present dispensation with these words in John 14:13&14: "Howbeit, when He, the Spirit of truth, is come, He will guide you into all truth; and He will show you things to come. He shall glorify Me; for He shall receive of mine, and shall show it unto you."

This same Holy Spirit is to manage our intercessory prayers as He makes intercession for the saints. Prayer that bears the burden for the lost reaches its deepest valleys when words are inexpressible and filters into nothing more than unintelligible groanings. The Holy Spirit understands groanings because He understands the mind that seeks His mind and will. When the Holy Spirit finds a mind that seeks His mind, the glory is transferred to man's Savior who paid the price to bring lost man into that Oneness of mind. What the Holy Spirit promotes pleases the Godhead and is the mind of the Trinity.

Jeremy Taylor approached prayer in these words: "When we pray for any virtue, we should cultivate the virtue as well as pray for it: the form of your prayers should be the rule of your life; every petition to God is a precept to man. Look not, therefore, upon your prayers as a short method of duty and salvation only, but as a perpetual monition of duty; by what we require of God we see what He requires of us."

PRAYER IS A SAINT MAKER.

Prayer can ready the soul for each circumstance in life. Prayer develops spiritual consistency. Saints are those who are redeemed and obediently called "the holy ones, the godly ones." Which is always applied to the Body of Christ by the virtue of their personal relationship to Christ.

Could Stephen have had the depth of Holy Spirit's grace needed when the hypocritical religious people cast him out of the city, and then applied their death's crushing blows. What if he had not prepared a prayerful spiritual foundation before the death blows came? In his dying breath, God's grace so flooded his soul in the midst of their cowardly act, he prayed: "Lord lay not this sin to their charge." Only a saint could so pray for those who committed this ungodly act.

The saint's prayer is an affirmation of God's holiness. What is the character of a saint's prayer? It is redemption in action that sets apart, a separation from willful sin. As the Godhead is separated from that which He has created, so mankind is separated as a human innate apart from all other creation, but man can participate in what the Godhead has created. The saint has a personal relationship with the Creator by personal choice and God's redemptive action, which is man's only redemption for his sin problem. No other religion can actually deliver man from sin. Thus, prayer becomes the conversation between the saint and his Creator.

God Himself is separated from His creation, is not in nature to be worshiped, but lives apart from His masterpieces. His creation is not to be worshiped, only the Godhead is to be worshiped.

Standing in the midst of massive pyramids in Mexico where the altars were stained with the blood of human sacrifices who were offered in worship of the Sun and Moon gods. They were worshiping creation as god and not the God of creation, much as the New Age movement. Worshipers travel miles to pay homage to their idols.

A saint sees life as a necessary will to conform to God's will if he is to be referred to as "being a child of God." Is not the Christian life a continual conforming to God's holy character? Prayer is the tender that consistently brings this relationship into focus each day. God demands human holiness and righteousness to complete the intimate relationship.

Saints have the privilege of evaluating from the Father's perspective what is holy or unholy, and walking in the His Light. But what is right or wrong is assessed in the prayer closet with the open Bible in hand.

The martyrs have exhibited sainthood throughout the course of history. But sainthood is not limited to the martyrs alone. There have been multitudes of believers who would have gladly chosen martyrdom over the daily persecution that ruined their reputation, robbed the family of its standing in the community, placed lasting labels that are ugly, mean and insensitive. Whereas the martyr's prayer (like Stephen's) can be quick and simple and immediately pass into eternity and suffering is over. But there are those who are spending a lifetime in prayer's agony to give daily victory over the continual onslaught of vicious attacks or are thrown in prison and without mercy and totally unjustly. Under these circumstances, prayer is carving out saints.

My heart is humbly crushed to think how insufficient my prayer has been when it comes to building sainthood. I ask, as many do, how has my prayer life changed circumstances. It is not that I aspire to be a Daniel or a Stephen, they saw action immediately, but is it not true that there is no way to know the true impact of prayer as far as the average Christian is concerned until he or she walks through heaven's gates?

Does sainthood arrive without the saint knowing it? I think so, in that being aware of its accomplishment would lessen the desire to approach the unconquerable, and create an attitude that the pursuit of the high calling of God in Christ Jesus is no long an absolute necessity. The soul's prayer must sharpen the desire to forge ahead in the more excellent way.

John Hus much like Stephen stood chained to the stake while his persecutors prepared fuel for the fire, and a paper crown with painted devils. To which Hus said: "My Lord Jesus Christ wore a crown of thorns for my sake. Why should not I, then, for His sake, wear this crown, be it ever so ignominious? Truly I will do it, and that willingly."

When the crown was set on his head, the bishop said, "Now we commit thy soul to the devil."

"But I," said Hus, lifting up his eyes toward heaven, "do commit my soul into Thy hands, O Lord Jesus Christ." This saint's final prayer reveals who he was.

PRAYER IS AN APPEAL FOR THE FATHER TO REVEAL HIS GLORY THROUGH YOU.

Is it possible without personally possessing Him to walk into His glory? I think not. To personally possess His glory is one thing, which only the possessor can know, and quite another thing to see His glory in the beauty of the heavens, and all of nature. As a lad, I had a paper route in the rural area that covered about fifteen miles. In the winter, the walk would extent into night hours. I can remember the crunchy snow under my canvas boots and the bitter cold that chilled to the bones, but beyond all that there was the magnificence of the starlit heavens that so thrilled me that it took away the sting of the harsh blast of the biting wind. Something would leap within me that tried to engulf the glory of the present, but that glory did not continually linger with me. Yes, it was etched into my memory, but

He who made the glory that revealed all this splendor was not a part of my inner being. To be God's love slave allows prayer to be tuned to God's glory that floods the soul. It becomes a part of him. Man's glory is but a shadow while God's glory is constant and everlasting, which passes the wear of time. Prayer's power is the pathway to the sea of God's glory. His glory is the flame that fires prayer. What would prayer be without God's glory within?

Prayer and mediation transports the soul right into God's glory. But as LaFountain says: "no flowery road leads to glory." It is only the prayer's cross that does. God's glory gives strength, while man's glory wears a shroud. The child of peril's prayer leads to seeking God's glory. What is this glory? Moses expressed it best in his words in Exodus 24:17: "the sight of the glory of the Lord was like devouring fire." When that fire is within, it is the fire that continually fires the soul, without which our prayers are mere sounding brass and tinkling cymbal. Our praise and glory must be filled with eternal gratitude that spills into prayerful service and caring concern for the lost. His glory fills and consumes the soul.

The mysterious power of prayer grasps heavenly treasures that are unique to the Christian's needs. When these needs are released and realized, the Christian's response of praise is linked to glorifying God as an acknowledgment of His loving care. Praying His glory down is the ultimate in the Christian's experience.

Biblical praying acknowledges the holy Deity and His demand that His people are to be holy. Hebrews 12:14 makes this declaration very forcefully: "follow peace with all men, and holiness without which no man shall see the Lord." The condition of prayer is a holy people acknowledging the holy God. Adam's Fall has compromised that condition considerably by placing great limitations on the relationship that the Creator did not intend. Man was created to be a little lower than the angels, but the Fall dropped him to being open to moral corruption. Therefore, man is left with a faulty judgment, available to being biased, dishonest, deceitful, lying, fraud, treachery, and all kinds of duplicity. God sought to redeem man from the lost estate and Calvary was the remedy. But redeemed man still is bound by the limitations of judgment, the physical is dying by degrees daily, our restrictions are confined by our limited abilities, our faults are more than marginal, leaving man helpless to rise above himself.

Prayer of the believer gives mankind contact with the God who is everything man is not, and what man longs to be. God's perfection is attractive, for there is stability that man does not have as a result of the Fall. In our God there is all purity that is unstainable, with complete and holy justice, is sinless, and has our welfare at heart, Almighty God in every aspect, is completely reliable, with unmeasurable mercy whose benevolence reaches to the lowest of the low.

With these attributes our God reaches down to take the believer's struggling hand in life's battle against an invisible enemy who attacks at the most inopportune time. O what a glorious privilege. Prayer in Jesus' name opens the door to endless power that will never change or forsake.

Because of His holy love and who He is, I can hang my life and hope for eternity on the living God, who has shown He qualifies to meet every human need. I may question His method but never His decision. Are some of His decisions difficult for my finite mind to comprehend, certainly, but do I know the beginning from the end as He does? Prayer allows me to work through my tragedy and rest on His never failing love for me. Prayer sends my heart cry that has imperfect knowledge and shortsightedness to an all knowing and understanding Savior.

Does not the lifelong decision come down to the fact, to whom can I trust my life, myself with all its fragile abilities, and frightful limitations; OR to the righteous holy God who cares for His own? If the holy God is chosen, then His purpose and concerns for my life must be known. How? Through the Light of His word and the prayer closet. Now the question is, how much do I want to know Him and His purpose for me? That answer can become a reality only by the amount of time I spend in the study of the Bible and the time I spend in prayer. Then how do I take the light received and place it into daily action?

THE PERSONAL PRAYER LIFE WILL DEFINE THE COURSE TAKEN.

The effectiveness of prayer will depend upon how surrendered the whole being is to the complete will of God. Prayer can go no further or higher than the degree of personal surrender. Prayer, to be complete and fruitful, must always be not my will be done, but Thy will be done. Prayer to reach the achievement sought must abandon all self agenda.

Prayer gives a Godly tone to life that affirms assurance to meet the challenge of the day. Prayer is the harmony within that is inserted regardless of what the circumstance is. Prayer gives the quickened cadence to the step of the weary journeyer, making a pleasant overtone to the unpleasant. Prayer permits a proper emphasis on life's situations from those that need a calm moderate undertaking, to another occasion that may require a blast of holy anger as our Lord expressed when with a whip he drove the money changers from the temple.

Each individual has a tone that reflects attitude, motive, and godly decision making. Prayer gives these attributes a heavenly ring and sets heaven's music resounding in the soul. Paul exhibits the musical ring in his words to the Philippians: "by prayer and supplication with thanksgiving let your requests be known unto God." There is the joyful praise approach in thanksgiving that encompasses heaven that the saints are broadcasting on heaven's wavelength. Some are thanking God for the grace received when thrust into heart wretched conditions that have crushed the soul; while others are pouring out theirs in thanksgiving and praise for their unmeasurable blessings received; others for God's loving care for loved ones who are half-way around the world; while others extol Him the only true God for who and what He is, for Calvary and His blood-bought privileges.

PRAYER HEALS THE FRACTURES LIFE PRESENTS.

Prayer copes with the chasm which seems impossible to cross. Prayer reinforces faith that is challenged by the unknown rocky road, tuning the soul into heaven's melodies that encircle the burdensome conditions.

Praying that is inconsequential produces light-hearted conviction that reveals an indifference that can be frightening. Routine praying, in most cases is no more than routine praying, usually resulting from a shallow Christian life. An undisturbed prayer that has little passion has lukewarm concern written all over it. James 4:3 is seeing the problem this way: "ye ask, and receive not, because ye ask amiss," which can include any number of things such as that which was just mentioned. Prayer without fervor is moved only by a cool interest chilled with hidden trivialities.

Lukewarmness is spiritually fatal, which is revealed greatly in the depth to which prayer will be effective. Is this type of unmoved apathetic praying going be no more than words?

Cold apathetic prayer can be a weak attempt at wanting to cover Christian duties and mediocre effort for the superficial witness. For such spiritual condition there is always a cause. Without doubt, it is concealing some contraband that is against God's law. The Psalmist (28:9) writes: "he that turns away his ear from hearing the law, even his prayers shall be an abomination." No matter what the appeal is, God can never go against Himself. Jesus loved the rich young ruler that came to Him with all his potential, but Jesus could not violate His own self by making an exception in this young man's case.

Let us imagine that this rich young man had a family and his little girl became very sick, the most skilled doctors in the country were summoned and each said she was going to die. Then he thought about the miracle he saw Jesus perform, he would go to Jesus. But something in him was a constant reminder that his riches were his god, and that he had made that choice years ago. Will the Lord answer his prayer if he ignores that sin of rejection? Again think of the words of the Psalmist, "sin an abomination" before God. His rejection blocks communication. Many lukewarm people are still praying when their concealed garbage needs to be cleaned out. To attempt to pray over willful sin is impossible.

The prayer of repentance is the first thing needed to right the privilege of prayer's open channel for the personal relationship that will make prayer fruitful. When forgiveness comes and there is nothing behind the soul and the Savior, prayer will take on a new passion.

Prayer is our impregnated force, especially if there have been years of prayer as a foundation for the present crisis. Prayer establishes faith that is based on what our Lord said: "He that believes on me, he shall do greater works, because I go to the Father; and whatsoever ye shall ask in my name, that will I do." (John 24:13) The Lord is giving power that we do not have on our own, but the condition is, asking in faith. But does our Lord answer prayer without giving the power for what is needed to be placed into action? There is a motto which reads: "You can do more than pray after you have prayed, but you cannot do more than pray until you have prayed."

Prayer without being impregnated by God's power is worthless. If not, prayer stops with the individual with no power to reach beyond the self. To every excuse for weakness, lack of ability, difficult obstacles, or the certainty of failure, Jesus would repeat the words in John 14:13. We can do nothing that impacts the human race and the social structure with righteousness without His empowerment. It was related of Lord Clyde, states the Rev. E. J. Hardy, chaplain of the forces, that on one occasion he asked his offices to pick him the bravest men from his small army needed for the desperate attack. It was Sunday evening. "There is a prayer-meeting going on now in the camp," said the officers, "If you go there you will find all the bravest men." Why? Because these men would draw on Infinite power outside themselves to accomplish what ordinary men could not.

God is not a servant to our own comfort, but He is very interested in what we need to better serve Him, because God's servant made himself servant of the Lord's need.

Prayer not only teaches, but endues with power that strengthens the resolve to approach the labor with His blessing. Is it not true, work will demand more prayer?

PRAYER ACTION IS QUESTION IN MANY CHRISTIANS' MIND.

The following are a few that need immediate action.

* States cannot prohibit partial-birth abortion.

* Voluntary prayer banned in all school activities.

* Flag burning is a constitutional right.

* The government is allowed to engage in race discrimination in college and job appointments.

* The Boys Scouts discriminate because they refuse to allow homosexuals to be leaders.

* The words "under God" deleted from our Pledge of Allegiance.

* Same sex marriage.

* The homosexual agenda in our schools and on our air waves.

It would not be difficult to continue to list the continual invasion on our Christian liberties. Do these and many more need dedicated prayer and the laborers to stand and work for Biblical truth?

D. L. Moody displayed the ethic of prayer and work in this way: upon one of his journeys across the Atlantic there was a fire in the hold of the ship. The crew and some volunteers stood in the line to pass buckets of water. A friend said to Moody, "Mr. Moody, let us go to the other end of the ship and engage in prayer." The evangelist replied: "Not so, sir; we stand right here and pass buckets of water and pray hard all the time." There is no way a completely dedicated Christian can separate prayer and work.

Prayer is the Believer's most useful and powerful instrument in his spiritual warfare.

PRAYER MUST BE INVOLVED IN EVERY SITUATION LIFE MAY PRESENT

When Lincoln was in sore straits as to what course to pursue during the Civil War, he went to God in prayer, and often remarked that he could not have succeeded in his great task without Divine guidance.

During Mr. Wilson's struggle in International Affairs he arrived at a cabinet meeting, his face wore a solemn look. It was evident that serious affairs of the nation were on his mind. He said to the cabinet members: "I don't know whether you men believe in prayer or not. I do. Let us pray and ask help of God." And the president of the United States fell upon his knees with members of the cabinet, while the President offered a prayer to the Almighty God for help.

Christ is the liberator even when trapped in circumstances beyond personal control. Many times the web is woven by the soul's enemy or by human choices. Regardless of how it happened the impossibilities are ravishing mentally, leaving the ingredients of the soul exhausted. The unyielding persistency torments and harasses the psyche with unimaginable doubts and temptations. Like, God does not care. Suggesting others' struggles are simply not compared to yours. But are not these unsolvable situations that which will bring the aching soul in touch with the Master that so loved that He gave Himself for such a vexing occasion.

Prayer is not the milk toast halfhearted praying, not the five-minute kind, but the time consuming, agonizing prayer that unlocked the closed doors and entered into belligerent hearts. Too many Believers fail to use their most important protective tool because it is without purpose, without appreciation, getting rusty, neglected, and used only in case of an emergency. These could be the reasons the believer is constantly running into unmanageable conditions. Does God allow troubling conditions to remind us of our human limitations, and how powerless man is?

PRAYER GIVES GRACE TO FACE THE UNKNOWN .

Prayer ready's the soul for death if necessary. Dare I use Daniel again to give the stature of the man who walked with God! Daniel knew the king's decree was signed, stating that no other god could be worshiped or petitioned for thirty days or decree would be fulfilled and "he shall be cast into the den of lions."

Jealous men made a conspiracy against Daniel, unknown to the King. They had studied this man Daniel, who lived for God with integrity and consistency. The only thing they could find was his faithful prayer life, which was so unswerving and dependable that they were certain this decree would trap him. The next day they watched in anticipation, knowing his prayer schedule. They waited for him to open the window that faced Jerusalem and pray three times a day. They were right! When Daniel knew the decree had been signed "he did as foretime," knowing the consequence was to be thrown into the lions' den. Willingly, he walked into the jaws of death, rather than compromise his prayer time and his faith in the living God.

Is it not right to ask the question, what is the average believer willing to risk? Death, or is it too easy to avoid and compromise and not open the window to pray knowing the results. Prayer had brought a relationship with the living God that Daniel prepared to lay down his life if necessary. What communion, what fellowship tied and united the living God, with His child Daniel. My heart is humbly crushed when I think how insufficient my prayer life has been in building a sainthood equal to Daniel's. My long prayer list is inadequate to match the saintliness of a Daniel, nor will my writing on the subject be compared to Daniel's faithfulness that changed a nation and many hearts through centuries. The opportunities for faithful prayer can have an impact that will be incalculable. Prayer builds a structure that has a foundation on which all of life will be ready for the agonizing times, even the bitter circumstances will be anchored in a prayerful faith. Rest assured the climactic event will come, and only prayer's consistency day in and day out, will create the fortified soul. Then sainthood will arrive without the saint knowing it.

What Pastor does not know the death choking discouragement that shakes the foundation of faith, when carnal people desire the things of Egypt, while the Pastor is calling for them to push on to the land of milk and honey that Canaan has to offer. Carnality cannot tolerate self-denial, or sacrifice that cuts into their personal comfort zone. Carnality brings with it lamenting, a disgruntled spirit, and dissatisfaction. Paul said, "are ye not yet carnal?" There is nothing more contentious than carnality. Most believers do not know carnality is a part of the problem, or their personal problem.

At one point in my life I prayed an unwise prayer. This kind of prayer can be used as a cop out. But my church needed a revival, the kind where holiness prevails. My soul was drained with my pleading that seemed to have little results. There is a danger in a desperate unwise prayer, there is no way to know the mind of God. With Him being in control He may have other ways that He wants to use. The believer has a big, "I want immediate action." Is not God still God?

Moses was not the only one caught in this despair. Elijah after his battle with Baal slipped away and found a juniper tree and prayed: "it is enough, now, O Lord, take away my life; for I am not better than my fathers." Both of these men were overcome by a defeated people and did not want to deal with their carnality any longer.

But our God did not punish their limitations nor rebuke their rash outbreak in their anguish. He knew their motive. Dejection is a part of the battle, and in time, He speaks to Elijah, "what doest thou here Elijah." It is needful that the believer rises above the murky overcast. This is a step forward because there is more man can do. Now it is time to turn it over to the Lord. In these cases, the Father did not chastise, but gave His counsel and comfort.

What the prophets found true, men who shaped our country also found true when the unknown needed to be faced. When General Grant was slowly dying of cancer an old friend, General Howard, was visiting him. He was speaking to Grant of the distinguished service he had rendered to the country, and how he would always be held in high esteem for his service in preserving the Union, but Grant waved all this aside; he was thinking of other and higher things. He knew the piety of his old comrade, General Howard, that it was as geninue as his valor. "Howard" he said: "tell me something more about prayer." He wanted know the place prayer would take when facing the unknown.

PRAYER IS AN APPEAL FOR GOD'S TOUCH, THAT HIS GLORY MAY BE REVEALED .

Moses and Aaron "fall upon their faces, and the glory of the Lord appeared unto them." (Num. 20:6) Is it possible just to walk into His glory? I think not! The heart needs proper preparation and openness to God's will. The wonder and beauty were like setting the soul free.

God's glory is self manifestation. Then how can man hope to explain that glory. God's glory is exhibited in His works; in His character; in His power to create; in His attributes no man can duplicate; His splendor can not be looked upon and crowned in His honor. Notice, everything about God's glory is intangible except His creation.

Prayer has its own beauty and glory. Moses says: "the sight of the glory of the Lord was like devouring fire." (Ex. 24:17) Prayer opens the door to unknown glory. Prayer elevates insight to its highest level of Spiritual experience. Prayer fills the soul with eternal gratitude that spills over into glorious adoration. Prayer gives the believer spiritual fullness that immortalizes God's image that our Creator had in mind when He first made man a living soul. Prayer is that which contacts the intangible God because its spirit just like his Creator.

The glory of God activates spiritual excellence in man. So many times when reading the scriptures about the glory of God, the word "filled" dominates, "the glory of God filled the house." Even if the glory of God is intangible all who were there were aware and experienced that the house was "filled" with His glory. His glory lives beyond time and magnifies His righteousness and holiness in man. Dare we do any less!

PRAYER APPEALS TO THE DEMAND THAT EVERY SOUL SHALL BE HOLY: " WITHOUT HOLINESS NO MAN SHALL SEE THE LORD."

Definitely, the statement is very clear. How then can man communicate with the holy God? Holiness is a state of separated conduct and motive that are befitting for man to meet with the Lord God. Holiness is the right relationship that is wholly separated from living in willful sin by a pure motive that is completely devoted to God's will. Holiness means being delivered from defilement and living a God life which is the highest good, wrapped in willing obedience. Willful sin is the disconnection to our God.

How does holiness relate to prayer? It is a must to live a consistent holy life for our God to hear prayer from a holy people. Isaiah 15 & 16 gives the reason prayer is unanswered if unrepented sin is harbored . . . " when you make many prayers, I will not hear: yours hands are full of blood. . . Cease to do evil." There is nothing new about this scriptural message, the whole Bible rings with, "he that has clean hands and a pure heart." (Ps. 24:4&5) There cannot be any halfheartedness when it comes to the believer's prayer life.

Prayer must not be dishonest, but must be clothed in moral excellence. Does our God know when the believer approaches His throne with any can of impropriety in the motive life? Praying is not just a personal agenda, but it is to allow the Lord to work through prayer to accomplish His will, and His will only. It comes down to the fact, does the believer's prayer want the Lord to handle the situation, or take his life in his own hands in spite of knowing the limitations in his fragile abilities. Who but God knows the beginning from the end? The prayer of obedience is willing to place human restricted qualifications in God's hands, who is fixed in His holy attributes. The prayer life is one of the deciding factors, that will determine the course the believer takes. The prayer life cannot climb any higher than the personal surrender. All self agenda is crucified, and yielded when spiritual victory is completed.

Paul's philosophy of prayer gives a godly tone to life. Prayer gives the soul a firm assurance to meet the challenge of the day. Paul writes to the

Philippians: "Be careful for nothing; but in everything by prayer and supplication." (Phil.4:6) Do not be anxious, but let God carry the burden. Can you change the future events? Someone said: " Prayer is an acknowledgment of faith; worry is denial of faith. Prayer is putting my hand in God's, trusting to His loving guidance; worry is withdrawing my hand, and denying His power to lead me. Prayer leads through the door of faith into the presence of God; worry leads through the door of anxiety into the darkness of loneliness and discouragement. If prayer rules the life victory results." (Selected)

Each life has a tone which reflects attitude, motive and the depth of quality. The prayer of faith is like a child that believes whatever happens to him, his parents will supply what is needed. He is not concerned about his physical needs, his father will tend to that. He comes to his father when he is troubled, never doubting that his father will care, and encourage him. Will our heavenly Father do less? This philosophy of prayer has a musical ring: "in everything by prayer and supplication with thanksgiving." The tones of the prayer with "thanksgiving" will engulfs heaven, and bring its radiant sound of praise to the Father's ears. How quickly these praises of thanks will crush the conditions that have distressed and alarmed the weary traveler. The disquieted soul's rest is answered in the privilege Calvary brings to the redeemed soul.

Life is fractured in so many ways, the chasms that looked impossible to cross, must not be apprehensive when the whole being has the Father's assurance that He has the solution. It is the believer's responsibility to: "be careful for noting; but in every thing by prayer and supplication with thanksgiving let your requests be made known unto God." This is the total submission to God's will for life, with thanksgiving for whatever comes. Our God stands guard over His own.

James discusses the prayer that misfires, "Ye ask, and receive not, because ye ask amiss" These words indicate the Father evaluates each prayer and also the individual who prays the prayer. Content is important and the condition of the heart motive is imperative. Prayer is not a triviality, but a connected communion with Omniscience that immediately appraises and acclimatized the positional state of prayer's fitness.

Solomon recognized that prayer had God's special interest. "He that turns away his ear from hearing the law, even his prayer shall be an abomination." (Prov. 28:9) These words again reinforce how the Father assesses each prayer with thorough scrutiny. Are some of my prayers "an abomination?" Is there a more condemning word than "abomination?" Is not "amiss" the same? These prayers are unfit and did not stand the test.

Prayer is a test of who the prayee is, and that which is considered to be the want of the prayee. Our God still has His irrevocable standards, even in the area of prayer. Somewhere along the prayer line, faith did not stand the test, on every occasion the choice was for righteousness or unrighteousness. "Amiss" is crossing the line, and being disqualified by the test and found unfit.

What causes unfitness? The blemishes, as the blemishes on the lamb made the lamb unfit to be the sacrifice to our Holy God. If prayer is offered with blemishes in the prayee's motives, with an impure heart, the prayer does not meet the test. God does not accept anything less than a pure heart, unless the prayer is from a repenting heart, asking for forgiveness. God's call is: "be ye holy, for I am holy." "Follow peace with all men and Holiness without which no can see the Lord." (Heb. 12:14) If there is an unclean motive, which will not properly display the dispositions of prayer, then prayer will be "amiss." Prayer requires spiritual fitness.

The reason blemishes can ruin the prayer are many, which will vary with the individuals. Only God and the individual can know the motive of the heart. Usually it is the sins of the Spirit such as: the sin of omission, unforgiveness, greed, bitterness, covetousness, lust, jealousy, self-interest, or wrong attitudes. These sins of the Spirit are usually secretly hidden, and the prayee would be very embarrassed if others would know what is buried in the inner most being. The cover-up does not escape God Almighty. Sins concealed is prayer "amiss." The Psalmist said: "If I regard iniquity in my heart, the Lord will not hear me." (Ps. 66:18)

THE PRAYER OF BEWILDERMENT AND DISTRESS!

In I Samuel 15:11 God is speaking: "it repents me that I have set up Saul to be king; for he is turned back from following me, and hath not performed my commandments, and it grieved Samuel; and HE CRIED UNTO THE LORD ALL NIGHT." How can the mind and emotions deal with "the anointed one" (the loved one) who has betrayed God's trust?

The torment can drain physical strength and can sorely distress mind and soul. This fallout can go beyond bewilderment and frustration.

Saul was a wash out, a miscarriage of God's plan which He had for Israel. God's trust had been violated. Such distain is never limited to one person but this dishonored trust spreads like volcanic lava. Disobedience to God is always destructive. In God's plan for mankind, He will eliminate those He has anointed, and appoint another to replace the obstinate self-willed person.

When Samuel received God's decision: "it grieved Samuel; and he cried unto the Lord all night." Samuel's heavy heart was a prayerful cry that needed to succumb to the likes of a cold blast of winter. That prayer cry for the reprobate king or one of His children fills the valley with the turmoil of tears. Unruly wounds are harsh disappointments that harass the distressed situation. Prayer spills out from the anguish of a bleeding heart for an indictment for one who had lost his way that has nothing do with Samuel. Without doubt, the question that was on his mind was, had he done all he could to prevent this tragic end?

Samuel had faced many periods of trouble, but none had taken him to pits of dependency as much as Saul's sentence of elimination for his own lineage forever. Samuel's agonizing went on all through the night. Abraham Lincoln knew the heaviness of burdens when he wrote: "I have been driven many times to my knees, by the overwhelming conviction that I had nowhere else to go. My own wisdom, and that of all about me seemed insufficient for that day."

The soul that encounters broken promises, heartache and suffering would be wise to take the advice of an elderly Chinese philosopher given to a mother who had lost her son and wanted to know how to overcome her great grief. The old man said: "I can help you, but you must first bring me some mustard seed. But you must get it from a home where there has never been any loss or sorrow."

Eagerly the woman started the search, but in every home she visited there was someone who had lost a loved one or experienced some tragedy. Returning without any mustard seed, she exclaimed: "how selfish I have been! Sorrow is common to all." "Ah" said the philosopher, "you have learned a valuable lesson. Because you know sorrow, you can sympathize and comfort others and when you do, your sorrow will be lessened."

Personal sorrow and caring may not be shared with the disobedience of Saul, but the distress of soul has mounted to the degree that prayer is your only source, your only refuge that personal resources have. The raging storm inwardly needs calming. Spending a night in prayer and mediation will lift the anguish and the darkness that cause the tears to flow.

PRAYER IS A NECESSARY PART OF GOD'S FULLNESS!

The Psalmist uses the fifth verse of the twenty-third Psalm to flood the mind with the caring of the Sovereign God. The enemies are looking on as God supplies the abundance of food that the enemy wanted to deny. The table is filled with its bounty, David acknowledged whom the Provider is. The totality of the provisions gave delight and contentment to His faithful followers. It was a matter of standing back and watching the Father shower His blessings upon those receiving His perfect security. Through our inabilities and weakness the Father bestows all needs.

Prayer raises the joy of expectations. The hardship of sorrow and sacrifice of the hunted David, remembers the joy of prayer's blessing meeting with the approval of the Father. Then the cause will overrule the quality of the meat that is the main attraction of the feast.

Man is measured by his need; God is measured by His fullness which has no measure. God's fullness is filled with His virtue and completeness. God's filling man's emptiness allows God-given joy to embody the unfavorable as well as the favorable. The provision of life's necessities is rendered by our God's fullness. Is this not the captivated radiance that anoints the servant?

Then does not prayer's worth come from reflection on the person of our Lord? Prayer's intimate fellowship is the secret of joy and real peace. There is vast difference between the fullness of God's fellowship and the fellowship with man. Prayer is drawing upon God's fullness. Mankind can have an abundance of materialistic possessions but purposeless in the substance of things unseen.

Are not the words of the Psalmist: "my cup runneth over," an expression of exuberance? The soul could not contain the inner flow. The prayer of praise unlocked God's fountain of spiritual delight. The songwriter expresses the jubilation with the words: "I've found it, I've found it." The secret to man's cup running over is, God's imparted fullness, that your joy may be full. Prayer fulfills the connection that produces the relationship that leads the soul into the green pasture beside the still water. There is where the cup runs over.

PRAYER CARRIES MOTIVE!

How does prayer get God's attention? Attention involves motive. Some prayers are designed to use God for personal reasons. An overwhelming circumstance devastates the family and immediately prayer becomes imperative which would be natural for the believer who is active in daily prayer. But the circumstance can make the prayerless soul into a praying saint. It is called getting religious only when the need presents itself. Many prayers are used to manipulate God by attempting to set up a bargaining agreement with God. "Lord release the family from this predicament and I will do whatever God call's me to do." The prayer motive can be good or evil. It can be clothed in good attentions but with questionable ambitions. The Lord is always searching the heart to see what motivates.

How disheartening it must be to the Lord to have someone's behavior debase the privilege of prayer and the holiness of God to man's depraved ego! To pledge an impure motive is a lie that mirror's the true self. To belittle the sanctity of God to self-centeredness to the point of personal interest only, is the height of arrogance. Motive hidden is a hope for a reward that is not deserved.

Is it not God who propagates the instigation of life's conditions? Is it not man's obligation to meet God's conditions rather God meeting man's conditions? Is this not clearly presented in the Lord's prayer in Matthew 6:14: "For IF (the condition) ye forgive men their trespasses, (then) your heavenly Father will also forgive you?" It is not man setting up the condition; it is God. It is always man meeting God's condition, then He will act, but not until the condition is a part of pure motivation. There are multitudes who give head consent, but God looks on the motive of the heart when prayer is reviewed.

Prayer carries motive. Aleksandr Solzhenitsyn writes in; *One Day in the*

Life of Ivan Denisovich, how Ivan was faced with all the terrors of a Soviet prison. "One day Ivan was praying with head bowed and eyes closed, when he was approached by a fellow prisoner who scoffed in these words: Prayers won't help you get out of here any faster." To which Ivan replied: "I do not pray to get out of prison, but to do the will of God."

The prayer of God's will is a prayer of pure motive. God's will was more important than Ivan's terror of prison life and its abuses. How God-pleasing Ivan's prayer was. No disposition for personal benefit; no bargaining with God; no questionable motive; no demeaning attitude toward what God had allowed, only a complete surrender to God's will for his life.

PRAYER CAN DESTROY SATAN'S PLAN!

Paul wrote to the Corinthians in his second letter about the weapons that are available to wage this battle against the enemy's strongholds. Consider how the Amplified version presents this subject in 10:4 "For the weapons of our warfare are not physical (weapons of flesh and blood), but they are mighty before God for the overthrow and the destruction of strongholds." Christian forces are armed with more than the weapons of flesh and blood. Truth will prevail against the profane doctrine of secular humanism and its cohorts. The antagonist aliens that have defiled God's truth will encounter His might, even if it appears the power of darkness has won. The enemy has established positions that are deeply entrenched in the sub-culture. At every turn the adversary seeks to block any spiritual advance of God's truth. For success these hostile assailants must destroy the impact of the Christian church.

The word "destroy" according to Dr. Greenlee (my Greek professor) is made up of several parts. At its center the word means "work" or "deed". We observe Satan's "work" and "deeds." These must be destroyed by spiritual power. The second part of the word means, "not working." When something is destroyed, it is not working. The third part means, "utterly idle." It is not functioning. It is ruined, brought to naught.

The believer knows there is value in knowing the enemy's plans. This knowledge understands the fallacy of unscriptual dogma; the destructiveness of the liberal humanistic educational system; the brain washing of the unsophisticated student; political correctness that censors open debate in spiritual matters; moral values by liberals of Hollywood's following; the wearing away of Biblical Truth by the liberals who deny the doctrines of the church; the dismantling of the constitution by the judiciary; the robbing of society of the skills of the aborted child; and the obstruction by sinister forces like the ACLU that are determined to get God out of every segment of society.

This is the type of enemy the believer must confront daily. Rojas said what the believer needs to heed: "It is the enemy we do not suspect who is the more dangerous." While William James said it this way: "The deadliest enemies of nations are not their foreign foes; they always dwell within their own borders." Ungodly forces from within will bring down our nation, because they have the freedom to overwhelm man's depravity, if God's people do not have the will to press the battle in Jesus' name. Otherwise, the battle is already won until Jesus comes.

The spiritual battle will be won or lost in the prayer closet. There is an account given about the bastion of trenches, barricades and rolls of barbwire that fortified the enemy's strategic military position in World War II. If the allies would attack under these fortified conditions, it would mean thousands of lives would be lost, without the possibility of victory. The general dared attack without demolishing those protective barriers. The most powerful guns the general had were brought into place. Hour after hour the destructive shells rained on that invincible haven. Those powerful shells caved in the trenches, blew the barbwire into pieces, and utterly destroyed the barricades. After those deadly guns did their work, the enemy was routed, devastated and brought to naught.

Prayer is our big gun; when focused on the enemy's barricades the heavenly bombardments will be of such magnitude God's power will demolish every barrier, as we saw when the Berlin wall came crushing down. God's victory will go as far as the prayer closet will allow it to go. Is anyone concerned? Until prayer, the Christian's weapon, takes deep rootage, the forces of evil will continue to build their barriers higher. Fear can not control God's forces. The believer will be challenged by ungodly forces like the weak-kneed believer who said: " I don't believe in abortion myself, but the other people should have the right to choose for themselves." How magnanimous! There is no stand for right. No stand is a good safe stand; that way it is easy to fit in anywhere. Tolerance can push the believer into the gutter. Can anyone imagine Jesus straddling the fence. How forcefully He faced the religious zealots. It is either right or wrong according to the scriptures. Simon Cameron said it correctly: "a man who makes no enemies is never a positive force." Prayer is our positive force for the Lord. Every believer must pray through this kind of superficial slush. Accountability rests with the believer's stand or no stand.

PRAYER ALLOWS THE BELIEVER TO DWELL IN THE SECRET PLACE OF THE MOST HIGH!

To dwell is to inhabit; to settle down; to have a fixed abode; to take possession of the privileges salvation gives. It is dwelling in the secret place of the most High. One occupies the prayer place, not just goes in and out.

The believer is surrounded by demonic forces. It appears to be like the pressure that is closing in all the walls that attempts to suffocate righteousness. The suffering clashes with the weary pilgrim who is tired of battling the forces of darkness, and who now is gradually embracing the questionable that does not cause the conflict that the holy life demands. How can this happen if the believer's dwelling place is in the secret place of the most High?

David evidently had experienced the same combatants that the believer faces today. He exhorts some very assuring words in the ninety first Psalm's, words that impel hopelessness into real hope.

The believer encounters the "snares of the fowler." The fowler builds "snares" that were to meet the demand for snaring birds. The fowler would devise all kind of decoys that would "snare" the prey. What an illustration of what wick people will do to change the traps in order to accomplish their sinister plans. There is always a decoy that appears to be something it is not. Life is filled with "pestilences" of plagues, famines, floods and the sword; multitudes will fear the nights as they walk in darkness, nor will they be able to bear the destruction that wastes in noonday. This type of world is filled with terror.

The Psalmist suggests there will be thousands that will fall under these unbearable burdens. But these circumstances will not come to the believer in situations that he cannot bear for he has taken refuge in the secret place of the most High. Moreover, the believer will personally see the reward of the wicked.

How is this turmoil going to allow the believer to escape this evil that will befall the wicked? By the believer having made the Lord his refuge, no plague shall come nigh him. He, the eternal God shall bear thee up, and more: "He shall give His angels charge over thee, to keep thee in all thy ways." 5:11.

No matter the situation, the host of angels are those that faithful prayer has available for any righteous endeavor. Regardless of the number of the enemy's forces, my God's forces are always present and more than adequate. Why? Because prayer will take the believer in the secret place of the most high.

> "When our souls are much discouraged,
> By the roughness of the way
> And the cross we have to carry
> Seemeth heavier every day.
> When some cloud that over-shadows,
> Hides the Father's face from view,
> Oh tis will to remember
> He hath blessed us hitherto."
> -Selected

Israel was at war with Syria. Elisha was guiding Israel around the Syrian trap. Dothan was encircled by the enemy. Elisha's servant arose at an early hour and viewed a troubling scene of which Elisha was unaware. Elisha needed to know the problem, but Elisha seemed undisturbed about the hopeless appearance of what appeared to be a murderous defeat. Elisha's words were baffling, "fear not." Then Elisha prayed and the Lord opened the eyes of the servant, and "he saw, behold, the mountains were full of horses and chariots of fire round about Elisha."

Elisha, through believing prayer, had God's availability that unleashed the armed heavenly host to rescue Israel from certain destruction. Fear can not control prayer, because perfect love casts out fear. The believer's protection does not rest on fear, but on a faith that is anchored in the impossible, and the Creator God is the God of the impossible.

PRAY AND FAINT NOT!

Luke uses the words, "faint not" that are connected to prayer. (18:1) "Faint" is not used in a medical way of unconscious fainting, but as weak, half-hearted resolve. It can also denote a lily-livered faith that fades when prayer is not immediately answered. To faint is to lose courage; to be weary and faint-hearted; and laboring under a despondent spirit. Prayer is shattered with doubt. "Who can endure a fainthearted man?" (Prov. 18:14) Families and nations are destroyed by the lack of moral strength by its men. A fainting influence is passed from one generation to another. Faithful prayer with the family anchor's the manhood that God intended men to be. So few men have the godly influence that a family can attach their faith and stoutheartedness on to their purity.

With the universal affliction on the masses and with the world leaders who struggle for power, prayer has become a useless weapon because of man's depravity. Spurgeon makes a needed statement for this present chaotic world: "Oh, brethren, be great believers! Little faith will bring your souls to Heaven, but great faith will bring Heaven to your soul."

Phillip Brooks writes: "Oh, do not pray for easy lives! Pray to be stronger men! Do not pray for tasks equal to your powers: pray for power equal to your task! Then the doing of your work shall be no miracle. But you shall wonder at yourself, at the richness of life which has come in you by the grace of God."

Men need to pray for the stamina to nourish their families with the potency of God's righteous power; and to maintain the Biblical lifestyle when the family is confronted with sinister blasts that this world's subculture will purposely force upon them. This toughness will not come by a half-hearted self-serving attitude. This stoutheartedness must have inner clarity that wills nothing but God's will for each member of the family. The place to find this fortitude is in the prayer closet, which will take firm daily discipline.

Prayer always intensifies as the burden increases if the heart does not faint. One thing about this prayerful struggle or warfare, when victorious, it will always enlarge spiritual capacity. But capacity will level off as prayerful resolve diminishes. Prayer will tune the soul for the insurmountable. "Men ought always to pray and faint not."

Jesus gives the parable about a widow who went to an unbelieving unjust judge who did not regard God or man. This judge was asked to avenge her adversary, but he gruffly refused. After a number of requests, the judge became irritated with her continual pestering. After thinking about her insistence, the unjust judge came to the conclusion if he did not grant her request, there would not be any other way to get rid of her. Her faithful importunity paid off. If an unjust judge will grant the request of an unimportant widow, what will the just judge of all the universe give to a praying persistent believer?

God will avenge the avenger when he comes again, but will He find faith in the prayer of those who call upon Him? Will the strength of God's people be drained because of the lack of enduring prayer? Let the believer's prayer be sealed in the faith where the impossible is possible, and faint not.

Henry Stanley, the well known African explorer, wrote: "On all my expeditions, prayer made me stronger, morally and mentally, than any of my nonpraying companions. It did not blind my eyes, or dull my mind, or close my ears; but on the contrary, it gave me confidence. It did more; it gave me joy and pride in my work, and lifted me hopefully over the 1500 miles of forest tracks, eager to face the day's perils."

Pray and faint not is a must in meeting any bewildering situation. Prayer is the stabilizer in the up and downs in life. Prayer releases God's power and fortifies the soul in the midst of any antagonist attack.

PRAYER IN JESUS' NAME!

"That at the name of Jesus every knee shall bow, of things in heaven, and things in earth, and things under the earth." (Phil. 2:10) And Paul again emphasizes these words to the Ephesian church: "Above every name, that is named." (1:21) While the Amplified version translates Acts verse 12: "And there is salvation in and through no one else, for there is no other name under heaven given among men by and in which we must be saved."

What an authoritative declaration that is impacted in imperatives! Who else but Jesus can command: "I am the way?" He, the very God is and shall be exalted. God's blessing cannot and will not be denied. Jesus is prophetically named by the angel when appearing to Mary with the words, "thy shall call his name Jesus." Man did not name Him. There is all power in that name.

Every knee shall bow in holy worship, recognizing Him to be Lord. That means everyone that had a foreign god; all in heaven; all in the earth; all under the earth; all in the infernal world; and every soul from the beginning of time will confess His Lordship. He alone is worthy of our worship. The one worlder, whose god is himself; those who emphasize all religions are the road to heaven; those who fancy themselves that intellectual, position or power gives them rights to the hereafter; those who branded the Bible-believing Christian as an arrogant bigot will bow their knees and confess that Jesus Christ is Lord.

My answer to the godless unbeliever is: "my experience verifies the Bible, and the Book verifies my experience. If there is any problem with the Bible, take the issue up with the author. This truth is relived in the heart of a multitude world wide.

This scriptural believer can, in the name of Jesus claim authority over all kinds of satanic dominion. Peter and John on their way to prayer time, were confronted with a lame man asking alms; their reply to the man was: "silver and gold have I none, but such as I have I give thee: in the name of Jesus Christ of Nazareth rise up and walk."

Why pray in the name of Jesus? Because prayer connects with all power in heaven and earth. Jesus' tomb is empty, while millions visit their god's graves, and their offering is placed on the dead man's grave. Jesus is alive. The tomb could not hold him. My soul requires that I pray to the living God, and prayer will be a vital link that gives a personal relationship. Alexander Marshall said: "Every blessing you need is treasured up in Christ. Young or old, rich or poor; may now obtain the blessings of forgiveness, justification, and eternal life "without money and without price," without groans and sighs, "good works" or religious observances."

PRAYER THAT ABIDES IN CHRIST JESUS!

Since mankind is the branch and our God is the Vine, what is the branch's part in our God's plan? When Adam willfully sinned, the tender branch was torn from the Vine. Adam's race became the fallen branch that was broken from the Vine that needed to be grafted into the Vine if the branch is to fulfill its Divine purpose and become fruit bearing. The Lord Jesus responded to that need by opening His wounds on Calvary. These wounds opened by the Vine now makes it possible for that withered branch (mankind) to be grafted into the Vine's wounded side to once again receive spiritual Life and the necessary fruitfulness that will glorify God. This engrafted union brought God and man back into this glorious Oneness. In John 15:5 Jesus gives the version that is to be the basis for man's relationship with his God: "I am the vine, ye are the branches; he that abides in me, and I in Him, the same brings forth much fruit; for without me ye can do nothing."

The branch needs the constant attention of the Vine Dresser, who prunes the useless suckers that would hinder and take nourishment that was needed for the production of more delicious fruit. The vigor of the branch depends on "the know how" of the one doing the pruning. The pruning will open wounds on the branch that will cause bleeding. Pruning the soul usually is hurtful, but necessary. The Husbandman will take great care that all pruning will be done according to His perfect standards. Where He finds no fruit, there was no real union with the Vine, and He must act if the other branches are to be fruitful.

Prayer that "abides" is in the present tense. Abiding means remaining, continuing in, tarrying, to wait, to endure to the end, otherwise there is no fruit. The Vine does not bear the fruit, it only supplies the nourishment for the branch for its fruit bearing. Each branch is under the inspection of the Husbandman, and the fruitless branch will be cut off and gathered for the fire that continually burns. Mankind can be attached to a belief about God, which means being fruitless and good for nothing. Abiding means continual abiding. Godet defines abiding: "It is the continuous act by which the Christian lays aside all he might draw from his own wisdom, strength and merit, to desire all from Christ by the inward aspiration of faith."

A family lineage can be spoken of as a vine and its members as branches. Jesus was a stem out of Jesse. The family leaves some kind of fruit, which may be good or bad. One thing is sure; the heavenly Husbandman will judge and inspect each branch for its fruits. He expects "fruit," "much fruit," and "more fruit."

All of this "abiding" is building up to the Amplified's seventh verse: "if you live in Me (abide vitally united to Me) and my words remain in you and continue to live in your hearts, ask whatever you will, and it shall be done for you."

This account of the vineyard laid the foundation for the condition of prayer. Fruitlessness has a dead end for any prevailing prayer. The whole condition for prayer rests upon a continual abiding in Him. Not for an hour, but day in and day out. Condition, "if," if what, "if you abide in Me." This means not yielding to temptation. Abiding in Him will reveal if unforgiveness, wrong attitudes, pride, or self-gratification is making the life fruitless. Thus, prayer will be as fruitless as the fruitless life. Then does not prayer mean a commitment to a fruitful ministry to others?

DAILY PRAYER CAN SEAL AN ETERNAL PARTNERSHIP WITH THE LORD!

Our daily prayer is the ladder on which faith must climb to take God's blessings. Prayer is the invisible rope that is attached to heaven's bell which rings in the Father's attentive ear. Daily prayer awakens the dry bones to new life; empowers a dormant mind; quickens the lifeless imagination; refreshes the dolefulness of reassurance; captures newness; conquers boredom; enriches thought; develops character; eliminates life's drabness; and develops greater capacity. Prayer enriches the daily atmosphere.

But daily prayer would fall short even if all the above is fulfilled, unless there is a compelling love that reaches to the deepest needs of others. This love must reach beyond the verbal expression and be placed in action with deeds that are a part of daily life.

Prayer has this declaration given by 1 John 3:24: "and hereby we know that He abides in us, by His Spirit which He hath given us." He is in us! This is that which we have heard from the beginning and which needs to remain a personal focus. Our Lord has given access to His Word, which opens the promises to confront the trials, difficulties and defeats with victory. Let us not depend on the rockets, the bombs and the equipment that carry their destruction to their destination. The living God must be our sufficiency, while all tangibles will pass away. God's myriad of blessings will continue with us into eternity. Every profitable blessing that God has will become our own. The Spirit bears His own witness of our hope. Is it not said: "because I live ye shall live also." This we know because the Spirit dwells in us.

This partnership has a common purpose signifying everything will be shared that is needful for this life and eternity. There is a spiritual agreement that travels from earth to heaven. Compare the believer's hope with an obituary that appeared in the Akron Beacon Journal. "She was a great card player, and consistently beat the pants off her family in everything from slapjack to bridge. She gardened and golfed, smoked a cigarette a month and told jokes. She loved spring flowers, the Indians, her Akron friends, big family meals, her husband, and bridge club. She proved there is life before death."

Imagine giving these credentials to the Lord as her passport to life forever. There is one thing for sure, "she proved there is a life before death." Evidently there was not much emphasis on the life after death.

Prayer will keep life centered on the prize in the next life. The Amplified version in 1 John 3:24 gives broader focus on the depth of living life in these words: "all who keep His commandments (who obey His orders and follow His plan, live and continue to live, to stay and) abide in Him, and He in them. (They let Christ be a home to them and they are the home of Christ.) And by this we know and understand and have the proof that He (really) lives and makes His home in us: by the (Holy) Spirit whom He has given us."

The Holy Spirit has sufficiently proven that if the believer seeks the Lord as commanded, He will move into his home. The depth of this relationship is beyond measure. Prayer is at the core of building this bond.

PRAYER IS USELESS WITHOUT WHOLEHEARTED OBEDIENCE.

Prayer uses God's Word as its standard! Genuine prayer will seek to prevent the spiritual Christian from conforming to the present day subculture. The word "conforming" has a continual impact upon the believer. The scriptural meaning of "conforming" is: to make; to render like; having the same form; fashioned after; changeable in the essential character; compromising the manner of life; to fashion oneself; to be made known; the usage of that which Christ Jesus had already abolished. While obedience signifies submitting to, by an act of the will to our Savior, conforming is an evolutionary process that absorbs the believer into the subculture by degrees.

"Conforming" has the allowance of an attractiveness, but having only the form of godliness. "Conforming" into the present state of things that gradually, and subtly has subconsciously accepted a form of religion that satisfies the personal wants, rather than the spiritual need.

What then is the spiritual description of this world? This world's atmosphere has been cast into deep spiritual darkness that is injurious to the soul. Revealing the hidden intangibles that control our culture, such as pride, covetousness and greed for luxury, the vanity and lust in dress, riotous living and sensual appetites, all are sinful, unbecoming and unacceptable to Biblical Christianity. The church has bought into what the natural man wants. Forget about the need for God's standard. Even though this humanistic religion is degrading it has taken over the religion of our educational system that has allowed its devious pressure to infiltrate into the church and the home.

How deeply has conforming penetrated into our society? A questionnaire about raising children was taken with parents concerning the time spent in various categories. One question was the time given to prayer, only 4 percent prayed with their children and just 1 percent gave attention to "integrity and good character." At this "conforming" rate secularism will take over in less than 2 decades. The Amplified version warns: "do not be conformed to this world (this age), fashioned after and adapted to its external, superficial customs."

Praying homes will not permit secular humanism to devour their Biblical standards. Bailey says: "prayer is the spirit speaking truth to Truth." This Truth guides the soul into all Truth. Conforming is impossible as long as prayer is holding to and obeying Biblical Truth. "Prayer purifies; it is a self-preached sermon." (Richter) Believers' homes need to be saturated with prayer if the homes are going to stand the adversity caused by the liberal Judicial system that is making their own laws, and other godless agendas.

Romans 12:2 goes from the deceptive "conforming" to "transforming"and obedience. There is a choice between "conforming" (to be fashioned after the world) and "transformation," which is God's way of reconstructing and remaking man's nature to the likeness of His nature. Transformation is conversion, being made new spiritually. Society has sought to make technology the transformer, but man still retains the depraved nature that controls the inner life.

The praying believer would ask the academia skeptic: "who calms the raging sea; who turns the hurricane from its destructive path; who laid the foundation of the earth; who hung the stars in space; who keeps the planets in their orbit; who has placed a thermostat on the sun? It is the same caring God who stirs the spiritual hunger of the human soul. It is that same God who transforms the evil heart of lost man. This living God works the inner being of man where no human being has ever been."

This God hears the pleading prayer: "God be merciful to me a lost sinner." This prayer's answer is the wonder of wonders, the burden rolls away, forgiveness rushes in to free from sin's shackles, God given joy bursts into the soul. This simple prayer transforms the soul from the world of human despair to the knowledge of knowing the Infinite God. The answer to this prayer supplants all human understanding. No scientist, no skeptic, no conventional religionist can duplicate this miracle. Mankind can realize this transformation by the simple prayer that believes Christ Jesus came to save every lost sinner that will come to Him.

Paul continues the second verse with: "but be transformed (changed) by the (entire) renewal of your mind (by its new ideals and is new attitude), so that you may prove (for yourselves) what is the good and acceptable and perfect will of God, even the thing which is good and acceptable and perfect (in His sight for you.)" (Amplified Rom. 12:2)

→PRAYER MUST UNITE WITH GOD'S WORD, AS ITS STANDARD.

Lost man may not know God's Standard, but the believing heart seeks His Standard. The believer positions himself by standing on the Divine inspiration of God's Word. To make prayer to be an assurance, the stand must be steadfast.

God heard this lost woman's prayerful plea when confronted with the gospel. She was a frightfully wicked woman working in one of the paper mills of Glasgow when converted (transformed) through the efforts of a city missionary, and became a person of great devoutness of character. She described the process of her salvation in these terms: "I was like the rags that go into the paper mill. They are torn and filthy, but they come out clear, white paper. That is like what Jesus is doing for me." (Rev. G. P. Eckman)

The power of God's Word is revealed daily in lives that have believed the message of its pages. The Bible is the standard that arouses God conscious awareness. Its principles never change and it becomes the leader of the lost.

"A Jewess of wealth and position noticed an advertisement of some article which she fancied, that would accompany the purchase of a Bible. She sent an order for the sake of what she wanted, and tossed the unwelcome book aside; but in an idle hour later, picked it up and turned its pages. The New Testament was unfamiliar and she glanced at it curiously, becoming intersted before she knew it.

She fought against belief, but it gradually forced itself upon her, and she found herself in deep trouble. Confessing her faith meant the loss of property and home, the heartbreak of father and mother, even separation from her husband, but she could not remain silent.

All that she feared was threatened in those awful days, but because the family loved her, and to prove to her her error, her family also read the despised Gospel. Earth's unending miracle was repeated; they found what she had found, and looked wondering into other's faces, a Christian household." (Forward)

PRAYER INDUCES BURDENS AND RELIEVES BURDENS.

Paul was on overload. The weight of natural man's depravity was troubling. Wickness abounded as a result of man's fallen nature. This suffering under the load had become a burden that was grievous. In a sense, Paul felt the torment that our Lord experienced in Gethsemane. He saw the sin sick world as Jesus saw it. Paul bore a compassionate faith for society's redemption which he saw being weighed in the balance and found wanting. His tent (body) was an element of decay, his time short. His responsibility was to lost humanity. Departing from the burdensome task would be far better. There was the thought of laying aside the tent for his mansion.

Paul's groaning was an out-pouring of the inner concern. Groaning implies the agony of prayer. Hear his words: "For while we still are in this tent, we groan under the burden and sigh weighed down, depressed, oppressed, not that we want to put off the (clothing of the spirit) but rather that we would be further clothed so that what is mortal (our dying body) may be swallowed up by life (after the resurrection)."

Paul's mind was set. Death is spoken of as being clothed, and yet being welcome. The dying thief cried: "Lord remember me." Jesus responded: "today thou shalt dwell with me in Paradise." Not some future time but "today." Paul spoke of being present with the Lord. Remember the soul is not in the grave. The soul is conscious after physical death. There is no way to bury eternal life. God put eternal life in the soul, and nothing can remove its life. Paul could hear the cheers from the balcony of heaven for he was "compassed about with so great a cloud of witnesses," very conscious witnesses. If these witnesses were in the grave, then Paul was greatly deceived. (Read Luke 16:19-31)

Prayer takes on new meaning when living under devious circumstances. If there is no or little concern, then this encumbrance spiritual battle will have very limited meaning. There will be no knowledge of knowing what Paul was talking about. Carrying a burden for the lost puts the soul under strain and stress with the responsibility that goes with intercession for carnal rejecters.

The praying believer can choose to take on an overwhelming pressure that costs prayer time, or he can leave the force of intense social decay for someone else. Not too many are lining up for a groaning prayer meeting. That calls for heartbreak and living with reaching the decadent, religious blind that are leading the blind.

Paul reveals the induced burdens, the true concern to relieve the burden of lostness from the unredeemed. When this induced burden is released, that will release Paul's burden.

DESPERATE PRAYER AROUSES THE NEED TO FAST!

Fasting is voluntary abstinence from food, a situation to allow inspection and purpose. Fasting strengthens the intensity of prayer that expresses a need that refuses to pamper the flesh by its self-denial. As the burden becomes intolerable, demanding drastic faith action, the weight is insisting on destroying any fleshly propensities. Fasting is a part of the crushing process, a continual crucification of tempting self driven encumbrances; Fasting exposes the weakest areas in the spiritual life; it is a fortification built in to protect from any subtle temptation to be misleading, allows time to concentrate on adequate personal faith; and witnesses to our Heavenly Father that this concern cannot be handled by the limitations of human effort. Fasting reveals to the Father that this prayer of desperation cannot be overlooked. The groanings are so critical that words are unutterable; fasting releases a faith that believes the Lord will do the impossible. It manifests an earnestness before God that He is first and is so honored, believes God cares and loves the believer; fasting carries a cost that is willing to pay any cost. The Psalmist in 109:24 cries a despairing cry: "my knees are weak through fasting and my flesh fails of fatness." How travailing and saturated such a plea is! His prayer is filled with anguish and wretchness. It is out of the hands of frail man, beyond human capacity, and now Lord, this my earnest plea. God's help is a must or the Psalmist sinks in the quicksand of despair.

An old Purtian called fasting "a soul fattening institution." Most strive for a lean soul, while the pursuer of righteousness hungers for the fullness of the soul that cannot be contained, as an artesian well. Spurgeon wrote: "I think many fairly ask you who are lovers of the souls, who have eyes which do weep, and hearts which can feel, to try my Master's prescription (fasting), and see if the most unmanageable devil which ever took possession of a human heart, be not driven out as the result of prayer and fasting, in the exercise of your faith?"

Fasting under a chastised burden is a necessity that marks the soul with its sense of urgency; always pushing beyond the ordinary. Fasting is the component history's spiritual giants have used as their weapon against overwhelming odds to transform social and spiritual structures. This type of praying is not caught, but sought.

PRAYER WILL MEET ALL PERSONAL NEEDS.
(Needs, not wants)

All my Christian life has been a faith walk that was beyond my personal resources. When I was called to preach I was still paying off my Electrical Education bill. In '39 started my electrical trade at 35 cents per hour, when there was work, very seldom did the weekly work reach forty hours. Then in '41 the company joined the union, and the hourly wage went to $1.50. Besides, I had married the owner's daughter and the business was going to be mine eventually. Then the call to the ministry came with such force that there was no escape. I tried every excuse. My dreams were shattered. I had gone through the great depression, and I had a goal to have some things I never had. The ministry demanded 7 years of College and Seminary, with no money, and books which were not my choice of activity. Both my wife's parents and mine thought I had lost all reason.

Of course, I never did have any money so that did not bother me, but the 7 years of nothing but books, that did. I was married, so it was necessary to think of more than myself. I knew there would not be any help from the family, and then someone asked me, "how I was going to pay the bills." I responded with the words the Lord flashed in my mind: "by faith." The reply was: "you can't eat faith." There were a number of laughs about my remark, living "by faith."

In those seven years there was only one time that I was late by two weeks with my tuition.

Were there trials? At times all we had was tomato soup; at Thanksgiving there was not one thing to eat in our one room. We told no one, but we prayed about our need and went to the Thanksgiving service. When we returned there was a bushel basket full of groceries at our door. It is living by faith. Faith is going to classes and painting hot metal roofs on the campus at 20 cents an hour.

I understood there are two schools the Lord has for His faithful children, expanding beyond learning through books, social structure and the educational environment, but there is the school of trusting God in a living faith that can do what none of the others learning tools can do.

This trusting faith is watching God supply the penniless graduate with the furniture for an eight room parsonage in his first full time church. While checking my car to see if it would make the journey from Kentucky to Ohio, the owner, who was not a Christian said: "Shaum what are going to do about furnishing that parsonage?" How he even knew about the parsonage was shocking because I had never expressed anything about my situation. That dear man said: "I will make arrangements with a furniture wholesale place in Louisville and you take my truck and pick out the furniture, and pay me when you can."

Prayer will open endless opportunities that could not be realized otherwise. Like our Home for Boys that was not underwritten by any organization, nor did I ever ask any one person for a cent of support. All needs were met by prayerful faith. It was our privilege to see my God perform miracle after miracle, and pay bills on time.

We talk a great deal about prayer and faith, but how many Christians know what it is to sell all they have, like my aunt who went to the foreign mission field with only a few prayer partners and no organization supporting her, not knowing anyone on that mission field; no place to live, no one to meet her; just there answering God's call.

Prayer that believes in the God of the impossible, will sell all, and go years without a salary knowing in his old age God will supply all his needs. And He will and has! That is the God that says, "trust me for everything that is needed." The good news is: "the eyes of the Lord are upon the righteous, and His ears are open to their cry." (Ps. 34:15)

PRAYER IMPRESSES THE PRAYER BURDEN ON THE BELIEVERS TO INTERCEDE FOR ANOTHER.

God spoke to the Pious Ananias about going to pray with Saul the known terrorist from Tarsus. Is it not interesting to see how God works through this righteous man. Ananias did question the wisdom of God's message, but his fear was overcome by the knowledge that this was what he was supposed to do.

What would have happened if Ananias had continued to question and procrastinate his willingness to obey? This same type of proposal enters into the spirit-led prayer life of every believer. It is so easy to just pray words and not stop long enough to listen to what God has to say. What God has to say to the believer is the most important part of the prayer! "God said to Ananias, Arise and go, . . . for behold, he (Paul) prays." (Acts 9:11) He went.

The prayer life of the believer predicts what the daily life will display. Be assured there will be a "watcher" that may have a godly mother and father who are praying for him. The believer's life will be measured by what the "watcher" knows to be true. Personal piety can be the answer to that godly mother and father's prayers. Verification came to the "watcher" because the believer's prayer life was on display.

But I wonder how many tragic experiences could have been aborted or solved if God's people were in such tune and connected with the Almighty God, that He could speak to the prayerful ear of the believer about someone who was desperate and needed prayer at a particular time. May God help me, if I am so engrossed in my personal prayer list that I am unaware of someone's crucial situation miles away. It is listening that needs our prayerful attention. I must ask myself, am I that sensitive to the prompting of the Holy Spirit when others are at the decisive point of their lives. Do I sense the gravity of missing the prayer that would have given hope? Then, if I do, do I pray?

John Paton's wife and baby were stricken with fever while a missionary to the New Hebrides. Both died from the disease. This is mentioned to question, was there anyone in the family, the church, that had the prayer line opened and sensed the urgent need of the Paton's family on the other side of the world? I do not want to judge, I only ask, is the Holy Spirit speaking to believers about grave circumstances of others that may be near or far? Am I in such a relationship to my Lord that I will not allow crucial needs to slip by?

It causes me to wonder if my unattentive spirit has resulted in some tragedy, that a prayerful spirit would have tuned the soul to make captive the need and responded. I must ask myself, how close to the Father does my prayer life take me? Does the Spirit move me to pray about that which is unknown to me? Will the Lord have a list of the tragedies that would not have happened if my prayer life had been listening instead of praying words? How thankful each believer should be that Ananias listened to God, and not his fears. God is still speaking. Let prayer position each one of God's believing children to spiritually hear. Prayer refuses to tolerate God's child living below his privileges and the Spiritual capacity that our heavenly Father provides.

Do I hear the cry of the fallen? Do I hear the plea of the sick bed? Do I hear the appeal of the afficted? Do I hear the agony of defeat and failure? What am I hearing?

PRAYER GIVES THE PRIVILEGE TO PRAISE GOD.

Who can be sure any praise is adequate? Emotions are involved, as they should be, but praise has a deeper depth. Praise is valueless, if God is not placed first. Is not real praise the cry of the heart that lasts after the emotions have faded, and when true oppression evolves? Should not praise be a part of a broken heart in that lonely night? " Praise is the best auxiliary to prayer; and he who most bears in mind what has been for him by God will be most emboldened to supplicate fresh gifts from above." (Henry Melville)

Dr. Johnson describes "praise, like gold and diamonds, owes its value only by its scarcity." The scripture states: "let everything that hath breath praise the Lord."

Praise is the commendation of God's character that cannot change. Praise to God for His sacrificial Lamb. Where would we be without God coming to rescue us in our lost condition?

PRAYER HAS THE PRIVILEGE TO SPIRITUAL POWER WHICH COMES IN PATIENCE AND GENTLENESS.

Great men have found that spiritual power has more might and persistence than any tangible force. Do not the intangible thoughts of God rule this world? Prayerful spiritual power keeps the believer from seeking the excessive power the fallen angels sought.

Prayer has the privilege of arriving in the midst of poverty and conquering its demeaning attack. No one is more strongly tempted to vice than that one caught in poverty. Only the prayer hearing God can understand poverty's weighty load, for poverty is heavier than the results of its chains. It is prayer that can reach from the depth of poverty's pits and lift from dependence to the confidence of trusting in the caring God.

Prayer has the privilege to prevail over church politics. The struggle for position, the dictatorial hierarchy, the apostasy of ministers that need to apologize to the founding fathers, the hypocrisy of the professors who claim the name Christian and deny the scriptural Truth on which Christianity is founded, and continue to brainwash their student body. Those who would stand for the church doctrine that has scripture as its base and would resist this ungodliness are appointed to some place in the wilderness where their voice is not heard. Prayer is the only thing that can keep heart and mind focused on the narrow path that leads to glory. No one has the power to assess the multitude of lost souls that are a product of a religiosity that has cut the anchor rope of faith and now their ship is caught in the storm with no scriptural answers. There is no escape, each one will be held accountable at the judgment. Pray for the lost shepherds.

Prayer gives the family privileges that need to be seized at the moment. These prayer privileges only last for a life time. Prayer keeps the family continually alive to seek new and higher ground if God's privileges are achieved. Many times these opportunities will be lost and regret always follows. There is always remorse when God's privileges are not fulfilled. This is clearly revealed in the account of the foolish virgins: " and while they went to buy oil, the bridegroom came; and they that were ready went in with him to the marriage; and the door was shut." (Matt. 25:10) There is something shattering about the door of opportunity being shut. God gave the privilege.

"A father sat at his desk poring over his monthly bills when his young son rushed in and announced, "Dad, because this is your birthday and you are 55 years old, I'm going to give you 55 kisses, one for each year!" When the boy started to make good on his word, the father exclaimed, "oh, Andrew don't do it now. I'm too busy!

"The young son immediately fell silent as tears welled up in his eyes. Apologetically the father said, "you can finish later!" The boy said nothing and quietly went away, disappointment written all over his face. That evening the father said: "come and finish the kisses now, Andrew." But boy did not respond.

A short time after this incident the boy drowned. His brokenhearted father wrote: "If only I could tell him how much I regret my thoughtless words, and could be assured that he knows how much my heart is aching." (Daily Bread)

We cheat ourselves if we settle for anything less than the excellence our heavenly Father has for us. It is always an anguished turmoil that arises in the soul when prayerlessness allows God's opportunities to slip by.

Prayer reaches for excellence; the area of our limitations and thoughtless-ness choice needs much prayer. Prayer opens and closes doors, no power but only God Himself can operate these doors if the believer is surrendered to His perfect will.

God always operates in His Omnipotence. He can not do other wise; while demons always operate under limitations that angelic beings are given by their Creator. Paul said to the Corinthians . . . "I came to Troas to preach Christ's gospel, and a door was opened unto me of the Lord." (2 Cor. 2:12). Again in (1 Cor. 16:9 Amp.) "For a wide door of opportunity for effectual (service) has opened unto me (there) one great and promising - - and many adversaries." Joseph Parker reflected on prayer's opportunity: "the face is made every day by its morning prayer, and by its morning look out of the windows which opens upon heaven."

Obedience is at the heart of the prayer that unbars doors or shuts them. But each door has its risk, because choice is involved. Life's values are weighed. Choice chooses the direction of life.

Two brothers, Ahmed and Omar, wished to do something to perpetuate their memory. Omar's choice was to cut from the quarry a great obelisk. He lifted it up beside the highway, and carved his name upon it, with many other inscriptions. There the monument stood for ages, a splendid monument, but of no use to the world. Ahmed dug a well beside the desert highway and plated palm trees beside it. And in the course of time the spot became a beautiful oasis where the weary traveler stopped to quench his thirst and feed upon the fruit and to rest beneath the shade of the tall palms. All who passed that way blessed the name of Ahmed the Good. The story illustrates two plans of life. One is to make for himself a great name, as high as the obelisk of Omar, and as useless. The other choice is to make his life like an oasis where the weary may find rest and comfort and refreshment.

The Lord can make a door accessible to all kinds of godly opportunities; self can open another door for personal ambitions. God's door opens to rich fulfillment living in God's domain; while the door of self-interest creates an emptiness that selfish effort can not exit. Any door will present "many adversaries." The door of self-interest will depend on personally solving the "many adversaries." While God's door also will have "many adversaries" but has God's eternal promises that will defeat all adversaries. Obedience has locked in it, the prayer power that will remove mountains.

The Russian revolutionary Vladimir Ilyich Lenin who opened the door of communism to the ignorant masses in Russia, spoke the following words about his faithful followers that would shame many Christians: "dead men on furlough." His dedicated followers were willing to die for the cause. That door has closed leaving endless misery to a godless people that know nothing of the intangible God who for years has been buried in the manure pile of materialism and socialistic communism.

If God is to open the door to the wonderful world of grace and mercy, it will require much prayer. Prayer allows the believer to face the unknown with its uncertainty, with certainty. With absolute faith, the Father will not leave his child on the other side of the door. Prayer may be uttered in the darkest night of the believer's life, but as in the words of the song: "somewhere in the shadows you'll find Jesus." The believer's next step has already been prepared. Prayerful obedience will complete the journey with the joy of God's fullness.

PRAYER ENCOUNTERS THE BURDEN OF THE WEAK WHO ARE UNAWARE OF THEIR WEAKNESS.

Paul forcefully addresses the proper approach to those who are vulnerable in Romans 15:1, "we then that are strong ought to bear the infirmities of the weak and not to please ourselves." Without doubt this statement implies more than prayer, but prayer is a must for the empowerment to live in a situation with the weak and impaired. It is more than a duty, Paul is saying, it is a calling, a design for each Christian to carry a burden for the weaker person's good.

Does our prayer life place all believers in the spiritual position to bear the infirmities of the weak? Who can tell the influence of a daily life that is viewed by some struggling Christian, or some rebellious young person? How do believers measure spiritual strength? Is it by activity; by appearance; by morality; by church going; all these may be good in themselves, but all of these are not the real core of a completely surrendered life that bears others burdens. The core of life is whether the believer willingly places his life in the midst of that battleground to free those caught in their powerless weakness. Is this kind of surrender possible without the undergirding power that comes from consistent prayer?

At our Home for Boys, my wife and I dealt with rebellion; with boys being unwanted by their parents, angry, having very little conception of what is right or wrong, stealing, lying, sneaking, cheating, running away, fires at home and at school, returning things that were stolen, there was little or no moral restraint to most of the boys. The anger would reach the point where one would punch the window out of the door, or punch a hole in the wall, or use a ball bat to go after someone, or knock a hole in the safe that had a concrete bottom. This is only the beginning.

How much strength is needed to deal with these, many times dangerous situations? Sanity is needed 24 hours a day, and 365 days a year. These boys were revealing all the strength they had in their rebellion against any type of authority. Their lives were regulated by their world of violence. They were fighting back against the hurts, rejection, and law breaking. This bitterness was their weakness, housed in their fragile morality. They were battle hardened, many could not, or would not cry, knowing little or nothing about tender love. They had to know how weak and vulnerable they were before they could be helped.

Prayer was the source of strength needed during these dueling circumstances. It was not done by brute force, or enduring stamina, but by prayer for the exposed wounds that inwardly cried for help. Prayer believed God for protection, and earnestly prayed for unconditional love for those who hungered for that love. That love needed will be revealed in sickness. Love would be shown when the vomit was cleaned up without complaint or when the bone broken happened at an inconvenient time and the doctor was a number of miles away and the trip was made. This is what Paul meant when said: "not to please ourselves."

Without caring for the debilitated, they would not be rescued and this scripture in Romans 15:1 would not be a part of Christian concern, the assailable masses would be thrown on society's trash heap.

OBEDIENCE PRAYER APPROVES GOD'S PLAN, EVEN WHEN THE RESULTS ARE NOT SEEN.

How many have said or heard someone say: "there is no use to continue praying any longer. Everything has been done that could be done." Weariness and utter hopelessness are flowing out in every look, in the body language, in the spoken word, and in physical exhaustion. Everything humanly possible has been done. Being brought to the end of human resources, is it not time to stop, and re-evaluate the prospect of God doing what human effort cannot do?

Prayer is always at its best when every human means has been depleted. Prayer has little purpose if the best physical effort has not been given, God will never do what human ability can do. New faith rises when the burden is completely turned over to the Lord, knowing that energies have extended to the highest degree of personal skills. God is ready to carry the burden.

However, it does not mean that the believer is resting on the oars and saying: "Lord, I'm through with giving a competent attempt." Prayer in this struggling valley is a pursing renewal of vigor when there is no awareness that God is intervening. Prayer arouses to a new faith that will quell subtle doubts of the enemy that would suggest that prayer is worthless, just give up the ship and allow the winds of disappointment to dash the spiritual life on the rocks of doubt and human inadequacy. Why continue on, because if God be for us, who is able to go against us?

The prayer of importunity is a shameless approach to the Father. This type of praying has the seeds of earnestness and an unblushing persistence that claims the boldness of what He has promised, and a significant sense of assurance.

Luther said it wisely: "Prayer is a powerful thing; for God has bound and tied Himself there unto." Prayer reaches beyond man's possibilities confronted by the test of personal faith. Read again the account of the man who went to his friend's house at the midnight hour to borrow bread for his unexpected visitor. Luke 11:8 "I say unto you, though he will not rise and give him, because he is a friend, yet because of his IMPORTUNITY he will rise and give him as many as he needs." Importunity has eternal rewards.

Some years ago a Nova Scotia town was burning. An old retired minister entered the church, and knelt to pray for its safety. The oncoming sea of fire was very near. His friends entreated him to leave, but the old servant of God prayed on and on. Then a strange thing happened. The great sea of flames parted in two streams. When it had passed the church and the few surrounding buildings the two streams of fire came together again, and completed their work of destruction and desolation. But the man of God was still on his knees in the church." (Christian Herald) Importunity at work!

PRAYER KEEPS THE BELIEVER FAITHFUL.

Nehemiah lived in an environment that demanded the need for both prayer and watchfulness. "Nevertheless we made our prayer unto our God, and set a watch against them day and night." (4:8) This recipe can be just as effective today as was in Nehemiah's day. The enemy is more subtle today by controlling the mind-set of society through today's technology. As a result society has become hardened because the individual has become hardened to the place where conscience and spiritual morality have little affect on thought or action.

A lady accidentally hit a car in which several men were riding. The men jumped out of their car and started to beat her. She managed to get her car started to cross a bridge. The men raced after her and boxed her car in, so she was trapped. The men pulled her out of the car beating on her with a tire iron and tearing her clothing off, while the crowd watched, many were encouraging the men. Finally, the battered woman pulled away from her attackers and jumped to her death in the river below. Not one soul came to her defense.

What does that say about these men, and this coldhearted crowd? Does it not reveal a depraved brutality that is satanic and even barbaric? It does not take too long for that heartless attitude to enter into the believer's mind-set, if there is not a prayerful watching taking place daily.

Paul Brown the Hall of Fame football coach made this statement: "we've got to be as good a football team as the CLASS of people we are." In other words, the football team will only be good as the class of people who play on the team. In most cases people will not rise any higher than their leader.

How many leaders have been prayerful and watchful! Where was the leader or leaders in that merciless apathetic crowd that watched a defenseless woman plunge to her death? Our society has very little interest in what is going on unless the circumstance affects them personally. There is no outrage about sinful activities. Leaders, ministers are silent, making sure they do not ruffle any feathers, lest they lose their position. Once this nation's pulpits lit the spiritual fires that formed a nation of sensitive, caring people.

Where were the prayerful, watchful guards that were on duty when the enemy was making the inroad into the homes of our country? Where are they now when future generations will reap the harvest of their sowing?

Prayer cultivates the heart of watchful caring that will be vigilant. Prayer is and will be actively watching and guarding the welfare of others. Prayer and watching is a custody that demands diligence in every hour of the day and night. Prayer is the watchman of the soul, even the soul of our native land. Prayer continually keeps on watching for the sin stricken, the needy, the outcast, and even the up and outer.

Spurgeon wrote these words: "Dost thou want nothing? Then thou dost not know thy poverty. Hast thou no mercy to ask of God? Then may the Lord's mercy show thee thy misery. A prayerless soul is a Christless soul. Prayer is the lisping of the believing infant, the shout of the fighting believer, the requiem of the dying saint falling asleep in Jesus."

A prayerless nation has lost its watchfulness, thus has become invaded by the enemy that destroys its soul. This is true of the home and the church, as well.

PRAYER ASSUMES ACCOUNTABILITY.

All teachers, including ministers must understand the power of words, and how they can affect others. One teacher I had in the seventh grade used to deliberately call on me to read before the class and my nerves would knot in my stomach, my mind would go blank, and my face would be burning with embarrassment, much to her delight. The fear of standing before an audience has been a battle across my lifetime.

Prayer allows us to think Godward, but we dare not fail to think manward. Before we think Godward, or manward we must think inward. What is inward is what comes out of the mouth! James's account in 3:1 evidently understood what could happen if teachers of the Christian faith could not handle the position if there was not a sound relationship with our Lord. The Amplified version has James saying: "Not many (of you) should become teachers (self constituted censors and reprovers of others), my brethren, for you know that we (teachers) will be judged by a higher standard and with greater severity (than other people). Thus we assume the greater accountability and the more condemnation."

What does this scripture say about these Ph.D.'s that are placed in powerful positions who follow Marx's line and openly desecrate the Biblical God in the University and Seminary classrooms of our nation? Now these captive audiences are spreading their anti-God views making everything spiritually generic, a worthless band-aid. These classes have now produced federal Judges on the Supreme Court that are interpreting their decisions on "international opinion" rather than our nation's constitution, allowing "international opinion" to overrule the constitution and our laws.

James speaks about these teachers of the law as "self constituted censors and reprovers of others." This dishonesty of trust is a disgraceful shame that is a deception to lead our nation of laws into the illusion of eventfully universal law, which means we will no longer govern ourselves.

Prayer will bring our Lord into the daily events and permit an evaluation of the encroachment on the spiritual principles of the founding fathers. Prayer allows the prayee to calculate spiritual direction, and separate idealism from reality. Prayer holds the prayee accountable for the spoken word, the scripture says "every idle word."

Prayer points out eternal responsibility that will become our accountability. Prayer makes God's man spiritually honest. Prayer exposes pride and reveals the true self. Prayer puts the heart of the gospel into daily action. Prayer emphasizes God's revealed truth. Prayer prepares the heart for the day and what it might hold. Prayer pushes the teacher to spiritual excellence. Prayer sets ambitions in their proper order. Prayer puts humility to work and lifts the cold heart into God's oven. Prayer will not permit the soul to live below piety's privileges. Prayer builds the scaffolding that fully supports God's teaching servant who has chosen the highway of holy living which our Lord has appointed. Prayer is the Divine channel our Lord has chosen to be an important guiding force to the affairs of life. Prayer defies spiritual defeat and lifts the broken heart to glorious victory. Prayer acknowledges that wherever the servant is called, there is and there will be accountability.

PRAYER SEEKS AFTER!

The scripture repeatedly entreats us to pray.

God calls us to pray. "Seek the Lord and His strength, seek His face continually." (1 Chron. 16:11) Prayer is not an afterthought when God calls His people to prayer. Can believers comprehend our God summoning His people to commune with Him the Almighty God, participating as members of His family? Believers are persuaded to receive His riches. To "continually" seek that which carries a constant consistance through unto the end. The intent is to finish without interruption by still abiding steadfastly. Seeking denotes thinking for meaning; to strive after the things of God. The thought out seeking is carefully done.

The Father invites us to fellowship with Him through prayer. "Ask and it shall be given you; seek, and ye shall find, knock and it shall be opened unto you." (Matt. 7:7) Prayer is seeking. Then how can the believer seek? He seeks by thinking and mediating who God is that can fulfill prayer's diligent pursuit. Seeking is how to ascertain prayer's meaning by searching thoroughly. Does it not require diligent searching? To be careless about responding to God's invitation would belittle our Lord's cost on Calvary and reveal a spiritual indifference that carries an anguished torment.

PRAYER IS GOD'S COMMAND.

"Watch and pray, that ye enter not into temptation; the Spirit indeed is willing, but the flesh is weak." (Matt. 26:41) "Watch" is a wake up call, "watch and prayer" are linked together, that makes both of them indispensable if there is to be victory over temptation. The word "watch" indicates a continual active spiritual alertness. The intent is to keep on watching by being vigilant. Watch what the eye is seeing; what the ears are hearing; what the mind is entertaining; and where the activity is taking you. This "watching and praying" is an endless accountability.

Prayer is not only a human plea, but also the Lord's plea. " He spoke a parable unto them to this end, that men ought always to pray and not to faint."(Luke 18:1) It is difficult to have God begging the believer to understand the absolute necessity "always to pray." "Always" has the design to be perpetually practicing prayer at every season and in every time zone. It is an incessantly imperative to be continually successive and on going.

As noted, scripture after scripture makes prayer a foundation for the present spiritual life and a certainty for eternal life. Prayer gives the wholeness of life.

Obedient prayer allows our Father's willingness to share all the ingredients that the soul needs. "Hitherto have ye asked nothing in my name: ask, and ye shall receive, that your joy may be full." (John 16:24) The fullness of prayer is joy, abiding joy that rides the waves of the storm; that refuses spiritual despair or defeat; because of joy there is that which enlarges the capacity to see the prize beyond the tempestuous turbulence of the age. The joy that exults the soul with exceeding delightful rest, makes a great contrast between weeping and sorrowing.

PRAYER GIVES US A SENSE OF URGENCY ABOUT OURSELVES AND THE LIFE TO COME.

Too many times, urgency is only thought of as an emergency such as Jehoshaphat encountered when the enemy surrounded him on the battlefield. God becomes our pressing necessity when the crisis develops. But when things are calm and collected, there is a tendency to relax in our Godly pursuit and the spiritual discipline slowly ebbs away. Prayer time and Bible study have given way to a personal agenda, and this agenda may be perfectly legitimate.

The enemy of prayer can find hundreds of ways to give logical reasons to interfere with the time planned for prayer. When I had the boys' home, it was on a farm. I had set aside some days to fast and pray for a meeting that was coming up. There was a knock on the door, something went wrong with the tractor. The holder for the throw out bearing had broken. A few minutes later I was informed, the manure spreader had broken. Later there was the report that the secondhand lawn mower back wheel twisted out of the frame. Then to crown the problems for the day, the field mower's piston rod had broken.

All these things needed attention now, while I was trying to pray. The devil said: "you need to fix this equipment now, everything will fall behind schedule." (I love to fix the manure spreader while others are relaxing.) It is certain the enemy of prayer will make it appear that it is reasonable and proper to quit praying and attend to the problems at hand.

The scripture has some phrases that are repeated many times, such as: "and it came to pass." That time of opportunity has been passed through. Many times there is a passing through a fixed gulf that can not be back tracked. Our prayer record is fixed, sealed by time that appears for the moment and then the journey is past tense. But as long as there is time, it is filled with opportunities that cannot disregard Divine forbearance that involves communion with the Maker of man.

There will be pressing circumstances holding the feet to the fire of testing. But lo though if I walk through death's valley, my past record (including prayer) assures me I can proceed without harm or fear, He will be my shield and strength. My prayer life that has enriched my spiritual life will continue to fulfill my deepest need as I step across the dividing line between time and eternity. "And it came to pass." It will be so.

Jehoshaphat stands as a monument of the passing of time. At one time he was walking in obedience to the Lord, but time passed and he became friendly with the scoundrel Ahab and before he could come to his senses, he was on the battlefield fighting Ahab's war. Suddenly, he is surrounded by Ahab's enemies, and "Jehoshaphat cried out, and the Lord helped him; and God moved them to depart from him." (2 Chron. 18:31)

Jehoshaphat's prayer of desperation saved his life. "And it came to pass" that God rescued him from his foolish decision. He became entrapped with Ahab's plea for help. Why link with a person that had sold his soul to his god, Baal? Without a continual prayerfulness, there are the possibilities of being ambushed by a godless friend in serious trouble. Daily prayer will give an awareness of the unknown pitfalls and will definitely alert the calamity of the ties to an Ahab. Regardless of the circumstances that surround prayer time, the obstacles are usually Satan's plan to hinder that needed time.

DAILY PRAYER PLACES A WATCHFULNESS OVER THE SOUL.

Prayer gives the spiritual attractiveness that bonds the soul to the hope of the heavenly prize. Prayer has a heartfelt compulsiveness that creates a holy atmosphere which allows a proper environment in which righteous decisions can be made. Prayer will give the necessary backbone to say "no" to any Ahab that may knock on your door. Prayer is the urgency of the present time that needs personal attention before it passes by. The "came to pass" can be grievous, or the "came to pass" can be an up-to-date spiritual victory that carries a conquering spirit.

Dr. Macartney said: "A student who had been urged to take a course of conduct that was wrong, not only wrong, but shockingly wrong. Amazed that one should feel it necessary to consult a minister, or anyone else, as the right or wrong of the suggested action, I said, "How does it seem to you when you pray about it?"

"Oh, then," came the quick answer, "it seems to be wrong."

"That is the great thing about prayer. It strips the mask from the face of the temptation. A temptation to succeed must have some type of disguise or mask. But prayer tears away the disguise and reveals evil in all its hideous features."

Watchful prayer will uncover the motive and desire to pursue a course of an unholy plan that someone may have mapped out for their personal desire. Or the desire could have been from personal carnality. Prayer is a sentinel that reports any masquerade.

PRAYER UNCTIONIZES GOD'S REVEALED TRUTH.

Unctionizing is a sacred anointing that is connected to the Holy Spirit's oil of gladness. Unctionizing is an anointing that enables the possession of the knowledge of Truth that equips for service. Spiritual fire accompanies the unctionizing of the message that the Holy Spirit wishes to reveal. Holy fire consumes the sacrificial offering, just as the fire consumes the believer's offering of complete surrender. This spiritual fire expands into the prayer life of every day living.

The altar was where the sacrifice was offered which contained a constant fire that burnt unceasingly, which is in turn symbolic for the believer to keep his spiritual fire unwavering. This unctionized fire in the human soul is uninterrupted worship and communion with the Father. Prayer is at the heart of this trusted steadfastness.

If the fire did go out on the altar of sacrifice the fire could not be lit from another fire. That would be "strange fire" which is unacceptable to God and it would mean certain death to anyone who uses "strange fire" to light the altar fire. The only fire that can be used to light the altar fire must be started by friction. When the unctionized fire goes out in the believer's soul, too many times the backslider will use "strange fire" (which is sure spiritual death, such as some cult, a false religion, or just dead religion) to create the unctionized fire. The only way to start the unctionized fire is through Godly repentance and forsaking that which put out the fire.

Truth becomes alive with the anointing of the Holy Spirit. Prayer speaks through His Word that imposes zeal that ignites the inner fire.

Spurgeon said it this way: "One bright benison which private prayer brings down upon the ministry is an indescribable and inimitable something, an unction from the Holy One...If the anointing which we bear comes not from the Lord of hosts, we are deceivers, since only in prayer can we obtain it. Let us continue insistent, constant, fervent in supplication. Let your fleece lie on the threshing-floor of supplication till it is wet with the dew of heaven."

As two men walked to their home in Emmaus, Jesus appeared out of the unknown and walked with them as they discussed the bewildering events of the past several days. The Lord was invited into their home to have something to eat after a long journey. When Jesus took the bread and blessed it, they recognized Him and He disappeared. Their words were recorded in Luke 24:32, "Did not our hearts burn within us, while He talked with us by the way, while He opened to us the scriptures?" Prayer allows God to talk to the believer.

Prayer gives audience with Jesus, and there is no way that the believer can be with Jesus and not have his heart burn within him. He opens the fountain of Truth and makes Himself personal and real. There may be logical theological correctness and sparkling rhetoric, but that will not take the place of the Divine anointing of the Holy Spirit that sanctions God's blessing for daily life.

Multitudes of believers live in a spiritual famine, not knowing the enrichment that the fresh enduring power gives. This relationship is an indefinable, indescribable anointing that is quick and powerful, piercing like a two edged sword. The Spirit is the discerner of Truth, giving insight and an enlargement of soul.

Inward fire is kindled by prayerful mediation when the Psalmist said: "my heart was hot within me, while I was musing the fire burned." . . . (Ps. 39:3) While Jeremiah 20:9 declared: "Then I said, I will not make mention of Him, nor speak any more in His name. But His word was in mine heart as a burning fire shut up in my bones, and I was weary with forbearing and I could not stay." Prayer brings the soul to this spiritual edge, unctionizing God's revealed Truth.

PRAYER CALLS THE BELIEVER TO BE IN THE RIGHT MIND-SET.

Prayer dares to invade the world of demons. Jesus directly addressed the demons. The demons recognized Jesus as God. "I know who You are, the Holy One of God." (Mark 1:24) The Gadarenen man was pathologically controlled by demons. Luke 8:35 "and they found the man out of whom the devils were departed, sitting at the feet of Jesus, clothed, and in his right mind, and they were afraid." Demoniac possession is a spirit acting in all idolatry; always a deceiver of men by the seducing believers. The Gadarenen man was given unusual demoniac power that could break chains. His actions revealed cause for mental derangement that produced his madness and destruction to himself as well as others. His home was among the tombs; living among the dead without the seat of reflective consciousness.

Prayer is challenged when encountering the mystical intangible power on which some soul's personal identity is lost because of demon possession. The faculty of understanding will be lost until Jesus transforms the mind and heart into godly righteousness.

Today the person of the bodily Jesus is replaced by the Holy Spirit, therefore today's prayer must have the empowering of the Holy Spirit to attack the deep seated problem of demon possession. Too many of us, (me included) have a fear to go into the shadows of the abyss. All must deal with tests, but this type of prayer moves into the demoniac world of torment. The abyss is the place where Jesus, hanging on the cross, dumped all our sins. Now the association with that kind of terror and ungodliness is distressing and alarming, even when confronted in the prayer closet.

Prayer and more prayers are needed to prepare the heart, mind and soul for this battle of the spiritual world. This prayer must be loaded with faith that has the right mind-set, even the mind of our Lord. Having this mind-set will move both God and man into a union that no demoniac force can defeat. Prayer of faith has the will that Paul admonishes the Philippian church to have: "let this mind be in you, which was also in Christ Jesus." (Phil. 2:5)

Prayer takes the mind to a new level; allowing the Holy Spirit to search every area and reviews all personal standards with Biblical standards. Prayer tells how and when to approach this world of chaos; and produces a faith that can deliver demons from the physical body. Jesus confronted this dreadful specter without any can of intimidation. Did Jesus not give his disciples power over demons?

Jesus gave the Gadarenen man the right mind-set, but this could not have been done without a new nature. Jesus not only had to deal with the demons within the man but with the people He disturbed; their terror demanded that He leave. He who does not have the right mind-set, will not take kindly to the prayee who intrudes upon his mind-set with its personal values. Prayer will allow the believer to overcome the evil force that instigate the war against God's man and the devil's heinous forces. Prayer moves the impossible.

PRAYER IS EFFECTIVE IN THE TIME OF NEED.

Jesus in Matthew 14:19 was in the process of feeding the multitude. This is the scene: "and He (God) took 5 loaves, and the two fishes, and LOOKING UP INTO HEAVEN, HE BLESSED and brake, and gave the loaves to his disciples and the disciples to the multitude."

These words "looking up into heaven, He blessed," captured my thought. Here is the expression of acknowledging the Sovereign source of all blessings. Even when the disciples protested that the material source of 5 loaves and 2 fishes were not sufficient to consider the task of feeding this multitude; Jesus insisted that which is placed in God's hands, is a source that is endless. Spiritual miracles are performed when life and its material substances are given to God for His blessing.

Prayer looking heavenward is a celebration of what is going to happen. Prayer is a pronouncement recognizing God's invoked blessing of virtue rendered benefits. What God blesses, God anoints. Prayer that God blesses pays homage to what God sanctions. Prayer that blesses is that which has the joy of unmarred care; it is pursued in righteousness while walking in integrity. Prayer brings the relationship between the Word and fact into action. God's kind of prayer invokes benefits on others with gratitude because this aid will advance their welfare. Prayer identifies and appreciates the blessed attribute of God's continued Goodness. Prayer that adheres to the Father's commandments will receive His favor.

The disciples surrendered what they had at the time and the multitudes were fed. What if they had said the 5 loaves and 2 fish are not sufficient for ourselves? Prayer and faith must have the ingredients that expect miracles that are bestowed on the necessary need. God will not toy with the prayer of the faithful believers when all is surrendered. Why? Because our Lord will bless what He receives, and because faithful prayer knows where the needed resources are stored.

Because of prayer's blessing upon the limited material resources that was given to our Lord, the multitude ate their fill. As always, there was more left over, than they had in the beginning. How like our God, when He blesses, it is always more than expected. L'Estrange said what we so often think: "We mistake the gratuitous blessings of heaven for the fruits of our own industry."

PRAYER CAN RESTORE SPIRITUAL LIFE AND POWER TO A DEAD CHURCH AND A FOUNDLING NATION.

Isaiah takes note of what has happened to the church by giving an indictment against God's called "watchmen" in 56:10, "His watchmen are blind; they are all ignorant; they are all dumb dogs; they cannot bark; sleeping lying; loving to slumber." This kind of preaching can blow the lid off the religious community, or any major denomination. What kind of courage would it take to charge a large number of the modern day clergy with being spiritually blind; being ignorant of spiritual conditions and discernment; being dumb dogs that cannot or will not bark God's message; the of love sleep instead of actively being involved in the spiritual battle; being ignorant shepherds that care little about the lost; loving the pleasures of the subculture and seeking favor for gain.

Thank God that not all the "watchmen" are asleep and passive about the church and social conditions that are an insult to our holy God. We read about the struggle with infidelity and sexual sin in the church. Who is going to address the lust that craves for the excitement of infidelity? How can the "watchmen" become alive to the horrors of the sex crazed nation that has saturated our social structure? The sinister intent has invaded God's house, but first it had to invade the home and the heart.

First the corrupt spiritual condition must capture the believer's heart that will cause the soul to actually drive the believer to the prayer closet for the Almighty interior minister to search for any lukewarmness that may have subtly taken up residence. It is so easy to excuse oneself and say, "the immortality is not affecting me," even though the children have become prodigals.

Pray for the "watchmen." Pray for recovery of the cost of sin, that will awaken the sleepers. Pray for the vigilant "watchmen" that trumpets the Truth and then support their efforts. Pray for these "watchmen" of the Truth that they will not suffer any lockjaw disease when threatened by the hierarchy or church boss. Pray for the insidious crowd who pushes the anti-discrimination laws that include "gender identity" regardless of behavior. Pray for the godless educational system that destroys Biblical faith and produces gnosticism, and atheism. Pray for the major denominations that have been taken over by the liberal establishment and have betrayed their Biblical foundations and church discipline powers.

This prayer must have the cry of a John Knox: "give me Scotland or I die" in the face of terrifying tyrants and Queen Mary. Baxter filled his study walls with agony of prayer. A praying Wesley reached into the gutters and slums and rescued the multitude from sin's slavery, and saved England from a bloody revolution that still has tragic results in France.

Does God's people want to spiritually restore our nation to its founding Fathers' vision or watch the disease of materialism and secularism be these vampires blood suckers that slowly drain our spiritual life? If so, it will takes more than a half-hearted prayer campaign that soothes the conscience, delight's Satan and moves or convicts no one of their sins. Did our God raise up this nation out of its wilderness to disintegrate into the lowest type of filth? It is necessary to feel that the nation's destiny is in our disheveled hands to pray for its resurrection, or to leave it to plunge into its own abyss?

Physically, our efforts are limited, but spiritually, prayer is our battleground, and there needs to be the knowledge that the prayer time has met God's expectations. This is our personal accountability.

Dr. Guthrie speaks of prayer and its necessity: "The first true sign of spiritual life is prayer, prayer is also the means of maintaining it. Man can as well live physically without breathing, as spiritually without praying." The labor of prayer is God's way of restoring the spiritual power of a nation, a church and a home that has lost its vital spiritual soul winning life.

PRAYER DELIVERS US FROM BECOMING SLAVES TO MATERIALISM AND ITS SECULAR COUNTERPART.

Our Lord in Matthew 6:33 made it quite clear how this demon of materialism and secularism can be subdued. "Seek first the kingdom of God, and His righteousness and all these things will be added unto you." Our Lord's statement is self-evident, unmistakably transparent. "Seek FIRST," what, "the kingdom of God," which means first is not second, but first in order; first in obedience; first in our chief concern; first in importance; first in rank; first in our spiritual welfare; first from the beginning; and first by becoming His love slave. "First" is the essence of discipleship. How else can there be a dedicated disciple?

But what is the believer to "seek first?" Our Lord did not confuse His pronouncement, but identified what was to be first; "the kingdom of God and His righteousness." The kingdom of "God is RIGHTEOUSNESS, which is God's righteousness not our righteousness. Righteousness unites with holiness; righteousness has no part in sin; righteousness can not be righteous if there is no justice; the will for righteousness leads to justification; righteousness is right; righteousness alerts a sound mind and a social justice; righteousness is imparted into man's soul through His act of Atonement; God given righteousness is to be engrossed entirely; righteousness renders rightness which is reliable; righteousness seeks the God of righteousness above all else; and righteousness permits the believer to rejoice in the riches of eternity now.

Seeking and finding the imparting of His righteousness is the real liberty all mankind longs to experience. Prayer is seeking; prayer is the "must" if God is to be first; prayer opens our God's store house; prayer is a matter of a righteous and pure heart; and the power of prayer will be manifested in motives that drive the seat of authority in every human being.

If prayer is to be effective, prayer must be liberated from the second seat. All too many professing Christians have prayer positioned in a self-serving placement, or in a malfunctioning location. Why is the matter of prayer so carnally bound? The comparison is like the resurrected Lazarus, alive but still bound in his grave clothes. The unsurrendered carnal Christian is constantly fighting the dead burial garments that are holding the carnal Christian in bondage.

Jesus said to those who stood by Lazarus, "loose him and let him go." Believing prayer will plea for the power needed to be released from secular materialism's grave clothes. Only Almighty God can do the releasing when there is seeking for righteousness that is first. Materialism has a strange appetite that hungers for more and more of the fleshly subculture. All the while the soul is crying out, "enough is enough, I demand my liberation from my grave clothes now."

The prayer for the emancipation from the desiring carnal mind, that can be a death trap, is a must. It is the impure lasciviousness that has chained and claimed secular materialism for selfish purposes. These sinister grave clothes still have the smell of eternal death.

Prayer is at the heart of putting our loving Lord first and seeking His righteousness. Prayer will be no more than what the heart allows it to be.

PRAYER AND FASTING ARE NOT A MEANS TO BRIBE GOD, OR TO EARN SOME EXTRA BLESSING.

Fasting is a topic that is not discussed in conversation or books. I have a number of books in my library on prayer. I went through fourteen of them without finding anything on fasting. Much is written about prayer, but very little about fasting. Daniel wrote about his experience in 9:3 "and I set my face unto the Lord God, to seek by prayer and supplications, with fasting, and sackcloth and ashes."

Daniel's act was a voluntary resolve to abstain from food. Fasting would increase prayer's ardor because of the trying circumstances that had caused considerable emotional distress and misfortune as reason to plead for God's mercies. Jesus said; "this kind comes by prayer and fasting." "This kind," this particular kind that bears the crushing burden that is too heavy for man to carry. "This kind," which only a few know its weight and acknowledge the apostasy disaster of church and state. "This kind," that discerns the heresy that defies and denies Biblical Truth. "This kind," of loaded burden is so serious that it demands the denial of food to avert calamity.

Fasting is of little use if faith does not saturate the prayer. Prayer and fasting develop faith; together they develop a caring burden, that rises to the need of higher achievement. Fasting is a yearning to allow the soul to reach the maximum spiritual growth. Fasting, prayer and faith are placed right in the center where the soul, "pours out the heart like water."

Jesus clearly mastered Satan's appeal when, after fasting 40 days, Satan suggested turning the stones into bread. There was a legitimate hungry appetite that was a justifiable need. Fasting disassociates food to permit the Spirit to control a God given appetite. Fasting brings the body into submission and the Spirit into focus. This self-denial concentrates on the deepest concerns of the heart.

To define a spiritual burden of this magnitude that Daniel carried for Israel's captivity, requires more than genuine caring. The overload cannot be satisfied by the ordinary. Fasting expresses there is no doubt that the spiritual problem extended the concern, even to the denial of the absolute necessities of life. All temporal concerns must be willingly sacrificed to seek God's intervention.

The one who is climbing the mountain takes only what is necessary. It is called "a lean pack." Fasting carries only the essential load; which is not done to impress our Lord, but is a voluntary separation from the life's basic needs for a period of time. Fasting is not an appealing activity but a dedication to pay whatever price necessary to reach for God's will and excellence. With each battle that is won a prayerful faith is developing a larger capacity.

PRAYER KEEPS THE SOUL SELF-DISCIPLINED, RESULTING IN SELF-DENIAL.

Prayer undergirds self-enforced practices, which admonishes the training of a sound mind. Self-discipline is contracted to the governing mind to used at God's pleasure. Disciplinary self-control is a covenant between God and man with the object of sharing His glory. Without self-discipline to carrying out the compact that retains Christian faith, man's relationship with God would be impossible. Prayer would be a mere fantasy.

If the believer becomes out of control spiritually and becomes obsessed with self-induced appetites; by falling into temptation with undesirable associates that are enslaved by harmful habits, expect the harvest that the self-willed life sows. These associates are indiscreet with their families and abuse the families by their disgraceful will to hinder the family desire to pursue a faithful relationship with the Lord. This willful disobedience is a risk that can become an accident just waiting to happen.

The remedy is found in a repenting prayer that gives a willingness to allow the Lord to control all self-discipline and self-abasement. Self-will that does not have the blessing of the will of God, is not real repentance, which is the foundation of personal salvation. Without honest repentance all the self-discipline and self-abasement will be in vain.

Self-abasement and denial have the element of being God's slave servant. Self-denial seeks the high way of holiness that reaches out to the struggling believer who needs a strengthening embrace. Self-denial will not neglect carrying a cross that has splinters that pierce the flesh. Self-denial's interest is glorifying the God of all glory; while denying oneself of personal interest and renounces the apostatizing Biblical teachings that are hidden under the cloak of religion. Self-denial rejects liberal heresy that paganizes Christianity by their unbelief in the inspired word of God and persuades followers to do the same. Self-denial in the Biblical sense affirms the "narrow way" and is willing to pay any cost to perpetuate Christianity's historic faith.

Prayer can be the fortitude that will be the undergirding forces that gives the spirit the moral strength to attack any force of evil. Prayer draws the resolve from heavenly resources that are always adequate for the situation. This is not minimizing the cost, by making the cost appear to be trivial.

Consider value of prayer in Mr. Li Ying's case who is spending 15 years in prison for working for an "unofficial" Christian magazine in China. Or Rhanja Masih's life sentence in prison, being accused of throwing a stone at an Islamic sign in Pakistan (very tolerant). Or the self-denial of Sung Seo Pao, an evangelist in Vietnam, sentenced to 11years for preaching the gospel, who was obeying God rather than man. What gives these men the fearlessness to deny self-comfort for a prison life of hard labor. Without doubt they have nothing but prayer that gives the tenacity to bear this cross of human suffering. Denying themselves of freedom, the joy of family, the love of fellow believers, and the ease of living apart for chains, the rigors of hard labor, and prison bars.

Prayer allows the believer to evaluate life in time as well as for eternity, knowing that self-discipline and self-denial may have a price of unknown consequences. Prayer (if the Bible is prohibited) may be the only power available to deal with the unknown. No one can stop the heart that prays. Living alone in filthy surroundings, like a caged animal, the imprisoned believer finds communion by praying to the God that has promised never to forsake His child. Prayer must be the superstructure for a tested faith, anchored in the providence of the living God. How else can the Christian face the overwhelming spiritual battle of the unknown!

PRAYER THAT WAITS KEEPS THE BELIEVER ON GOD'S SCHEDULE.

The Psalmist says to his soul: "wait thou upon God." Waiting is one of the most difficult things to do in this geared up society. Waiting can be light or heavy, it all depends on what the individual is waiting for. Waiting can expect a favorable reception, or it can be waiting at the bedside of a loved one. Waiting for the opportunity that has a promising future, hope rises, but in the reality treachery was used to get the individual in a place where he is always in debt and can never get out. Waiting has its rewards and its disappointments. Waiting, but ready to act by conforming to God's purpose.

How must His child pray while waiting? By mediating on who God is, and waiting for His counsel. Prayer has much to do with burden of waiting. Waiting for the very God of all gods who waters the hills from His chambers that the fruits may satisfy their thirst. Prayer permits the waiting believer to contemplate He who supplies all his needs according to God's riches in glory, and allows His child to consider his God who makes the clouds His chariot and walks on the wings of the wind. Ponder while waiting, the God who laid the foundation of the universe and covers it with His garments. Study while waiting on the God who furnishes the water for the mountain springs that flow to the valley's meadows below. Dwell on the Omnipotent God who stretches His curtain across the heavens, and still hears the groanings of the prisoner. Mediation is prayer in the deepest sense.

An unknown writer describes the plight of waiting for unanswered prayer: "Did it ever occur to you that if you do not hear God's answer to prayer, it may be not because He is dumb, but because you are deaf; not because He has no answer to give, but because you have not been listening for it? We are so busy with our service, so busy with our work, and sometimes so busy with our praying, that it does not occur to us to stop our own talking and listen if God has some answer to give us with "the still small voice;" to be passive, to be quiet, to do nothing, say nothing, in some true sense think nothing; simply to be receptive and waiting for the voice. Wait thou only upon God," says the Psalmist; and again, "wait on the Lord." (Selected) Mediate while waiting!

Prayer can be confused by misdirected legitimate energies and by unintentional distractions. It takes time to be holy and prayer always relates to fulfilling God's purpose for life. Meditative prayer aspires to what is more excellent, always defining God's will.

PRAYER CAN REMOVE SATAN'S TEMPTING OBSTACLES.

Too many times the believer does not deal seriously with temptation. Peter seeks to awaken the leisurely approach to temptation by illustrating the need for demanding careful thought by relating to what happened to the fallen angels when tempted to rebel against God. If God did not spare the holy angels that were tempted and sinned, and were cast into hell, how then can any believer hope to escape the same fate if the believer is not aware of the pitfalls of temptation?

Since the fall of man, temptation has been his thorn in the flesh. Whether temptation was the means of seducing Adam and Eve in the garden, provoking David to number Israel, commanding our Lord to turn the stones into bread, taking advantage of the innocent; or being tested by the appealing powers of vice, the lure of monetary gain, the lascivious attraction to the opposite sex; or whatever the temptation may be, make sure Satan will make the licentious opportunity available as he did in the case of David and Bathsheba.

Prayer fortifies any weakness, while prayerlessness invites temptation, which will eventually mean spiritual defeat. How serious is that!

Peter gives hope when he writes to the church: "the Lord knows how to deliver the Godly out of temptation". . . (2 Peter 2:9) All mankind craves deliverance; deliverance renders release, making free, to rescue from bondage; the deliverance from more imminent danger; liberation from imprisonment that controlled the will that resisted God's will. Deliverance has a force to it, as the shepherd rescues a lamb from the mouth of the lion. Deliverance is action.

Prayer is the warrior that goes to battle against an invisible enemy. Prayer is the connection to the invisible God who is the power that can bind the forces of evil that tempt. Only the Lord knows how to save the believer from the tempter's power. Nothing but Divine intervention through sincere prayer can liberate from the powers of the lost world. Deliverance is a prayer that hands everything over to the God who sets free the believer when under the power of the sinister deceiver.

All through history there has been that God of the universe, that has heard the cry of His people whether it was deliverance out of Egypt, or through the Red Sea, across the wilderness into the promised land. It always has been liberation out of the temptations of peril and hostility. Temptation is an open door, but not with devoted prayer that believes in the endless power of God. The believer's spiritual motives are molded by prayer's connection to Omnipotence, because it is through prayer that God prepares the heart for life's tests.

PRAYER SHATTERS FEAR WHILE ENERGIZING THE SOUL FOR THE DAILY SPIRITUAL BATTLE.

Dr. S. Parkes Cadman, tells of a Georiga cracker sitting, ragged and barefooted, on the steps of his tumble down shack. A stranger asked him if he could get a drink of water from his well. The man gave his consent and between swallows he asked the man: "How is your cotton coming on?" "Ain't got none," replied the cracker. "Nope," said the cracker, "fraid of boll weevils." "Well," said the stranger, "how is your corn?" "Didn't plant none," was the reply. "Fraid wasn't going to rain." The stranger went to another question. "Well, how are your potatoes?" "Ain't got none, scairt of potato bugs." The stranger said: "Really, what did you plant?" "Nothin, I jest played it safe," replied the cracker.

Multitudes, as well many Christians, are just playing it safe. Fear can dominate life. Professing Christians on the whole know little about stepping out on nothing but faith. Most professing Christians have to have a guaranteed salary before venturing beyond certain material security. This type of faith can be expected from the secular humanist, but when the gospel proclaimer needs the guaranteed material security, it reveals a clear lack of God loving faith. Is this not operating on no faith at all???

It is not difficult to find someone who is fearful of something or some person. Fear is a destructive fever that terrorizes, extorts inward peace, and intensifies an evil fear that gives anguish to mind and soul. Fear is a paradox that dreads to face God's displeasure, but dares to abide under the shadow of the Almighty. There is fear for God, yet the believer loves God. Fear is to worship God with reverent awe, yet fear can so control that the worshiper can become a coward when faced with compromising Biblical Truth in order to attain a higher position.

What are the issues when one is living a fear filled life?

1. Vicious intimidating adversaries.
2. Loss of job, and wondering if the pension will be adequate for retirement and medical problems age will bring.
3. Fear of not meeting the expectations of people, especially in the ministry.
4. Fear of death, the unredeemed need to have that fear.
5. Fear of failure, in business, family, or friends.
6. Fear of displeasing God by being unable to think through personal salvation and know faith's security.
7. Fear of being blackmailed by the hidden past.

This list is only a few of the fears that are deeply registered in the mind. These and more like them are the destructive fears, but Solomon writes: "the fear of the Lord is the beginning of knowledge." (Prov. 1:7) In other words, the beginning for anyone is the fear of God unto repentance. May I dare to say, this then is the true start of knowledge. Misplaced fear only creates havoc and despair.

Prayer can bring all these tormenting fears to the Lord. Prayer refines and perfects the fears that distress. Prayer mounts a capacity to engulf the full purpose of God through complete deliverance from the agony that fear manufactures.

Esther overcame her fears when she prayed and fasted and then went in to the king without an appointment saying, "if I perish, I perish." Overcoming fear in Esther's critical hour is the solution for any fear ridden soul. There is no way for spiritual victory from the horrors of fear, by playing it safe. The cost is prayer and fasting. Meeting these conditions will connect the soul with the never, never failing God.

PRAYER GIVES VICTORY OVER SPIRITUAL DEATH.

Paul gives the contrast between being "dead" in sin, and "alive" in Christ Jesus when writing to the Roman church in these words: "Likewise reckon ye also ourselves to be dead indeed unto sin, but alive unto Christ Jesus our Lord." (Rom. 6:11)

Dead in trespasses and sin; human depravity is a part of the human nature; the will is willed to sin; that which is dead cannot produce life; sin is the nature of being dead; dead refers to the spiritual condition of the unsaved; sin is real and the cause of spiritual death; but "that which is yielded to sin can also be yielded to God."

Alive is a union with life; it is eternal life now; God sharing His life with the obedient child of God; this alive gift is beyond human personal achievement; "He is the way the truth and the Life." His alive is self giving; ponder the change when He permeates life. Being alive is having fellowship with the living Christ as He is now making intercession for His child. This is trading death for life, free from the law of sin and death. Can any of the "dead" match the benefits that being spiritually "alive" gives to the genuine believer?

Prayer is at the center of this battle with life and the dead. The unredeemed claim to be alive, but are entrapped in hidden sins. Willful sins dominate the motive that is buried in the soul that drives the daily action and carnal appetite. Inner sin, such as unforgiveness, greed, self-centeredness, hatred, rebellion, covetness, and lust are self deceptive while being concealed. Outwardly such lives can be respectable by carrying on daily duties, which could be church duties.

If this hidden Phariseeism continues this shameful insincerity; there will be very little prayer. Prayer would be self-convicting. No prayer will throw open heaven's door if the sins of the spirit are willfully ignored. The sins of the spirit are just as condemning as any willful outward act. In fact, the look can be sinful and covered sins may not be evident, but it will take more ingenuity to keep the disguise of the inward mask than it does the outward sin. There is the fear of having the secret self revealed.

The self-satisfying sin is why it is so difficult to pray loved ones into the kingdom. Usually when their outward life is congenial and giving, there is little need to seek salvation. Praying through contentment and materialism that has brought the comforts of this life to the family, their view is, what more is needed? Praying for those who do not know they are dead in trespasses and sin, is demanding, especially when there appears to be no spiritual movement. The call is to be faithful with prayer regardless of the lack of spiritual understanding and sin's consequences.

E. M. Bounds said: "The gospel moves with slow and timid pace when the saints are not at their prayers early and late and long."

PRAYER CAN LEAD FROM DISTRESS AND MOURNING TO VICTORIOUS PRAISE.

Who has not felt the pain of distress and mourned the calamity that has settled in the pit of the stomach? Sometimes it reaches to a loud wailing, while other times there is an inexpressible heaviness that cannot be removed by self-effort.

Lincoln described this inward grief to a friend during the Civil War. Lincoln told how often he was driven to his knees, because there was no place else for him to go. The load of a country he loved was divided in a vicious war, the weight was too heavy for him to carry; help was needed beyond the limitations of man. Divine intervention was his only hope.

The Ninevites were gripped with the impending judgment when Jonah told them of the coming of the judgment of God if they did not repent. They sought sackcloth and ashes in their lamenting over the tragedy that loomed over them. The Egyptians moaned in their lamentations as the death angel destroyed the first born when God rescued the Israelites from their slavery. What about the average person who knows the utter despair that rages in the soul when a loved one is slipping into glory. Helplessly, all is out of hand.

The Psalmist pours out his heart in these words: "Hear, O Lord, and have mercy upon me; Lord, be thou my helper. Thou hast turned for me my mourning into dancing; Thou hast put off my sackcloth, and girded me with gladness; to the end that my glory may sing praises to Thee, and not be silent. O Lord, my God, I will give thanks unto Thee forever." (Ps. 30:10-12)

Then Almighty God steps into the situation when prayer pierced the heavens and turned the mourning into gladness and praise. Mercy and grace are poured into the anguish that attempted to crush hope. Prayer is the rewarder of a trust that has results of righteousness' fruits that brings eternal benefits out of tribulation. Prayer that is tied to His promises has an expectancy that overcomes circumstances that were devastating. That praise may not be a thunderous praise, but a love that is so deep it is silent.

Prayer that praises God for His endless benefits encourages and builds more faith; exalts mind, soul, and spirit; and replaces the burden with His honor and glory.

PRAYER PERSONALIZES THE SCRIPTURE.

When Biblical words are connected to vital prayer this motivates expectancy that coincides with God's Word. Every promise in the scripture is personalized for each believer. God's promise is a solemn assertion on His part that He will perform as promised. The prayer that personalizes His promises usually has a particular promise that catches the mind and the heart. When the prayer of faith captures the whole inner being, then all God's mercies are at the believer's disposal. Prayer has little on which it can be activated if it is not based on God's promises. The prayer that embraces God's promises has an impressive trademark which asserts: "I never disappoint."

There is the prayer that is personalized for deliverance. The Psalmist wrote: " Many are the afflictions of the righteous; but He deliver him out of them all. He keeps all his bones; not one of them is broken." (Ps. 34:19&20) He not only delivers, He (God) emancipates and frees. There is no escape from the curse of adversity for "the righteous," but there is liberation when prayer vitalizes faith to claim what God has promised. Then the soul is allowed to rest on His Word.

Who has not felt the spiritual emptiness of the weak and the sick? But once again God has made provisions that personalize His concern: " The Lord will strengthen him upon the bed of languishing; Thou will make all his bed in his sickness." Pain takes so much energy that there is no strength left to pray. Someone stands by the bedside and takes the hand, while lifting the distressful soul in prayer and gradually feels the hand release its grip, relaxing in the midst of misery. It is God's promise not to forsake the weak and the sick. Prayer brings back the connection that pain threatened to disconnect.

Prayer reaches God's comforting presence: "when thou passes through the waters, I will be with thee; and through the rivers, they shall not over flow thee; when thou walk through the fire thou shall not be burned; neither shall the flame kindle upon thee." (Isa. 43:2) Prayer gives assurance when caught in the whirlpool that terrorizes faith and inflicts doubts. Prayer permits the believer to move beyond the intimidating circumstances, and to watch as the Lord removes threatening obstacles. Consistent prayer brings His promises to converge on the believer's personal care.

Paul wrote the Roman church: "and we know that all things work together for good to them that love God, to them who are the called according to His purpose." (8:28) It is difficult to see this truth in its entirety in this life. But it is God's personal promise to each believer who obediently loves God. God through prayer works with His child to fulfill His ultimate purpose. God presses all adversities and afflictions into His child's fulfilling purpose as prayer presents them.

I shall never forget what the late Dr. A. C. Dixon of Spurgeon's Tabernacle once said when speaking upon this theme of prayer. I can not quote him verbatim, but the substance was this: "when we rely upon organization, we get what organization can do; when we rely upon education, we get what education can do; when we reply upon eloquence, we get what eloquence can do;" and so on. Nor am I disposed to undervalue any of these things in their proper place. "But," he added impressively, "when we rely upon prayer we get what God can do." (The European Harvest Field.)

PRAYER ENLISTS THE HOLY SPIRIT'S AID IN OUR INFIRMITIES.

There is the lack of knowing how to pray as we should, and the need of God's wisdom to make intercession out of our groanings when words fail. Our infirmities lack the ability to search our hearts, that we may know our hearts; and by knowing and understanding the mind of the Holy Spirit. Our infirmities reach out to know the will of God and how to live with the limitations that the "Fall of man" has given us.

How leisurely prayers are lifted without comprehending how meaningful each prayer uttered by the saints is to God the Father! Revelations allows the saints to sit in on the scene of what happens to the saints' prayers. "And another angel came and stood over the altar, having a golden censer; and there was given unto him much incense, that he should add it unto the prayers of all the saints upon the golden altar which was before the throne. And the smoke of the incense, with the prayers of the saints, went up before God out of the angel's hand." (Rev. 8:3&4)

God commissioned the angel to validate the love in the petitions as mankind's best and to mix them with incense on the Golden Altar (God's best) and the smoke of the mixture ascended before God. The pleasing odor radiated throughout heaven. The Golden Censer and the Golden Altar were used only on the day of expiation; the act of making an atonement which was made by the Son of God, once and for all times.

Prayerful communion with the Father is priceless. Prayer is not only for our benefit but delights God our Maker. How painful it must be to hear so little from those who say they love Him. Visiting in the nursing home, it will reveal, in part, what the feeling God must have, when people hang on, because no one comes to see them. They have not heard from those that say they love them. Does God just hear from those believers when their hearts are crushed and their anticipations have lost hope?

Dare we place insignificant concern on the matter of prayer when God places the prayers of the saints on His Altar to relish and to rejoice in the pleasure these prayers bring to Him! Obedient prayer pleases our God. Do we have the time to delight the heart of God? Is the desire of the God of our salvation worthy of our daily concern?

PRAYER IS CONFRONTATIONAL.

Prayer is in the center of faith and it clashes with the depraved human nature. Prayer must confront those who burn with jealousy and will compromise Divine favor in order to achieve their envious goal. Jealousy drives the inferior character to court superiority, always seeing another through a magnifying glass. Colton said: "of all the passions, jealousy is that which exacts the hardest service and pays the bitterest wages. Its service is, to watch the success of our enemy, to be sure of it."

Knowing the king had signed his death warrant, Wesley said: "Daniel did not increase his prayer out of hypocrisy, nor did he try to conceal it out of fear." He prayed at the same time by opening a window that faced Jerusalem. Daniel would not allow any decree of any king to hinder or interfere with his prayer time.

Prayer gives fortitude to defy a king's order and challenge those who would devise such a scoundrelly plot. Prayer contends with the cowards that seek shelter in their ungodly unbelief called humanistic intellectualism. Prayer gives spiritual courage and assured rest in the confrontational demands to face the forces of ideas that conflict with Biblical Truth and holy alliance to Almighty God. Prayer will defeat the powers of darkness when fearless tenacity is displayed at any cost. Daniel and a great host of others have proven that.

Prayer confronts the elements. "The tin-roofed tabernacle in Waterloo Iowa, roared under the driving rain when Charles Fuller stepped up to the microphone to pray, "Lord, if you don't stop the rain the Old Fashion Revival Hour will not be able to go out over the air. For Jesus sake, please stop the rain." Within three minutes the rain stopped abruptly and the program was broadcast without interference. But five minutes after the service was over there was a down-pour that drenched the home going crowd." (Sunday)

PRAYER IS THE CONDITION OF RECOGNIZING OWNERSHIP.

The world is saturated with seekers for personal satisfaction. But few seek after God the source of Life. Money will buy pleasure, but not joy or peace; a bed, but not sleep; books, but not understanding; food, but not an appetite; jewels, but not inward beauty; a house, but not a home; medicine, but not health; luxuries, but not heart purity; a cross to hang around the neck, but not a daily godly walk; and a church pew, but not heaven.

Such a seeker does not recognize who owns what. His goals are centered upon what he can get, but not upon Who gives every good and perfect gift. This seeker thinks he owns what he can touch and see. His thoughts are on present possessions and those material things which he hopes to acquire in the future. But he appears to be entirely unaware that his future is not in his own hands. "As a man thinks in his heart, so is he." This seeker has never gone beyond the incubator stage in comprehending who he is. He thinks he is his own self-appointed god.

Can this seeker possibly assimilate that he is made in the image of God Almighty, and His likeness? Can he absorb the fact that God breathed into him the breath of life, making him an existing entity forever? Thus, making him accountable as to how he invested his life of probation.

Honest prayer will siege the seeker and cause him to evaluate his real purpose for living. If his ship is on the wrong course, it will be dashed upon the rocks. This type of prayer will truly assess life and its values. Did not our Lord say: "come let us reason together." Prayer brings God and man together in His counsel chambers for full appraisal with every area of life placed on the table for careful consideration. Prayer will bring the seeker to deliberate his personal destiny. Prayer is man's door to understanding his unique need of a personal relationship with the Savior and His designed purpose for the seeker's life. Prayer sets up the seeker's recognition of his true ownership. "Yea are not your own, yea are brought with a price."

PRAYER IS ALWAYS ANSWERED.

Jean Ingelow once said: "I have lived to thank God, that not all my prayers have been answered." Why? How can that be known? All obedient prayer is answered in one way or another. What reason could the Holy God give for acknowledging the prayer that would be harmful in the future? It probably could be added that which appeared to be unanswered, had a "no" as its answer. Our Father never just looks at the immediate, but always considers the whole life, even into eternity.

If the child would ask for a pair of powerful reading glasses to enlarge the print to make it easier to read, and does not need them, would a father allow her to continually use them? No, because it would weaken her normal eye sight so that she would eventually have to depend upon the use of the powerful glasses for normal reading. The dependency would grow with time. Her request to use them for the moment does not appear to be a big deal. But the "no" was not made for the moment, but for the future. Does not the Lord view each request in like manner?

Is this not the reason prayer should be, not my will, but Thy will be done? Praying for God's will puts prayer on a level beyond personal priority. Praying out of the will of God leaves the believer in a wilderness with endless problems with nothing but personal skills to handle the unforeseeable. But praying for God's will allows Omnipotence to work out His full purpose for the believer. For prayer to be fruitful, the believer dare not have any other frame of mind. Unanswered prayer will teach in unusual ways.

"General Gordon said: the Confederate troops prayed for victory before the battle of Sharpsburg. He said he felt satisfied that the Confederate forces would sweep the Union lines, and would be on their way to Washington within a week. But the next day the battle resulted in one of the most crushing defeats the Confederates received during the war. General Gordon was shot five times, men were discouraged. But he told me years after that the prayers of the Confederates on the day before that battle were best answered by defeat; that if the Confederates had captured Washington and defeated the Union our nation would now be far down the scale among the weaker nations of the earth." ("How to Live the Christ Life") James Hastings.

God's foreknowledge willed to form a nation that would honor Him and be used to send His message around the world.

PRAYER IS AN INSTRUMENT OF HEALING.

Isaiah had just given Hezekiah the shocking news: "put your house in order, thou shall die and not live." "Then Hezekiah turned his face toward the wall, and prayed unto the Lord and said: "remember now O Lord, I beseech Thee how I have walked before Thee in truth and with a perfect heart, and have done that which is good in Thy sight, and Hezekiah wept sore." (Isa. 38:2&3) It is certain, most people would react just as Hezekiah did when tragic news comes without warning. Such news can shake the very foundations of faith.

Years ago, I developed some nodules in my armpits. Naturally, this concerned me even though they were not painful. A doctor in my church examined the nodules and said I had cancer in the glands. Because I felt healthy, this diagnosis was unexpected, sending a shock wave through my whole system. After further medical investigation, doctors determined that it was some fine flakes from sanding fiberglass that had worked their way into the open pores in my armpits and had infected my glands.

I had purchased a boat for five dollars, which had a large hole in the bottom. I took on the project of rebuilding the boat and then covering the wood with liquid fiberglass for strength and to make sure the boat did not leak. The sanding to smooth the uneven places caused the trouble.

I think I know a little about what Hezekiah experienced. I did some praying, as did Hezekiah. Does God ever change His mind? He did in Hezekiah's case, and gave him fifteen more years.

Why is not every prayer answered that appeals for healing? I do not have the answer, but I know that God does respond to the plea for healing. A number of times in my ministry I have seen God's healing touch in hopeless situations. Then again I have seen, even though earnest prayer was lifted, where God has not responded to many prayers in the way requested. Does this mean, what will be, will be? Not in the least! Hezekiah had already received the summons, but the case that was closed, was reopened because of personal prayer. There was a new beginning.

The value of prayer cannot be measured, even when the meaning is hidden and the request appears to be denied. God evaluates prayer up until the last minute, and what was closed can be opened.

"Prayer is the pulse of the renewed soul; and the constancy of its beat is the best test and measure of the spiritual life." (Octavius Winslow)

CONSTANT PRAYER IS NEEDED, IF -

Paul writes to the Roman church: "I beseech you therefore, brethren, by the mercies of God, that ye present your body a living sacrifice, holy, acceptable unto God, which is your reasonable service." (12:1) Prayer must be the center piece if this scriptural Truth if it is to be lived out each day. The word "beseech" has a heart-warming appeal to every believer. It is a call for one's aid, an exhorted desire that magnifies concern for that fulfillment that will produce a particular effect. There is no other way to claim the mercies of God.

Paul relates the necessity of personally presenting one's self, that is to be offered freely, which means complete yielding, a sacrifice at any cost. Only this will be acceptable to the Lord God. "Acceptable" is freely welcome to any task that our Lord would bestow upon His servant. This acceptably is self promoted action that is favorable toward the most unassuming call.

This is "service" that is wrapped up in the body, soul and spirit. This service is a completeness that includes all that His child is or ever hopes to be. All service is an acknowledgment that God is fully worshiped with all honor due Him. The whole being is to be an instrument in His hands for righteous service by a voluntary act of the will.

"Reasonable" has the rationale that is just and fair. It is not excessive, but right being proper and prudent toward God's Word and His service. What is more reasonable for any child of God, than to become a living sacrifice to the One who breathed the image of God into the soul! It is said of Caleb and Joshua: "they have wholly followed the Lord." This is the most reasonable service any true child of God can do. There can not be this kind of committed dedication without prayer being the central part of this walk with the Lord.

We are not talking about a one day deal, but a constant daily walk that has spiritual victory in the moment by moment relationship. Prayer will place you in full focus when living this scriptural appeal. Prayer will give discernment when separating man's standards from God's standards. Prayer will give the Holy Spirit the proper opportunity to direct the decision making.

One of the heartbreaks of life is to listen to the Christian who has professed to be Christian for years. Their shallowness and gullibly is unbelievable. Sitting in a Sunday School class, the class was asked to define sin.

One of "the saints" said: " that is difficult today, because what we called sin thirty years ago, we do not call sin today." Why? Has God's word changed? If God has not changed, who has? Another said: "clothing worn today, thirty years ago would have been considered to be indecent."

A minister's wife spoke to an unsaved woman about accepting Christ. The woman's reply was: "I do not wish to become a Christian, but if I did, I would never appear in God's house with such clothes as you wear."

Do you think vital daily prayer would have allowed such spiritual desensitizing. When prayer has become a forgotten mission the soul dries up spiritually. How degrading is the present day understanding of the leadership of the Holy Spirit and the problem of sin. How inadequate is the thought that is given to our influence, the fruits of the spirit and spiritual living standards in all areas of life. Honest prayer will never belittle holiness and its Biblical standards in any way.

How could those mentioned above and their kind ever begin to understand what Paul was writing to the Roman church? God said, the lukewarm He will spew them out of His mouth. It is certain a disciplined prayer life would be the fountain needed in their dried up soul.

HE PRAYED WHILE OTHERS SLEPT

Mark simply states: " and in the morning, rising up a great while before day, He went out and departed into a solitary place, and there prayed." (1:35) This act has the liberal Theologians raising numerous questions, such as, if Jesus was God, why did He need to pray? Man's knowledgeable limitation is shocked into a reality that has never existed before. Logic defies the possibly of Jesus being both man and God. How could God be housed in man? If God can do the impossible, why not? Who can question believers who believe that which is called a miracle is suddenly a reality? But is it possible for the human to comprehend? The fact that every believer that is "born again" has experienced the transforming miracle that has completely changed all of life. Explainable, no, but very real. Does not the Holy Spirit live in the believer now? Did He not say the believer's body is the temple of the Holy Spirit?

Our Lord's physical body was subjected to every detail that all humanity has ever experienced. Our Lord was disappointed with the lack of dedication; He required sleep; He wept; He suffered disillusionment when His disciples were asleep in the garden when He was sweating drops of blood for their sins as well as the agony of the weight of the whole world's sins. He was facing the greatest travesty of human justice that history would ever record, without support from those who had dedicated their very lives to Him.

How does human flesh stand this type of pressure? His physical capacity would falter under the unbearable load if there were no outlet. Prayer was His refuge and the reinforcement of physical strength. How did He end His burdensome prayer: "not my will but Thy will be done." Prayer pulled the physical through this uncompromising situation, knowing the hour was at hand, and the cross was ahead.

Jesus revealed that prayer must concur with God's character and must present the spirit of reliance and submission to the Holy Spirit. The Holy Spirit is the interpreter of faithful prayer. When the motive is approved by the Holy Spirit, prayer delivers the desires of the heart. The Word of God becomes alive, promises become a reality, enrichment is satisfying, nothing is dead and dry; the Word gives a chart for the uncharted course, and guidance that is anointed.

Prayer gives a thirst for more of God's grace which can not be satisfied outside the perfect will of God. Prayer enlarges capacity that gives the soul new worth that inspires more approved goals. Rowland Hill related to prayer as: "the breath of a new-born soul, and there can be no Christian life without it."

When it was suggested to the professor that the class pray for guidance; he blurted out: "Pray! Who needs to pray? We are men. We can solve our own problems." How sad for such a soul that could not add one inch to his stature. He can only operate in the littleness of his materialistic concept and never know the availability of God's unlimited grace. The mind is closed to the infinity of God. His empty soul drips on his students who are asked to pursue excellence, but has the door closed to life's answers that have eternity involved.

Prayer unlocks the privileges of the supernatural that our good professor denies his students.

PRAYER HUMBLES "THE WISE"!

Prayer's capability will leave brilliance feeble and vain. But the prayerless soul will base reality on what one wishes life would be; causing the dream to be mesmerized by self interest, making human effort the center of cause and effect. All because there is a fragile relationship with his personal Creator. Neither man nor the earth is the center of the universe as the elite would have us think. The world does not whirl around the selected, the self-absorbed intellectuals which are capturing the mind of the eager student. Shakespeare has Cassius saying to Brutus, "the fault, dear Brutus, is not in our stars, but in ourselves, that we are underlings." The fault is in the home and the educational system that has pushed God out into the dumpster.

Prayerlessness allows intellectualism to supercede the Almighty God. Prayer gives discernment and the Lord his proper place in our lives. The scientific world is considering taking organs from animals and transplanting them into human beings. There is no conscience in crossing the distinct creative line that has made the human being who was created in the image of God a part of a souless animal. Is the scientific world seeking knowledge to prolong human life or is it to allow the ego to experiment, hopefully to outwit God? "Self," says William Law, "is not only the seat and habitation, but the very life of sin. The works of the devil are all wrought in self. It is his peculiar work-shop."

Of course being crucified with Christ is a must if the self life is to be crucified. Prayer is necessary if the crucified life is to be lived out daily. Prayer is the empowerment that intercedes for the limitations of man, which permits God to become God. Prayer gives clear-sightedness when dealing with those who try to substitute the intellectual mind for God. Saadi said it this way: "I fear God, and next to God, I chiefly fear him who fears Him not." Prayer is the humbling process that graciously respects God in His realm, which is Omnipotent, and man in his realm which is restricted to mortality, making skills and understanding confined to temporal bounds. Prayer instantly travels to heaven and around the world.

Without prayer and saturated Bible study, man can exterminate himself while blindly trying to save himself. There is nothing more pitiful than to watch the intellectually blind leading the blind. Prayer is appropriating all God can and wills to bestow in order for us to be His obedient child. "How can He grant you what you do not desire to receive." St. Augustine.

PRAYER SHARPENS THE CONSCIENCE BY OPENING THE INNER SANCTUARY OF THE SOUL!

The scriptures speak often about the conscience, and the "good conscience." Paul writes to Timothy: "Now the end of the commandment is charity out of a pure heart, and of a good conscience, and of faith unfeigned." (I Ti. 1:5) Also in 1:19: "Holding faith, and a good conscience; which some having put away, concerning faith have made shipwreck."

What is a "good conscience"? A good conscience is God motivated; God's law is written on the soul, controlled by the apprehension of God; it instructs what is sin and what is Divine duty, and it is holy when it is free from sin's guilt.

How is the "good conscience" in depraved mankind to become a good conscience? The conscience must be purged, made clean, and cleansed by our Lord's precious blood. This treasure is that which cannot be found apart from Christ Jesus as Lord of all of life.

A condemning conscience gnaws and galls under the donation of distressful guilt. It is like the shadow that follows regardless of the path taken. This punishment disapproves and denounces the present way of living. The doctors' offices are filled with unsettled personalities that cry for help, but the doctor's pill is only for the moment while the emotional system continues in turmoil. All kinds of adjustments are attempted to quiet the uproar. Some have sought to solve the conviction by indulging in action, which may or may not be good or evil, but its anguish is still there.

Mrs. Hale writes concerning a convicting conscience with these words:

"He fears not dying - tis a deeper fear,
The thunder-peal cries to his conscience, "Hear"!
The rushing winds from memory lift the veil,
And in each flash in his sins, like spectres pale,
Freed, from their dark abode, his guilty breast,
Shriek in the startled ear- "Death is not rest.""

When prayer is a constant daily necessity, the "good conscience" seeks harmony with the soul walking in His Light. Prayer alerts the conscience; the conscience is awakened to acknowledge the true condition of the soul; probing the soul to enlarge its capacity; reviving the dried up spiritual life; pursuing holy maturity with godly passion; demanding scriptural discipline; and opening an inquiring mind to new Bible treasures .

Prayer sharpens the conscience to a fine edge, keeping the soul from shipwreck and shame. A "good conscience" can only remain good as long as there is a vital prayer life. Prayer's negligence diminishes and debilitates daily revitalization of the whole spiritual process. Prayerlessness will clog the spiritual arteries that feed the conscience.